EVERY CHANG

# EVERY
# CHANGING
# SHAPE

Elizabeth Jennings

*'And I must borrow every changing shape*
*To find expression . . .'*
T. S. ELIOT—Portrait of a Lady

# CARCANET

First published in Great Britain in 1961 by
Andre Deutsch Limited

Paperback edition published in 1996 by
Carcanet Press Limited
402–406 Corn Exchange Buildings
Manchester M4 3BY

A CIP catalogue record for this book
is available from the British Library.
ISBN 1 85754 247 9

The publisher acknowledges financial assistance
from the Arts Council of England.

Printed and Bound by Antony Rowe Ltd

*For*
*Aelwin Tindal-Atkinson* OP

MY GRATEFUL ACKNOWLEDGEMENTS are due to the editors of the following magazines and periodicals in which versions of some of the following chapters originally appeared: *The Aylesford Review, Blackfriars, The Dublin Review, The London Magazine, The Month, The Twentieth Century.*

# ACKNOWLEDGEMENTS

Grateful acknowledgement is made to the following for permission to use copyright material in this book:

for quotations from *The Diary of a Country Priest* and *Joy* by Georges Bernanos to the author, The Bodley Head, The Macmillan Company, New York, and Pantheon Books Inc. New York;

for quotations from *Language As Gesture* by R. P. Blackmur to the author, George Allen & Unwin Limited, and Harcourt, Brace and Company, Inc., New York;

for quotations from *Prayer and Poetry* by Henri Bremond to the author and Burns and Oates Limited;

for quotations from *The Cloud of Unknowing* to John M. Watkins;

for quotations from *The Collected Poems of Hart Crane* to the author's executors and Liveright Publishing Corporation, New York;

for quotations from the works of T. S. Eliot to the author, Faber and Faber Limited, Harcourt, Brace and Company, Inc., New York, and Farrar, Straus and Cudahy, Inc., New York;

for quotations from the works of Gerard Manley Hopkins to the author's executors and the Oxford University Press;

for quotations from John Frederick Nims's Introduction to his translation of *The Poems of St John of the Cross* to the translator and Grove Press, Inc., New York;

for quotations from Julian of Norwich's *Revelations of Divine Love* to Burns and Oates Limited;

for quotations from *Julian of Norwich* by Paul Molinari to the author and Longmans, Green and Company Limited;

for quotations from *Sonnets to Orpheus* and *The Duino Elegies* by Rainer Maria Rilke to the author and The Hogarth Press Limited;

for quotations from the poems of Edwin Muir to the author's executors, Faber and Faber Limited and Grove Press, Inc., New York;

for quotations from the poems of Wallace Stevens to the author's executors, Faber and Faber Limited, and Alfred A. Knopf, Inc., New York;

for quotations from *The Life of St Teresa* translated by J. M. Cohen to the translator and Penguin Books Limited;

for quotations from *Waiting on God* by Simone Weil and from *Simone Weil as We Knew Her* by J. B. Perrin and G. Thibon to the authors and Routledge and Kegan Paul Limited.

# CONTENTS

# FOREWORD

IN 1961, AFTER Elizabeth Jennings had written her first three collec-
tions of poems – *A Way of Looking, A Sense of the World* and *Song for a
Birth or a Death* – she published her most substantial critical work. Of
*Every Changing Shape*, a series of related essays, she writes: 'I am
concerned with three things – the making of poems, the nature of
mystical experience, and the relationship between them.' She was thirty-
five years old, working full time at a publishing house in London as an
editor and reader, and on the threshold of a psychological crisis which
was to beset her for twenty years. She wrote this book 'at the pitch of
poetry', with an entire concentration and clarity of purpose.

A spiritual element in her critical stance is her insistent knowledge of
continuities in the language of poetry, its inescapable contingencies.
'Poets work upon and through each other,' she declared, using terms
more plain and credible than Harold Bloom's. The natural, inevitable,
interdependence between poets and poems is 'the real meaning of tradition and influence'. This is not far from T.S. Eliot's sense of the contem-
poraneity of all literature, and thus of its transcendence. For her this
transcendence is not, as it is for the early Eliot, an aesthetic but a spiritual verity. The connection between Herbert, Traherne and Vaughan is
more than a literary matter. It entails profound affinities not so much of
temperament as of spirit. Her own connection with Eliot and with
Hopkins, with Muir and Christina Rossetti, with Charlotte Mew and
Rilke, is as patent as her loving inferences from Saint Teresa of Avila
and Julian of Norwich are. If the book, for the sake of convenience,
follows a chronology, it is to provide a sense of the changing contexts
within which continuities are sustained. 'If there is, as I shall try to show,
a connection between poetry and mysticism, then it will be found as
easily in the fifth century in Italy, as in the fourteenth century in
England or the twentieth century in France,' she wrote in the original
Foreword. It will be noted that all her subjects are AD.

In the end she comes down to a preference in poetry for a language of
embodiment, containing rather than describing meanings: 'With this
ring I thee wed' rather than 'I give you this ring as a symbol of our
marriage'. Such containment, or enactment, in language – a function of
rhythm, word-order, diction – can impart a spiritual dimension to work
by secular writers, so that poems mean more than a poet intends, as if
they have been touched by a grace which the poet inadvertently

9

accesses and then cannot deny. For the religious poet, crisis comes when such grace recedes, as in Vaughan and Cowper, St John of the Cross and Hart Crane, and from time to time in Jennings herself: the anxiety of disconnection is potent and can be fatal.

Elizabeth Jennings is a Roman Catholic and makes no bones about her belief and her doubt. Yet without resort to the politic and bland strategies of ecumenicism, she finds enabling energies outside her own church and even outside faith itself. In taking her title from Eliot's early poem 'Portrait of a Lady', she indicates the Protean nature of the spirit eluding embodiment in an age of doubt. In choosing Eliot she also signals her debt to the great Modernists, a debt some of her readers prefer to overlook when they approach the generally tidy stanzas and traditional forms of her poems. To miss the modernist thread in her poems – as in the work of her contemporaries Philip Larkin and Thom Gunn – is to misread or to shortchange them.

There are mystics in her book, there are religious writers, and there are those whose approach is more oblique, for whom the given structures of faith are drained of meaning, but who continue to surprise – in Larkin's famous phrase – 'a hunger in themselves to be more serious'. This hunger is not always expressed in brilliant poems: it can be wrestled for in tortuous prose, it can be almost grasped and then escape again, like Proteus in the cave. Language is a net made by men and women, its weave too coarse or too fragile to snare and hold the transcendent meanings it is after. Mystics write about the experience of mysticism, striving to express what it is and how to attain it, what they learn. A poet makes a poem, and 'What the poet says about how he made it is always a falling away from the experience itself; it throws a backward light. The poet's explanations are approximations at best.' How much more so the critic's, who has access to the product but not the process, unless that critic is a poet.

What is mysticism for Elizabeth Jennings? She puts it simply to begin with: the 'experience of loss of self and union with God'. In her first chapter she develops this rudimentary definition into something more nuanced and diversely serviceable. A mystic's prose meditations cast 'a forward light' on the experience, unlike the poet's critical retrospect. If the word 'mystical' emerges with definite meaning from this account, so too the words 'inspiration', 'intuition', 'vision' and 'revelation' shed their impressionist haze and acquire actual valencies.

In her original Foreword she concedes a degree of arbitrariness in her selection of authors but claims that her approach, her terms and definitions, her very manner of reading, can be applied to other writers. She draws attention to three particular gaps in her account: Dante, Blake and Yeats. Dante, to whom many of her later poems pay tribute in their deployment of *terza rima* and in their spiritual topography, she omits simply because he is too enormous, demanding a study on his own. Blake does not belong in her essentially *Western* mystical tradition (one senses an unease on her part with the arbitrary and personal nature of his symbolism, with his idiosyncratic discipline and his private angels). Yeats, whom she has loved and understood more than most of her contemporaries, she leaves out because, however much he 'talked and wrote of "visions", he was a shaper of systems, a creator of "myths", rather than a man who wished to lose himself in God.' These absences help define the areas of her concern.

And the concerns of this book are the chief concerns of Elizabeth Jennings's poetry. She has written philosophically, but philosophy only takes her to a threshold; it can be a pathway or a set of stairs, but it does not by itself arrive at the point of mystical experience. What matters is what happens when the 'I', the insistent first person of the early poems, the conscious 'mind' with its intractable definitions and flaws which recurs with such frequency in her books, including those written during her illness, reaches the point of 'communion'. Like the great writers of the eighteenth century who wrote out of mental and spiritual distress, out of nightmare, and towards the common light where men and women walked and worshipped and spoke a vulgar tongue, Jennings's work strives towards a norm. But for her, as a Roman Catholic, that norm has a crucial spiritual sanction.

Characteristically, she writes in this volume a series of essays which are intended, as her poems are, to function cumulatively, to build towards understanding. They do not aspire to a coherent structure but to a coherent meaning. They are tentative and do not over-reach, do not make claims too large. Nor, when they come up against contrary evidence, do they try to hide it. 'I have attempted to reach the centre of each writer and mystic by a careful reconnaissance, have tried, in effect, by indirection "to find directions out".'

Our own age is a secular one and the concerns of the poetic imagination – as Donald Davie argued so persuasively in *Thomas Hardy and British Poetry* – have been trammelled in a world of contingencies. Since the early 1930s, for most writers, history has seemed to displace the transcendent concerns of those poets from whom the large figures of the past took their bearings. David Jones, R.S. Thomas, C.H. Sisson, Donald

Davie, Geoffrey Hill and Elizabeth Jennings herself are awkwardly out of place in their difficult adherence to an older order.

The post-modern is in the ascendant and language itself beleaguered on all sides by those who deny that it possesses the nominal properties in which a religious poet's faith is grounded. Yet on reflection, reading the book thirty-five years after its original publication, many will find the content timeless, seriously standing apart from fashion, like the stable liturgies of the Book of Common Prayer and the real, the perennial truths of St John of the Cross, George Herbert and – though flickering and tentatively held – of Rilke, Charles Péguy and Wallace Stevens. Elizabeth Jennings is a Christian poet whose writings on nature, love, friendship, family, death and mental turmoil, spring from a questing and a doubting spirit. This is not a book written for academic advancement or for academic readers, though it will bring students up against salutary obstacles that most critics are happy to skirt or ignore. It is timely to re-issue it now, in part because it has proven a durable act of exploration and witness, in part because it is exemplary in its candour and directness of purpose. Elizabeth Jennings is not an ironist, and this too sets her apart from her generation and those that have followed it. She speaks of 'bold humility and a disinterested intelligence'. No intelligence is disinterested – that much can be conceded to the post-modern bias of the age. But the quality of interest here is different in kind from that which emanates from most seminar rooms. Elizabeth Jennings concluded her original Foreword with two lines of another Modernist, Ezra Pound, taken from the *Pisan Cantos*, acknowledging that she has wrenched them from their context. Yet they express her failure, as they expressed his, in a doomed enterprise that was vast, noble and worth the candle:

> to have gathered from the air a live tradition
> or from a fine old eye the unconquered flame.

MICHAEL SCHMIDT

# 1. DEFINITIONS AND WITNESSES

## Introduction

---

*Let the new faces play what tricks they will*
*In the old rooms; night can outbalance day,*
*Our shadows rove the garden gravel still,*
*The living seem more shadowy than they.*
YEATS – The New Faces

'MYSTICAL' IS ONE of the most misused words in the English language. In this book I shall be using it in a limited, precise and, I hope, lucid way. But before I define my own usage of the word, I want to indicate some of the abuses of it, if only to show the meanings it will *not* be burdened with in the following studies. The word 'mystical' is often appropriated to denote a sense of vagueness both on the part of the speaker or writer and also on the part of the thing described or spoken of. It is, in fact, employed to cover up an unwillingness to define meanings and feelings; it is a counter for the inchoate, a cipher for the half-understood. It is also used to hint at moods, experiences, apprehensions which are felt to be either religious or aesthetic. In this connection, one is reminded of Humpty Dumpty's remark – 'Words mean what I choose them to mean, no more and no less.'

The word 'mystical', then, tends to appear at almost any moment in thought or speech when definitions seem elusive and precision impossible. In the use I myself shall make of it, I hope not to align myself with Humpty Dumpty but rather to restore the word to an exact meaning in literature and religious experience; and as this book is essentially a study of the Western Christian tradition of mysticism, I shall now give the definition of the word supplied by Dom Cuthbert Butler in his exhaustive and invaluable work entitled *Western Mysticism* – 'The mystic's claim', he says, 'is expressed by Christian mystics as "the experimental perception of God's Presence and Being", and especially "union with God" – a union, that is, not merely psychological, in conforming the will to God's Will, but, it may be said, ontological of the soul with God, spirit with Spirit. And they declare that the experience is a momentary foretaste of the bliss of heaven.'

Put quite simply, mysticism is the study of direct union with God, a union which reaches beyond the senses and beyond reason. This is the essence of mystical experience. From it spring all the subtleties and complications which have exercised writers and philosophers for centuries. And it is in these complexities, these fitful sparks which the central illumination sheds and scatters that I intend to search for the connections between this particular sense of union with God and the making of poems.

In the history of English poetry, the word 'mystical' has perhaps been used most appropriately and with most clarity in the criticism that has accumulated around the seventeenth-century so-called Metaphysical poets. The great representatives of this group of poets are, in fact, not metaphysical at all; on the contrary, they are mystical poets. Vaughan, Herbert and Traherne were not primarily interested in the nature or study of being, the true meaning of metaphysics; they were concerned with making direct contact with reality or God, and with expressing this in their verse. Indeed, it is rather ironic that the use of the word 'metaphysical' as applied to these poets is just as vague and imprecise as the use of 'mystical' in other contexts.

It must, however, be stressed from the outset of these exploratory studies that a poet can write strictly mystical poetry without being fully conscious of what he is doing, whereas the mystic, in attempting to describe his contact with God, is usually perfectly aware of what he is striving to express. This phenomenon applies to all poets and all poetry and it explains why criticism of poetry so often sounds either arbitrary or contrived. For one of the purposes of criticism is to explain and to elucidate and, if it is to achieve these ends at more than a superficial level, it must of its very nature make conscious and explicit what, in a given poem, may be unconscious and implicit. Criticism does not exactly *make* something out of something else; if it is just and honest, it brings to the surface. But the problem of criticism often is that simply by bringing to the surface it alters and even destroys. The fish is caught, yes, but it is a dead fish or, at best, a gasping fish. What the perfect critic must do is catch the fish, examine it carefully, and afterwards return it to the water unimpaired. Criticism, then, is the application of a scientific method to a free, spontaneous activity and achievement.

The articulate mystics, on the other hand, have usually been their own best critics. Most of their written work is an attempt to explain, a skirmishing round a point where mysticism and poetry meet. It is for this reason that Bremond has declared that the findings of the mystics may throw light on the activities of the poet.

To illustrate just how deeply the word 'mysticism' has sunk to the level of the inchoate, the undifferentiated, it may be useful to examine one or two remarks made by a number of otherwise fastidious stylists. Sacheverell Sitwell, in his recently published *Journey to the End of Time*, delivers himself of this rather startling statement – 'Perhaps our greatest mistake lies in thinking that holiness is the most likely means of communication with the greater consciousness. If we take only the last hundred and fifty years . . . the seers in our midst have not been men of religion but scientists and persons of exceptional human gifts, Blake, Tolstoy, Beethoven, Rimbaud.' Though the word 'mystic' is not used here, 'seer' is certainly a substitute for it. Mr Sitwell has, in fact, fallen victim to a current fallacy – he has relegated to some vague area of 'mystical experience' something which he is not himself prepared to define more exactly.

Even the fine discrimination and clarity of Albert Camus's mind became clouded when he considered the relationship between religion and art and he was betrayed into some extremely confused remarks in *The Rebel*. It must, however, be said in fairness to Camus that he was not so much enthroning ecstasy as examining it. He built up only to destroy, it is true, but he finally found that total destruction is not possible and so was left with, as it were, humanity on the one hand, and abstract definitions of rebellion on the other. The tragedy is that he died at the very moment when he seemed to be reaching towards some kind of synthesis. In the work he has left, it is his humility which saves him from absurdity, as well as his joyful sensuousness. Here is an extract from the chapter called *Rebellion and Art* in *The Rebel*: 'Religion or crime, every human endeavour in fact, finally obeys this unreasonable desire and claims to give life a form it does not have. The same impulse, which can lead to the adoration of the heavens or the destruction of man, also leads to creative literature which derives its serious content at this source.' Camus does not mention mysticism here but he is certainly hinting at it. For him it is, along with religion, only one more attempt by man to impose order upon chaos. And for Camus ecstasy was almost always another name for escape or self-deception.

If Camus was confused, at least he was diffident about formulating absolute laws out of his confusion. In his thought there is none of the self-confidence which we find so frequently in the Existentialism of

Sartre. Most of his statements are questions and for this he must be greatly respected. I have considered Camus at some length because his ideas have had a potent effect on the contemporary attitude both to the purpose of literature and to the validity of religious experience. Yet, though he may appear to regard ecstasy as just one more possible experience, he is also acquainted with suffering, as we see in *The Plague* for example, and when he speaks of asceticism he is not simply indulging in a facile play of words.

It is perhaps noteworthy that those men and women whose written testimonies would seem to show that they have had the sort of mystical experience to which Dom Cuthbert Butler refers are themselves extremely reticent about using the word 'mystical'. Pascal's silence is, for instance, more resounding than the current Beat Generation's noisy avowal of attachment to Christ. Furthermore, some of the writers who were not Christians but whom I shall be considering in this book often reached towards an experience which appears to be similar to that which the orthodox Christian would call contact with God – but they refused to speak of it directly. And they refused because poetry or heightened prose always demands both precision and honesty – two names, perhaps, for the same quality.

Again, those men and women who have been mystics first and only writers afterwards are always notable for the stringency of their definitions, for their exhaustive ransacking of language and imagery in order to find the right, or at least the approximate, terms for their experiences. The vague may disarm the reader momentarily, but only the exact, and this often means the concrete, grasps and holds his attention and his credence for long.

If 'mystical' is often employed to connote the vague, it is also at times summoned as a substitute for 'imaginative', 'immaterial' or 'abstract'. Again, and paradoxically, in reference to writers like Wordsworth or D. H. Lawrence, it sometimes serves as a synonym for union with nature or a love of the earth; in the hands of the theorists 'mysticism' quickly takes on a spurious precision if it is replaced by the word 'mystique'. Thus Lawrence's plea for a more instinctual life becomes both a mystique of the earth and also a cipher for the word 'vision'.

A year or two ago Professor Zaehner, in his careful study *Mysticism Sacred and Profane*, introduced a large measure of clarity to this subject by dividing mysticism into three specific kinds – first, a sense of union with the created world, second, a belief in the self as the Absolute

Reality, and third, a direct, supra-rational union with a personal God by means of love. It is this third definition which I shall be employing throughout the chapters which follow. If such a definition is strictly a theological one, my use of it will be mainly literary. For, though the studies in this book are chiefly interpretative and evaluative, I have no desire to apply my definition of mysticism too rigidly to each mystic or writer with whom I shall deal. To appraise or pass judgment in this way is often to miss the chief point of certain writers. This is particularly true in the case of poets like Rilke, Hart Crane and Wallace Stevens, men who were not Christians but whose work seems to me to be moving towards some vision that has much in common with that of more orthodox visionaries; and 'visionaries' here, as elsewhere in the pages which follow, is a synonym for 'mystics'. It must be added, however, that my definition of mysticism will remain adamant and constant even though I may apply it now in one way, now in another.

What I am perhaps most concerned with is an illuminating paradox which I have discovered in my study of various poets and mystics. It has seemed to me that poets often come nearest to the full expression of a mystical experience when they are least inclined to admit it openly. On the moral plane, this is a kind of humility, and, on the plane of literature, yet one more indication that poets often write more profoundly than they consciously intend. This is not to say that there is a lack of lucidity in the greatest mystical verse but rather that the writing of such verse often leads the poet into an area which is dark with 'excessive light'; it is, after all, light which dazzles and blinds, not obscurity. To have captured and held such illumination seems to me to have truly ensnared a vision in its completeness, not in its fading or aftermath. Some words of Simone Weil's are relevant in this context; 'A poem,' she says, 'is beautiful to the precise degree in which the attention whilst it was being composed has been turned towards the inexpressible.'

As I have said, mystics, when they attempt to write about their experiences, generally know exactly what they are about; this is undoubtedly true when they write prose, even if that prose is extremely intense and bare. On the other hand, when they write poetry, they often write greater than they know. This fact explains, I think, the paradox whereby their poems describe experiences which their prose terms 'inexpressible'.

One of the purposes of this book is to demonstrate that mystical experience comes from a source similar to, if not identical with, that of poetry, but is also itself a perfectly suitable subject-matter for poetry. Poetry which is mystical in content is still, after all, poetry – something fashioned, designed, ordered. As Goethe has said, 'Religion stands in the same relation to art as any other of the higher interests in life.' But to make such a statement as this is to say very little. From a basic agreement with Goethe's remark I would myself go a good deal further than his own elevated humanism would have taken *him*. This book is concerned not only with the usefulness of poetry as a vehicle for mystical experience but also with some kind of demonstration, however tentative, that both mysticism (contemplation) and poetry (making) spring from the same creative source.

In many ways the present is a propitious time for an undertaking such as this. The literary climate is amenable now to a view of literature which gives twin positions of authority to the imagination and the intellect. We have reached a synthesis in literary criticism whereby words and images, or words and things, have struggled towards and, I believe, made peace with one another. Relationships are no longer a matter of passion only since, when intellect and imagination meet, reason or rationality is something acknowledged as well as something *felt*.

The inquiries and cautions of the mystics surely also have some affinity with the views held by the so-called New Critics in that both are concerned to test the truth and integrity of an experience by means of a stringent intellectual judgment. In the case of each, care for detail is a prerequisite of a generalization. A vision is, after all, only explicit, only communicable if it is an accumulation of detail, and we can only trust the whole if we have complete confidence in the parts.

Finally, I would like to touch on one more interesting misapplication of mysticism which does seem to be particularly prevalent today; it is not so much a linguistic misuse as a relegation to the wrong order, to an inappropriate level of being. I mean the kind of literature, usually fiction, which raises the sense of *place* to a kind of metaphysical contemplation. When man is felt to be belittled, when his grandeur seems to be diminished, he himself clings more fervently than ever to his roots and to his habitation. Household gods are cast out and subjective apprehensions take their place. Where divinity is derided or else ignored, human sensitivity assumes a kind of absolute validity since man is hungry both for certainty and for safety. The kind of sense of place, or the sense of the spirit of place, I am referring to is evident in, for example, the following statement from Elizabeth Bowen's novel,

*The Death of the Heart:* 'It is only in places where we have learnt to be lonely,' she says, 'that we have this solicitude for *things*.' And again, in Virginia Woolf's *To the Lighthouse*, we find the same adulation of human sensitivity, an adulation that has almost the strength of a personal religion. But no artist can turn inward for long, since the limits and interest of introspection are soon reached. Thus writers, such as Virginia Woolf, who make sensibility their approach to knowledge, attempt to find some kind of loss of self in the contemplation of natural objects and of things. This desire has some of the attributes of true mysticism though its end is very different. It would, for example, be easy to interpret *To the Lighthouse* in a strictly religious sense; but it would be *too* easy, and also more than a little dishonest, to do so. Nevertheless, this novel does represent several steps towards a vision that for ever seems obscure. Virginia Woolf remains in the area of uncertainty, creating her art both out of man's sense of separateness and also out of his unquenchable desire for peace and unity. The following lines from *To the Lighthouse* make a useful introduction to this book since they represent the mood and the moment, the intuition and the perplexity from which many of the poets and mystics examined here began their struggles towards God: 'It was some such feeling of completeness perhaps which, ten years ago, standing almost where she stood now, had made her say that she must be in love with the place. Love had a thousand shapes. There might be lovers whose gift it was to choose out the elements of things and place them together and so, giving them a wholeness not theirs in life, make of some scene, or meeting of people (all now gone and separate), one of those globed compacted things over which thought lingers, and love plays.'

# 2. IMAGES IN ABEYANCE

## Aspects of Augustine

---

*There was no movement in him such as wrath or desire, or any intellection;
nor was he, so to say, wholly himself, but as though in a rapture or
enthusiasm, he was wholly quiescent . . . in a condition of unmoved calm,
with no inclination outward from his own essence.*
PLOTINUS – Ennead VI

IN A PREFACE to his translation of St-John Perse's *Anabase*, T. S. Eliot
speaks of the relations between poetry and prose: 'Poetry,' he says,
'may occur, within a definite limit on one side, at any point along a
line of which the formal limits are "verse" and "prose". Without
offering any generalized theory about "poetry", "verse" and "prose",
I may suggest that a writer, by using . . . certain exclusively poetic
methods, is sometimes able to write poetry in what is called prose.
Another writer can, by reversing the process, write great prose in
verse. There are two very simple but insuperable difficulties in any
definition of "prose" and "poetry". One is that we have three terms
where we need four: we have "verse" and "poetry" on the one side,
and only "prose" on the other. The other difficulty follows from the
first: that the words imply a valuation in one context which they do
not in another.' Eliot goes on to explain just why he feels that the
prose poems which make up the *Anabase* are, in fact, poetry and not
prose: 'Its sequences, its logic of imagery, are those of poetry and not
of prose; and in consequence – at least the two matters are very closely
allied – the *declamation*, the system of stresses and pauses, which is
partially exhibited by the punctuation and spacing, is that of poetry
and not of prose.' Here, I think, he has probed to the heart of this
highly complex question. A prose poem is, firstly, declamation; it is
statement, not explanation; secondly, the syntax of the prose poem
is quite unlike that of prose; it is elliptical, allusive, in a sense dis-
integrated; and thirdly, stress, alliteration and repetition are employed
for the same purpose – that of attaining intensity of statement – as are

rhyme, rhythm and more regular form in poetry. 'Heightened' and 'intensity' are the key words to this whole subject.

The very term prose poem has fallen into disrepute in this country. It carries with it a suggestion of the decadent and the bizarre; it is also often regarded as the product of the poet *manqué*, of the man who can write neither good prose nor good poetry. But the success of both the prose poem and of 'heightened' or poetic prose can only be proved on the ear and the mind. If the effect on the reader (and here I mean the intelligent, well-read, accommodating reader) is the same as that of conventional poetry, we are justified in assuming that these kinds of prose are also kinds of poetry – different in degree perhaps but not essentially different of their very nature.

I have examined this question at some length because many of the mystics and visionary writers I shall be examining in this book employed a heightened prose to express their experiences rather than conventional poetic forms. The test of the success of their communications is the degree of intensity which they manage to attain; and this intensity depends in the first and last resort on cadence and imagery. Images, rather than simply words, are to the poet what colour is to the painter; they create a context and they either invite or repel. And if some form of poetic prose is employed to depict mystical experience – the direct encounter of man with God – it will be put to the utmost test; if it passes that test, if, in other words, it succeeds not simply in relating an experience but in re-creating, without devaluation, a moment of supreme intensity, it cannot, I think, be denied the name of poetry.

In Chapter nine of his *Confessions* St Augustine describes such an experience of awareness of God. It is a unique experience among those related by the mystics since it depicts a *shared* moment of ecstasy and illumination. The scene is Ostia towards the end of the fourth century and Augustine is talking with his mother shortly before her death. Augustine, of course, wrote in Latin so that we have his experience at one remove when we use a translation. Fortunately, however, Pusey's translation is one of those rare achievements in which the change-over from one language to another has lost nothing: the intensity survives, the images remain.

Augustine writes, 'We were discoursing then together, alone, very sweetly; and forgetting those things which are behind, and reaching forth unto those things which are before, we were enquiring between ourselves in the presence of the Truth, which Thou art, of what sort the eternal life of the saints was to be, which eye hath not seen, nor ear heard, nor hath it entered into the heart of man.'

The conversation between Monica and Augustine begins, then, with a consideration of time and with a meditation on the meaning of eternity. It is, in effect, the kind of preliminary to the higher forms of prayer which has, throughout the centuries, been considered an essential stage towards a closer union with God. The sense of the substantial presence of God (God immanent and transcendent) is already achieved. Augustine and his mother are moving towards what Eliot calls 'a closer union, a deeper communion', a contact of man with God by likeness and by humility – by likeness because, according to Christian doctrine, the soul of man is made in the likeness of God, and by humility because man can only confront God when all those elements in his nature which are the result of his fallen state have been cleansed and purified. Augustine is, in fact, seeking a contact of minds and the following passage vividly shows this: 'And when our discourse was brought to that point, that the very highest delight of the earthly senses, in the very purest material light, was, in respect of the sweetness of that life, not only not worthy of comparison, but not even of mention; we raising up ourselves with a more glowing affection towards the "Self-Same" did, by degrees pass through all things bodily, even the very heaven where sun and moon and stars shine upon the earth.'

This discourse started with Augustine's reflections on the nature of eternal life; he finds now that eternal life is more than the cessation of time, it is an aspect of God himself, and since God is 'pure being', timelessness is part of his nature, not simply a manifestation of his activity. Or, to be more exact still, with God, nature and activity are one and the same thing. And in this passage of the Ostia discourse, Augustine is rejecting all material images one by one. He is rejecting them, yes, but the very act of renunciation illuminates the experience. The power of poetry is that by simply naming it can illuminate. Thus by naming, even if only to reject the things named, Augustine is coming closer and closer to a full portrayal of an experience beyond the senses and the reason. The senses and the imagination are like the lower rungs of a ladder; if they were missing not only could the higher rungs not be reached but the ladder would itself be only a travesty of a ladder, would be a denial of hierarchy. Augustine, then, rejects the things which appeal to the senses not by destroying them but by leaving them behind. As we have already seen, he spoke at the

beginning of this whole discourse of 'those things which are behind'.
Hierarchy is preserved not eliminated.

He continues, 'Yea, we were soaring higher yet, by inward musing
and discourse, and admiring of Thy works.' This phrase, 'admiring of
Thy works', is vitally important. Augustine sees God shining through
all things. What he longs to do is to pierce through things and find the
Being who informs them and keeps and balances them both when they
are in motion and when they are at rest.

Now Augustine moves inwards, into the powers and resources of
his own mind. His mother does the same thing, and it is an indication
of the extraordinary closeness and affinity of these two people that
they could reach and sustain *together* so lofty an experience. 'And we
came to our own minds and went beyond them, that we might arrive
at that region of never-failing plenty, where Thou feedest Israel for
ever with the food of truth, and where life is the Wisdom by whom all
these things are made, but is, as she hath been, and so shall she be
ever.' Wisdom is God, eternal, unchangeable; she is also the Word of
the first chapter of St John's Gospel – 'the Word was with God and
the Word was God'. Augustine is still appropriating scriptural language
and imagery. 'We were discoursing and panting after her', he says,
and here he uses words of uncompromisingly physical energy and
desire. He goes on to describe the 'touch' of God, that contact for
which the Christian mystics have always employed the sense of touch –
not sight, hearing or even tasting, but *touch*. From this 'touch', which
was only slight and momentary, Augustine moves into the marvellous
passage which describes not only the pervasive sense of God's presence
united with him in his own soul, but also the stillness and peace of
everything in the universe. This is a peace where desire and fulfilment
become one. It is a subjective stillness in two senses – first, because it
exists in the mind of Augustine and second, because its presence there
seems, for a moment, to enforce peace on everything outside him. This
sense of order is like that of the poet who, when he has completed a
poem, feels the order and design in his poem overflowing into the
universe. He understands by intuition not by reason.

Augustine describes how everything has become 'hushed' – his own
strivings, imaginings and even his intellectual efforts, and also the
whole natural world. But he admits that these things can never be
'hushed' or pacified for long in this life; and he employs the word 'if'
to denote his own humility and frailty: 'If to any the tumult of the
flesh were hushed, hushed the images of earth, and waters, and air,

hushed also the pole of heaven, yea the very soul be hushed to herself, and by not thinking on self surmount self, hushed all dreams and imaginary revelations, every tongue and every sign, and whatsoever exists only in transition, since if any could hear, all these say, We made not ourselves, but He made us that abideth for ever – If then having uttered this, they too should be hushed, having roused only our ears to Him who made them, and He alone speak, not by them, but by Himself, that we may hear His Word, not through any tongue of flesh, nor Angel's voice, nor sound of thunder, nor in the dark riddle of a similitude, but might hear Whom in these things we love, might hear His Very Self without these (as we two now strained ourselves, and in swift thought touched on that Eternal Wisdom which abideth over all); – could this be continued on, and other visions far unlike be withdrawn, and this one ravish, and absorb, and wrap up its beholder amid these inward joys, so that life might be for ever like that one moment of understanding which now we sighed after; were not this, Enter into thy Master's joy? And when shall that be? When we shall all rise again, though we shall not all be changed.'

This vision of all things in abeyance contains the steps towards contemplation which later mystics were to systematize and turn into a method of prayer; 'by not thinking on self surmount self', 'hushed all dreams and imaginary revelations', 'not through any tongue of flesh . . . nor in the dark riddle of a similitude' – all these rejections are compiled and then set aside so that the touch of spirit with spirit, the 'one moment of understanding' may be attained. Augustine denies absolutely that such understanding can be achieved for more than a moment in this life. And, so great is his humility, he speaks tentatively throughout this passage as if he himself were unworthy of that 'moment of understanding'. As with all true mystics, his humility makes him elusive, reticent, hard to pin down. He speaks with a splendour that goes far beyond rhetoric, yes, but he refers to his own experience in oblique terms, and he also links his mother inseparably with that experience. But to be able to visualize, to imagine the perfect union of God with man, the attainment of the Beatific Vision, is surely to partake, however remotely, of that union; we are reminded of the profound words – 'Only those seek God who have already found Him.'

There is nothing passive in the acquiescence of Augustine in this scene at Ostia. On the contrary, the stilling of his passions, the disciplining of his imagination, were won only by vigilance and asceticism, by torment and struggle. The scene ends in silence and tranquillity. The world which, to Augustine and his mother, seemed for a moment to be halted moves again; the sea is rolling in along the shores of Ostia, the stars appear in their appointed places. This sense of images in abeyance, of emotions and passions utterly quieted, was a gratuitous gift certainly – 'something given and taken in a lifetime's death in love' as Eliot describes it. But such an experience was preceded by 'ardour and selflessness and self-surrender'.

Augustine's life had never been easy; indeed, it is perhaps his restlessness, his uncertainty, his unquenchable search for truth, which make him such a sympathetic figure to us today. Born in Africa with a Christian mother and a pagan father, he combined an intensely passionate temperament with a cool, appraising intellect. Order and chaos fought out their battle in Augustine's own personality. Like many passionate, sensual men, he longed for some experience in which the senses could be overruled and the disorderly emotions be brought into subjection. Augustine felt desire but what he wanted was love; his natural impulses were directed towards possession – even the possession of truth – while his deeper self longed to be dispossessed. He sought several different answers to his problems but they were provisional answers only. For a time Manichaeism held his attention – that heresy which taught that all matter was evil and that the things of the flesh were of their very nature malign. But this philosophy could not satisfy a realist like Augustine for long; tormented as he was by his desires, he could not really believe that the physical world was bad *because* it was physical. The neo-Platonism of Plotinus was more in accord with his temperament. He longed for a hierarchy at the summit of which absolute truth and absolute beauty might be encountered and embraced. The following passage from Plato's *Symposium* would have attracted Augustine strongly and, indeed, it describes an experience similar to that which he shared with his mother at Ostia : 'But if it were given to man to gaze on beauty's very self – unsullied, unalloyed, and freed from the mortal taint that haunts the frailer loveliness of flesh and blood – if, I say, it were given to man to see the heavenly beauty face to face, would you call *his* . . . an unenviable life, whose eyes had been opened to that vision, and who had gazed upon it in true contemplation until it had become his own for ever ?'

But even neo-Platonism could not satisfy Augustine; he wanted something more than abstract ideas, however lovely; he needed to invest abstractions with a personality, to find a God who was three persons as well as 'the act of pure being'. And so he turned at last to

Christianity. What held him back now was not dogma or doctrine but his own weaknesses, especially his own lusts and sexual pleasures. He describes the grip upon him of these pleasures most vividly: 'Very toys of toys and vanities of vanities they were, those ancient favourites of mine which detained me; they caught at the fleshly garment of my soul and softly whispered, "Dost thou cast us off?" and "Can it be that henceforth we shall not be with thee for ever?" But those things which they suggested by their "this or that", what was it they suggested, O my God? Oh may thy mercy guard the soul of me thy servant, from all the filthiness and shame they meant! I heard them indeed, though now far less than half their former size, not daring to withstand me to my face; but softly muttering behind my back, and plucking slyly at me as I went from them, as if in hope of making me look round.' A little later, in a garden in Milan, Augustine, after hearing the voices of some children crying 'Tolle, lege', 'Take, read', read the words of St Paul beginning 'Not in rioting and drunkenness, not in chambering and wantonness . . . but put ye on the Lord Christ', and was instantly converted.

From this time on he sought to dedicate his whole life to God. Called to the priesthood, he led an immensely active life in Africa of teaching, writing and preaching, yet he always found time for prayer and contemplation. His life was, in fact, a model of the life of 'mixed orders', a mingling of the active and contemplative elements to make a perfectly balanced whole.

Profound and far-reaching as his theological writings are, Augustine made no *systematic* study of mysticism. He formulated no method of prayer to correspond with those of the religious writers of later centuries. As E. I. Watkin has put it, 'The fact of the matter is that mystical theology, understood as the scientific study of infused prayer, was as yet non-existent. Neither St Augustine nor any other primitive saint thought of answering questions which it had occurred to nobody to ask. Enough that in some very real sense a direct intuition of God was possible in this life, and that he, Augustine, had enjoyed it.' With Augustine, then, we have the mystical experience concentrated, un-trammelled and bare. It has not yet been confined within terminologies and systems; it is concentrated but also free, so that his expression of mystical experience is, in some ways, like the poem which stands freshly achieved and finished, not yet placed in the hands of the critics to be assessed and afterwards accepted or discarded. This very lack of a systematic theology of mysticism means that Augustine's descriptions of the ineffable are unselfconscious yet entirely personal. For it is surely true that later mystical writers, such as Julian of Norwich or John of the Cross, worked from a preconceived pattern of how mystical experience should be described, even though they each made their personal and original contributions to the subject. With Augustine there are no concessions, no approximations. He is writing purely from the overflow of his own ecstasy. The *Confessions* may be an extended meditation on things past but they are written in a spirit of excitement which catches the very momentum of the initial experiences. And it is by means of his imagination much more than by his reason that Augustine reclaims his moments of vision and transforms them into literature. The passages in his *Confessions* which record these experiences are the most eloquent in the book; they are heightened prose, intensely rhythmic, crowded with images. But the images are only rungs on a ladder; they are necessary stages towards an experience which transcends imagery.

I think it will be illuminating at this stage to compare the flights of eloquence such as we have analysed in the scene at Ostia, with a poem by a young American poet, Anthony Hecht, in which he transcribes that experience and re-creates it in a poem of regular, formal rhymed stanzas. In the first six stanzas of this poem, which is called *Ostia Antica*, Mr Hecht creates the scene by describing the place:

> . . . the broken wall
> Is only itself, deeply accepting
>     The sun's warmth to its bricks.

.            .            .

> Each hanging waterdrop burns with a fierce
>     Bead of the sun's instilling.
> But softly, beneath the flutesong and volatile shriek
>     Of birds, are to be heard discourse
>         Mother and son.

The next two stanzas are crucial to this argument for in them Mr Hecht uses Augustine's own words but rearranges them to fit the formal pattern of his poem. There is no sense of strain or restriction, one does not feel that the words have been forced into a pattern; they *make* the pattern, it is not imposed upon them. The shape of the poem is felt to be dynamic, not a barrier to the content but a blossoming of the content. Mr Hecht writes:

If there were hushed
To us the images of earth, its poles
Hushed, and the waters of it
And hushed the tumult of the flesh, even
The voice intrinsic of our souls,
Each tongue and token hushed and the long habit
Of thought; if that first light, the given
To us were hushed,

So that the washed
Object, fixed in the sun, were dumb
And to the mind its brilliance
Were from beyond itself, and the mind were clear
As the unclouded dome
Wherein all things diminish, in that silence
Might we not confidently hear
God as he wished?

This is no facile re-creation of another man's experience, no diluted
rendering. Mr Hecht has preserved both the intensity and the mystery
of the prose translation. He has certainly omitted words and phrases
of the original but he has altered nothing. The poet, after all, works
by a more rigid principle of selection than the prose writer, even the
writer of poetic prose or the prose poem.

Mr Hecht's poem is, then, an account of Augustine's experience at
Ostia at two removes. First we have the Latin, then Pusey's careful
and imaginative prose translation, and finally Mr Hecht's rendering in
strict stanzaic form. The remarkable thing is that the two English
versions are so vivid and so true. The area of Augustine's experience
has not been circumscribed either by poetic prose or poetry itself in
another language; it has, on the contrary, been exposed and illuminated.
The precision of the Latin has been retained yet the uninflected English
translations have provided a fluidity, a subtlety that are entirely
faithful to the sense of wonder which informs Augustine's mystical
experience. But apt language and skilful technique alone are not a
sufficient explanation of these remarkable re-creations. The translator
and the poet must be in sympathy and must participate, must, in fact,
catch the fire and fervour of the original. This they can only do by an
effort of the imagination. To imagine an experience of union with God
– a union which goes beyond the senses, the memory and the reason –
is an extraordinary feat of identification. Augustine incontestably

*rejected* the things of the imagination in his experience at Ostia yet, when he came to write down that experience, he appropriated not only every verbal skill but also every subtle intuition. And his translators have followed him.

It does seem, then, that the essence of such an experience as Augustine's can be carried over and transferred to another language. Neither Pusey nor Hecht has departed far from the Latin, nor have they altered Augustine's images; and while the rhythms of an uninflected language such as English are different from those of Latin, the translators have preserved Augustine's intensity in, as it were, a different mode. In an essay on Augustine's *De Musica*, the American critic R. P. Blackmur has some illuminating things to say both about the literature of Augustine's time and also about his approach to poetry. 'The fourth century,' Mr Blackmur says, 'towards the end of which Augustine wrote his treatise, was not an age of poetry, or at any rate not an age of what seems to us great poetry; and it does not seem to have been to Augustine either, for his citations are from Virgil and Horace and Catullus chiefly, who were for him about as old as Chaucer for us. What survived, apart from the old poetry itself, was the procedure of poetry, its theoretic form, which had the name and seemed to have the habit of numbers . . . It was the study of this numerical aspect of verse which gave correct control of variations of sound, and it was the numbers themselves (as we should say the rhythms) which were the vestiges, indeed the manifestations, of the reality in the intimate core of being from which poetry or music drew its power.' This last phrase about 'the intimate core of being' would seem of exceptional importance in a study of Augustine's transmission of his mystical experience. Mr Blackmur would appear, I think rightly, to be suggesting that for Augustine poetry, music, indeed all art, sprang from the very centre of the human soul, that centre which, in the mystical experience, knows the direct contact of God. Mr Blackmur enlarges on this conception when he says '. . . for Augustine, the patterns of number in poetry and music, served as reminders of the skills of thought which have nothing to do with the language of words. For him the meaning of words were arbitrary, and by human authority, while the meanings of things, such as those which numbers moved, were true. The music or the meaning, to paraphrase Eliot, is what goes on after the words have stopped; to Augustine the numbers made the form of the meaning according to laws which, with licenses of silence and elision allowed for, were absolute, were of interest in verse

because of universal application, and were themselves a kind of limit
to human knowledge. This is his way of claiming poetry as a form of
knowledge, a form of being, or a form of revelation; claims to which
we are sufficiently used in our own time.'

The meaning of 'things', and poetry as 'a form of knowledge' are,
then, as seen by Augustine, a kind of foretaste of the claim which
Aquinas made much later when he said that though, in its ordinary
activity, the human mind could only know universals, there might
nevertheless be a direct, concrete knowledge of things made possible
by mysticism and perhaps by literature also. While Augustine could
find a symbol of infinity in mathematics, and hence in music, he could
also trace the revelatory power of poetry to the *things*, concrete not
abstract, for which words were only the counters. His hierarchy of
being is, of course, entirely Platonic but it is a Platonism anchored to
human experience; and since Augustine's vision was a unified vision,
with God as its centre, all knowledge, however secular in its immediate context, was part of the knowledge of God. Plato's ideas and
shadows were not sufficient for him, he wanted things in themselves.
And the cave of Plato's symbolism was, we may justly say, sealed off
for ever for Augustine when he surrendered to Christianity.

Mr Blackmur concludes his valuable analysis of Augustine's attitude
to poetry by quoting Augustine himself – 'Number, the base of rhythm,
begins from unity. It has beauty by equality and similitude, and it has
interconnection by order . . . All is due to the supreme eternal presidency of numerical rhythm, similitude, equality, and order. If this
presidency of mathematical structure is taken from earth, nothing
remains. Clearly God in the beginning made earth out of nothing
at all.' Mr Blackmur's comment on this passage is – 'It would seem
from these patchworks, drawn from this synopsis, that Augustine
thought poetry itself an increment to creation, at least under the right
presidency.'

From his examination of Augustine's *De Musica* Mr Blackmur
appears to have reached the same conclusions as we have come to
through a study of the Ostia scene in the *Confessions*. In other words,
art is exalted to a high place, words represent without debasing, and
direct experience of God can not only be expressed in poetry or poetic
prose *after* the experience is over, but the very writing of poetry or of
exalted prose is itself a kind of contact with God. And it can be a
contact with God because all art is a participation in the eternal act of
creation. All these things seem to be affirmed in Augustine's literary

practice. It would, however, be a grave error to suppose that he equated art itself with the mystical experience; indeed, he says almost the opposite in the Ostia discourse. But there is no moment in his writing, even at its most elevated, when he repudiates language as an instrument of truth and as a way of knowledge. To use an image I have already appropriated – language and imagery are, for Augustine, rungs on a ladder which reaches towards ultimate truth. But each step has to be climbed and we shall fall if we do not rest on each rung as we come to it; this is the important thing and this appears to be Augustine's own belief about the relations between making and mysticism.

# 3. THE SOIL OF SANCTITY

## *A study of* The Cloud of Unknowing

---

*Just as language has no longer anything in common with the things it names, so the movements of most of the people who live in cities have lost their connection with the earth; they hang, as it were, in the air, hover in all directions, and find no place where they can settle.*
RILKE – Worpswede

To UNDERSTAND PROPERLY the spirit of fourteenth-century English mysticism, we must re-examine our definitions of, first, discipline and second, sensuousness. Until we do this we cannot understand the conception of imagination as it was employed by the anonymous author of *The Cloud of Unknowing*. Discipline, since it took sides with Puritanism, has become a term of opprobrium; it has also taken on an almost autonomous power, a power which is divorced from nearly all the other qualities and activities of the human personality. Today, discipline tends to mean the opposite of delight and thus to be regarded as a cold abstract rule which urges limitation not wholeness, negation not affirmation. For the author of *The Cloud* the word had quite a different meaning; it connoted not a casting out but a gathering together, not exclusion but inclusion. Like all the orthodox Western Christian mystics before and after him, he is concerned not so much to constrict imagination as to bring it under rule. In Chapter sixty-five of *The Cloud*, he writes, 'Imagination is a power through the which we portray all images of absent and present things, and both it and the thing that it worketh in be contained in the Memory. Before ere man sinned, was Imagination so obedient unto the Reason, to the which it is as it were servant, that it ministered never to it any unordained image of any bodily creature, or any fantasy of any ghostly creature: but now it is not so.' In other words, imagination in itself is a valid instrument of knowledge and perception; it has only become untrustworthy since the fall of man disrupted it along with all the other faculties of human nature. But it is always subservient to reason since reason is an activity of the intellect and it is in his intellect and his will that man bears the image of God.

32

Thus it is not imagination of its essential nature which the author of *The Cloud* distrusts but rather the 'curiosity' of the imagination, and this curiosity is, he adds, especially active in those who are beginners in the life of prayer. 'For,' he declares, 'before the time be that the imagination be in great part restrained by the light of grace in the reason – as it is in continual meditation of ghostly things, such as their own wretchedness, the passion and kindness of our Lord God, with many such other – they may in nowise put away the wonderful and the diverse thoughts, fantasies, and images, the which be ministered and printed in their mind by the light of the curiosity of imagination. And all this disobedience is the pain of original sin.' Imagination, then, is not to be exiled but to be controlled. It is to be disciplined so that its deepest potentialities may be realized; it has, in effect, its own irreplaceable use in the approach to mystical experience.

*The Cloud of Unknowing*, as Evelyn Underhill has said, 'represents the first expression in our own tongue of that great mystic tradition of the Christian neo-Platonists which gathered up, remade, and "salted with Christ's salt" all that was best in the spiritual wisdom of the ancient world'. *The Cloud* thus descends in an undeviating line from the mystical experience which we find in the *Confessions* of St Augustine. But there is this difference – the august conception of God's relationship with man which is exemplified by Plotinus and his followers has, in the fourteenth-century English version of mysticism, become tempered by a warm and compassionate humanism. In *The Cloud* we find a humanism that is truly attentive to the needs of humanity, a spirit remote, indeed, from the earthly idealism of the Renaissance. For where Renaissance artists and writers longed to make men into gods, the author of *The Cloud* wants to make men *like* God. And though his book is in many ways a textbook for the instruction of beginners in the spiritual life, it is also a plea for wholeness and unity. It is both a map of life and a description of the journey through it.

The whole of *The Cloud* is shot through with sharp perceptions and earnest intuitions. The author of it is keenly aware of the possibility of his doctrine being misunderstood. For him, prayer is never a substitute for aesthetic delight, never a pseudonym for sensuous ecstasy. Indeed, in his penultimate chapter, he explicitly warns mere seekers after sensation not to attempt to follow his teaching – 'Fleshly janglers, flatterers and blamers,' he says, 'rankers and ronners, and all manner of pinchers, cared I never that they saw this book: for mine intent was never to write such thing to them.' His book is, he declares adamantly, for those who feel 'a very accordance to the effect of this work'. In other words, it is intended for those who are neither deceived by the senses nor swayed by the unruly images of the imagination.

*The Cloud*, in fact, traces carefully and systematically the difficult but by no means impossible journey towards God which will culminate in a direct apprehension of him in the mystical experience. Yet, austere as his teaching is, the author of *The Cloud* always employs clear, colloquial and vivid words and images in which to express his message. His psychology is deft and sensitive, he never forgets how easy it is to be a pseudo-mystic, to be one who mistakes 'consolations in prayer' for true union with God. In such terse phrases as 'nowhere fleshly is everywhere ghostly' and 'short prayer pierceth heaven' he gently repudiates the cloudy symbols of the imagination and the misguided fumblings of the untutored senses. Always he abhors anthropomorphism but even when he does this he uses the most homely images to enliven his exhortations: 'These men will with curiosity of their imagination pierce the planets, and make a hole in the firmament to look in thereat. These men will make a God as them list, and clothe Him full richly in clothes, and set Him in a throne far more curiously than ever was he depicted in this earth . . . Much vanity and falsehood is in their hearts, caused of their curious working. Insomuch, that ofttimes the devil feigneth quaint sounds in their ears, quaint lights and shining in their eyes, and wonderful smells in their noses: and all is but falsehood.'

The author of *The Cloud* is, in effect, as wary as Teresa of Avila was to be of the dangers of 'visions', locutions and delicious fragrances. And, like Teresa also, he never fails to find apt imagery for his teaching. His aim, like hers, is a sanctity based not on division but on unity. But the body, for him, is never simply flesh and feeling; always it adumbrates 'ghostly bemeanings'. 'Therefore,' he says, 'let us pick off the rough bark, and feed us off the sweet kernel.'

If God is not to be imagined in fleshly form, neither is the man of prayer, the aspiring mystic, to succumb to the facile physical expressions of piety. The author of *The Cloud* eschews repeatedly those who 'have it in custom to sit gaping as they would catch flies' or who 'set their eyes in their heads as they were sturdy sheep beaten in the head, and as they should die anon'. He will have no bargaining with the bogus and so constantly tells his disciples to beware of 'religious' people who 'hang their heads on one side as if a worm were in their ears'. Everything must be seemly, decorous and disciplined; those who seek God seriously must not 'row with their arms in time of their speaking, as them needed for to swim over a great water'. What they must have is 'sober and demure bearing of body and mirth in manner.'

Full of warnings and exhortations as it is, however, *The Cloud* is primarily a positive, an affirmative document. The author of it is concerned to pare away all that is superfluous and destructive, and he is concerned to do this because he is intensely eager to express and to share a direct mystical apprehension of God. The heart of his book is contained in the following passage – '. . . at the first time when thou dost it, thou findest but a darkness; and as it were a cloud of unknowing, thou knowest not what, saving that thou feelest in thy will *a naked intent unto God* [italics mine]. This darkness and this cloud is, howsoever thou dost, betwixt thee and thy God, and letteth thee that thou mayest neither see Him clearly by light of understanding in thy reason, nor feel Him in sweetness of love in thine affection. And therefore shape thee to bide in this darkness as long as thou mayest, evermore crying after Him that thou lovest.'

Here is the dark night of the soul, the purging of the affections which we find austerely tabulated in the writing of John of the Cross two centuries later. There is activity and there is passivity – activity because every man has the faculty of free will, and passivity because all men must allow themselves to be receptive to the grace of God. So the author of *The Cloud of Unknowing* continues, 'For if ever thou shalt feel Him or see Him, as it may be here, it behoveth always to be in this cloud in this darkness. And if thou wilt busily travail as I bid thee, I trust in His mercy that thou shalt come thereto.'

As I have suggested, the mystical teaching contained in *The Cloud* is fundamentally positive. It has all the warmth and humanity (rather than mere humanism) which we find later in Teresa of Avila's *Life* and in Traherne's *Centuries of Meditations;* but it also contains the cautions, the clear-sightedness, the abhorrence of false mysticism which illuminate both the prose works and the poetry of John of the Cross. The whole purpose of *The Cloud* is to enable the beginner in prayer to be 'oned with God', to find, in other words, union and wholeness. The teaching which it embodies is stern and relentless yet it is also compassionate and understanding. The author of *The Cloud* divides seekers after God into four groups – Common, Special, Singular and Perfect; yet even the Perfect cannot attain to a lasting union with God in this life for, he says, '. . . one thing I tell thee, that there was never yet pure creature in this life, nor never yet shall be, so high ravished in contemplation and love of the Godhead, that there is not evermore a high and wonderful cloud of unknowing betwixt him and his God.'

The spirituality of fourteenth-century England marks the full flowering of systematization and categorizing. But the systems are still lively and useful, they have not yet hardened either into formalism or mere abstractions. One reason for this liveliness, this reality, is the fact that the feeling and voice of the New Testament pervade the whole of *The Cloud of Unknowing*. Thus we are presented with the familiar but revitalized story of Martha and Mary to illustrate the differences between the active and contemplative lives – 'Lo! friend, all these works, these words, and these gestures, that were shewed betwixt Our Lord and these two sisters, be set in ensample of all actives and all contemplatives that have been since in Holy Church and shall be to the day of doom. For by Mary is understood all contemplatives; for they should conform their living after hers. And by Martha, actives on the same manner; and for the same reason in likeness.'

If, then, *The Cloud* represents that aspect of Western religious experience which stresses mystical union with God as a special vocation, its message is by no means confined simply to those who have dedicated their lives to God by taking the three monastic vows of poverty, chastity and obedience. On the contrary, it is full of wise advice and aphorisms which can be of immense help to those who want to lead a perfect Christian life in the world, whatever their callings or professions. So the author of *The Cloud* warns all those who feel their very existence to be 'a foul stinking lump' not to fall into despair, not to desire to 'unbe'. Every man must have a true sorrow for his sins, yes, but he must also both accept his own nature and be entirely acquiescent to God's dealings with him – '. . . God vouchsafeth for to learn to His ghostly disciples after His well willing and their according ableness in body and in soul, in degree and disposition, ere the time be that they may perfectly be oned with God in perfect charity.'

Charity is of paramount importance, that charity which, as St Paul says, 'envieth not, dealeth not perversely, is not puffed up, is not ambitious, seeketh not her own . . .' This charity, or love of God and one's neighbour, covers all vocations and every aspect of life; it is the *only* means and end of the Christian life. But it is perfected in mystical union with God, that union of personalities in which peace replaces passion and in which the presence of God is felt as a desirable invasion. Such a perfect union can only be achieved through self-mastery and asceticism. The body on its own is undisciplined and treacherous, therefore it must be brought into subjection. Yet *The Cloud* never advocates a severance between the body and the mind but rather a perfect co-ordination or integration of flesh and spirit. And the author of this book only distrusts the imagination, that faculty which works primarily on the findings of the senses, because it has such power to misjudge and mislead. Thus *The Cloud* is careful to differentiate between those who *need* 'consolations in prayer' – 'sweet feelings and weepings' – and those who 'can pick them comfort enough within their own souls, in offering up of this reverent and this meek stirring of love and accordance of will'. And, most important of all, he declares uncompromisingly that 'which of these be holier or more dear with God, one than another, God wots and I not'.

*The Cloud* represents both the grafting of all that was best and most life-giving in neo-Platonism upon the still uncontaminated orthodoxy of the mediaeval Church, and also the flowering of a branch of mysticism that was entirely *English* in character. If we find at the centre of *The Cloud's* message a discretion which had informed Christian spirituality since St Benedict wrote his *Rule* in the sixth century, that discretion has taken on a wholly English dignity and sweetness. A modern American poet, Robert Frost, has described artistic discipline as 'feeling easy in one's harness' and it is just this ease, this good sense which is the keynote of *The Cloud*. Thus in Chapter thirty-two, its author gives wise and essentially *sensible* advice about how to deal with temptations when they come: 'When thou feelest that thou mayest on nowise put them down,' he says, 'cower thou down under them as a caitiff and a coward overcome in battle, and think that it is but folly to thee to strive any longer with them, and therefore thou yieldest thee to God in the hands of thine enemies.' And he goes on, most tenderly, '. . . this meekness obtaineth to have God Himself mightily descending, to venge thee of thine enemies, for to take thee up, and cherishingly dry thine ghostly eyen; as the father doth the child that is in point to perish under the mouths of wild swine or wode biting bears.' But if the message is sweet, the language is never anything but vigorous and direct. This vigour and directness are also noticeable in the forthright and always orthodox theology which supports *The Cloud*. Reason, memory and sensuality are all analysed and assigned to their rightful places. Its author also slips easily into the already established tradition of categories of seekers after God and of the different stages of prayer. He systematizes, yes, but never coldly or from a distance; warmth and compassion glow in every sentence of his book. He wants to eradicate man's waywardness and self-will but never his humanity. The lofty vision towards which he wishes to draw his disciples is a vision made for men, body and soul, not for angels. The qualities essential for the attainment of this vision are 'meekness and charity'. Perfect meekness is exemplified by Mary Magdalen who 'hung up her love and her longing desire in this cloud of unknowing, and learned her to love a thing the which she might not see clearly in this life, by light of understanding in her reason, nor yet verily feel in sweetness of love in her affection'. It is, then, love and not simply sorrow for one's sins which produces perfect meekness. And in a further description of Mary Magdalen, *The Cloud* depicts the mystical experience itself, the direct confrontation of man's nature with God's nature, in words that foreshadow Teresa of Avila's experience of contemplation and Georges Bernanos's portrayal of a young mystic in his novel, *Joy*. The author of *The Cloud* writes – 'But to the sovereignest Wisdom of His Godhead lapped in the dark words of His manhood, thither beheld she with all the love of her heart. For from thence she could not remove, for nothing that she saw nor heard spoken nor done about her; but sat full still in her body, with many a sweet privy and a listy love pressed upon that high cloud of unknowing betwixt her and her God. For one thing I tell thee, that there was never yet pure creature in this life, nor never yet shall be, so high ravished in contemplation and love of the Godhead, that there is not evermore a high and a wonderful cloud of unknowing betwixt him and his God. In this cloud it was that Mary was occupied with many a privy love pressed. And why? Because it was the best and the holiest part of contemplation that may be in this life, and from this part her list not remove for nothing.'

I have quoted this passage at some length for two reasons. First, it illustrates perfectly the state of peace, quiet and recollection that have always been regarded as essential for the fulfilment of contemplative prayer; and, second, it shows how dexterous the author of *The Cloud* is not only in the appropriation of apt metaphor and analogy, but also in the selection of the *mot juste*. We may truly say that words never fail him. It never occurs to him that language might be inadequate in the description of mystical experience; he puts a complete and child-like trust in its power to express both the preliminary stages of prayer and also the heights of contemplation itself. He would certainly agree with St Paul that 'we see now in a glass darkly' but he does not shirk the difficulty of suggesting what it will be like to have the vision of God 'face to face'. He shares with the poet, in fact, that implicit faith which entrusts to language not only the most subtle states of emotion and being but also those experiences which go beyond sensation and ratiocination. He draws down no curtains, retreats into no protective shadows. If he emphasizes 'ardour and selflessness and self-surrender' as absolutely vital in the perfect approach to God, he never ceases to urge those who truly long for divine things to have courage and trust. 'Do thou on,' he says, thus showing the difficult but not impossible balance between activity and passivity in the mystical search for God. And for him, surrender is always a joyful thing, not a loss but a gain.

The generosity of spirit, the emphasis on charity, the firm but never inhuman urge to repent that shine like shafts of sunlight through *The Cloud* recall the warmth, sweetness and directness of an earlier treatise on mystical union. In the twelfth century, Hugh of St Victor, a Canon of St Augustine in Paris, wrote an exquisite dialogue between man and his soul in which, by means of discourse and argument, he presented the beauty and delight of surrender to God. Like the author of *The Cloud*, Hugh of St Victor first stresses the need for repentance and then moves far beyond this into an area of experience where everything is done out of love and not out of fear. He employs the kind of marriage symbolism which many mystical writers have used but, in his work, there is not a trace of cloying sweetness or unsuitable sensuousness. So, at the end of *The Soul's Betrothal Gift*, as the dialogue is called, Hugh of St Victor portrays, with a vividness and simplicity similar to those of *The Cloud*, the soul's possession of and by God: 'Truly it is your beloved that visits you; but he comes invisible, secret, incomprehensible. He comes to touch you, not to be seen by you [like the Holy Ghost of Hopkins's poem who comes 'to brood and sit']. He comes to counsel you not to be understood by you. He comes not to pour his whole self into you, but to offer himself to be tasted; not to fulfil your desire but to draw your love.' This last phrase reminds us of *The Cloud's* lovely line, 'With the drawing of this Love and the voice of this Calling.' Hugh of St Victor continues, 'He offers you some first-fruits of his love; he does not tender you the fullness of completed satisfaction . . . Now in the meantime be you consoled for his absence, inasmuch as you are continually refreshed by his visitation, so that you be not weary.'

If the symbolism of this dialogue is in a different mode and tradition from that of *The Cloud*, its message is nevertheless precisely the same. God may be glimpsed, tasted, touched in this life, but these experiences are fitful and momentary not sustained. Only in the next world can we

see 'face to face' permanently. In this world we move in a region of
signs and symbols and God became man so that these signs might be
flesh and blood not mere abstractions. Thus, the author of *The Cloud*
and Hugh of St Victor both make the Incarnation, the Word made
Flesh, the centre of their spiritual teaching. And if *The Cloud* distrusts
the idle 'curiosity' of man's imagination, it does not repudiate imagination itself. It is an invaluable step towards God in the early stages of
prayer although, in the final mystical union, it is the will, 'all holy
desires', which plays the chief part.

The main force of *The Cloud* lies both in its exalted presentation of
man's relationship with God and also in its entirely concrete, down-to-
earth and always precise imagery. If there is a 'cloud of unknowing'
above our finite beings, there is always firm ground beneath our
physical natures. The author of *The Cloud*'s achievement is to have
made that ground flower and flourish by means of a language subtle
enough to suggest those experiences which go beyond words, and
inventive and variable enough to make the austere life of prayer not
only alive but also dramatic and desirable.

# 4. THE VALUE OF SUFFERING

## Julian of Norwich

---

*The suffering hidden under gentleness.*
LAWRENCE DURRELL – On First Looking into Loeb's Horace

VAN GOGH, A painter who perhaps suffered more intensely than most other modern artists, said, in a letter to his sister, some very striking things about the relationship between art and religion: 'Sometimes art seems to be something very sublime and as you say very sacred . . . the crux of the question is that not everybody thinks about it in this way and that those who feel something of it and let themselves be carried away by it have to suffer so much – in the first place on account of not being understood, and quite as much because so often our inspiration is inadequate . . . There are times when it is far from clear to us that art should be something good and holy.' This clearly perceived but tentative assertion of the relation between religion and art, together with Van Gogh's emphasis on the necessity of suffering in the creation of a work of art, reminds us of the mystical teaching which Julian of Norwich based on a vision of Christ's suffering and death. Like Van Gogh, she saw that pain was inseparable from mystical union with God and, like him in his paintings, she surrounded, without concealing, the fact of pain with shining images and a radiant light. And since to suffer with complete submission demands a deep simplicity of heart, she shared Van Gogh's childlike sense of devotion and dedication. Just as he, in the silent medium of paint, could give a chair or a sunflower a vehemence of continuous creative energy, she could see in a hazel nut the eternal act of creation. She says in Chapter five of her *Revelations of Divine Love,* 'Also in this he [Christ] shewed [me] a little thing, the quantity of an hazel-nut, in the palm of my hand; and it was as round as a ball. I looked thereupon with eye of my understanding and thought: "What may this be?" And it was generally answered thus: "It is all that is made." I marvelled how it might last, for methought it might suddenly have fallen to naught for little[ness]. And I was answered in my understanding: "It lasteth and ever shall

41

for God loveth it." And so all thing hath the Being by the love of God.'

Thus, this fourteenth-century English anchoress saw in a hazel nut what Blake, several centuries later, was to see in a grain of sand. It is a vision in which image and meaning perfectly fuse, in which insight and love are inextricably linked. The concrete object is, in fact, the *raison d'être* of the mystical experience. But this joyful vision is found at the heart of suffering and just as Blake said 'Joy impregnates, sorrow brings forth,' so Julian of Norwich moves from her flash of insight into the significance of the hazel nut to an approach to God by means of the sufferings of Christ. At the centre of her mystical experience is the Incarnation of Christ and she achieves direct union with God by herself sharing in all that the Incarnation signifies.

Where there is accepted suffering there is always also compassion, and the keynote of the *Revelations* is sweetness and intimacy both with Jesus Christ and with all mankind. When she is presented with a vision of Christ's head, Julian says, 'In all this I was greatly stirred in charity to mine even-Christians, that they might see and know the same that I saw: for I would it were comfort to them.' If we compare this acceptance, surrender and desire to *give*, with Van Gogh's tempestuous rebellion and compassion, we can see, I believe, one of the essential ways in which mystical experience differs from artistic experience. In Julian of Norwich and-Van Gogh we have two deeply emotional, passionately committed people, but where Julian was content to let God work upon her own human nature, Van Gogh felt that only he himself, as a human being and as a man of genius, could work upon the visions he experienced and communicate them by means of painting. Quite as much as Julian he wanted to share, but the artist's desire to share is always a more active, more one-sided affair than the religious visionary's handing over of his awareness of God to other men. Van Gogh is an extreme case, of course, but *all* artists communicate impulsively rather than surrender with acceptance or resignation. Acceptance, in this context, is the key word in this whole inquiry, for where a necessary part of the mystic's task is 'waiting on God', the artist feels that everything must be done by himself and that 'dark nights' or barren periods are to be suffered rather than accepted. A painter or a poet, for example, can never really believe that his uncreative periods will lead him to new insights in his later work. As Auden has said, poets only feel they are poets when they have just completed a poem which they know to be good. During their bad times, indeed, artists are usually incapable of remembering even what it felt like to paint a picture or write a poem. With the mystics it is quite otherwise. Their sense of union with God is always recognized by them as a surprise, a gratuitous gift, something given not sought out. One 'touch' of God is sufficient to last a lifetime. For poets or painters, however, satisfaction with a completed work of art never lasts for long; always they must go on, creating more, discovering more; and there is good reason to suppose that every act of creation is a groping forward, a test not of strength but of truth, a movement, in fact (though few artists today would use such words or admit such a condition) towards ultimate reality or God. Art, then, is not a substitute for religion but an intensely passionate activity starting from the circumference of a circle whose centre is God; and this centre burns and transmutes. Thus it is not surprising that 'visionary' artists, those painters and poets who have tried simply through the medium of art to get as close to that centre as possible, have suffered so much and even, at times, gone mad.

These statements sound extreme and absolute and will, perhaps, swiftly arouse argument and opposition. Critics will leap to the dispute and cite countless artists whose lives were apparently serene and whose art approached a state of calm, stillness and wholeness not too remote from the transcribed visions of the most articulate mystics. There is certainly some truth in such a statement but I would, nevertheless, counter it with one tentative suggestion: there is, I think, a kind of calm and careful art which, within the limits of a deliberately constricted form, achieves a genuinely autonomous poise and power. Often such art is extremely secular. But where it achieves perfection, that perfection is often a matter of form only; as an example I would cite the abstract paintings of Ben Nicholson in which all human content has been removed and where one is left only with exquisite abstractions. Such a world of forms may satisfy the Platonic seeker after reality but it cannot for long sustain a complete vision of beauty or truth in the eyes and minds of other men.

At first sight, a world like Ben Nicholson's, in which 'the form is the reality', might seem to approach and express mystical experience more closely than those art forms or styles whose human and physical content is the most immediately noticeable thing about them. Myself, I do not hold this view and for the following reason: the centre of Western Christian mysticism has always been the Incarnation, Christ both as man and God. Abstract art has allegiances not with such a tradition but with the mystical experience as related in Plato's

*Symposium* or in the writings of his later followers, the neo-Platonists. A sealed-off world of perfect form has thus little in common with the struggles and surrenders of even the most austere Christian mystics; and it has little in common with their experiences because in abstract art, as in Platonism, so much is omitted.

Paradoxically, my detailed demonstration of the differences between artists and mystics is now leading me in the direction of their affinities. I am inclined to think, in fact, that just as reason fails and intuition takes command both in the experience and expression of mysticism, so sudden insights, rather than painstaking arguments, often reveal most vividly some of the likenesses between artists and mystics. Briefly, it is *because* artists approach what one can only and vaguely call reality in a different way from the mystics, that they can come near to the same conclusions; the differences, in effect, are in the means not in the end. And this whole subject is, I believe, more amenable to 'hints and guesses' than to rigid laws or coldly reasoned arguments. Insight and apt illustration may yield more fruitful results than generalization and a desire to formulate laws.

All these reflections may seem far from the mystical writings of Dame Julian of Norwich, but I hope that by laying likenesses and contrasts side by side I may illuminate not only her work but also the whole question of mystical experience. Just as one colour laid alongside another may reveal the unique quality of each, so, perhaps, the comparison of a particular artist with a particular mystic may throw into relief the especial message and achievement of each. What Julian of Norwich and Van Gogh share is a sense of the necessity of suffering and it is this sense, combined with an extreme yet uncontrived deftness in the discovery of apt imagery, that I want to examine in Julian's *Revelations of Divine Love.*

Paul Molinari, who is probably the greatest living authority on Julian of Norwich, has referred, in the following words, to three specific elements in her revelations or 'shewings': 'For a right appreciation of Julian's doctrine on prayer and contemplation it is useful and even necessary to consider not only the content of the Revelations but also her spiritual attitude before the time of the Shewings. First . . . there exists a real continuity between Julian's later doctrine on prayer and contemplation and the ideas and desires which typify her spiritual attitude before the Revelations. Secondly, and this is of great importance, knowledge of Julian's spiritual antecedents will eventually help towards formation of judgment concerning the divine origin of her

Revelations . . . Finally, Julian herself seems to consider some knowledge of her spiritual state necessary for those who wish to understand the true meaning of the Revelations. She says: "I desired three graces by the gift of God. The first was to have mind of the Passion of Christ. The second was a bodily sickness. The third, to have, of God's gift, three wounds." '

This passage is useful and explanatory. However, where Molinari is concerned primarily with the validity of Julian's experience and teaching, I am concerned with her vision, the language in which she expressed it, and her imagery.

With the unknown author of *The Cloud of Unknowing*, Julian of Norwich shares a directness, a remarkably flexible colloquial idiom, and a radiant generosity of spirit. And yet, simply because the author of *The Cloud* is anonymous and therefore a rather remote and shadowy figure, Julian has more in common with Teresa of Avila than with any of the mystics of her own century. Perhaps it is her feminine tenderness, her childlike audacity and her very personal and intimate approach to God that constantly remind one of Teresa's autobiography. Both women have a warmth that never degenerates into sentimentality, and a boldness that is too innocent to be mistaken for impertinence.

Dame Julian has also something of Traherne's confidence and accessibility. But there is this difference between her and the seventeenth-century mystic – where Traherne based his teaching on joy and delight in the created world, Julian found hers on a participation in the sufferings of Christ. Yet there is nothing masochistic about her life, and nothing pathological. The ease with which she communicates her experiences is both the ease of a completely balanced person and also the assurance of a born writer. Directness is, after all, an innate gift not a literary skill which can be acquired or learnt.

One of the signs of Julian's sanity and clear-sightedness is manifested in the following statement which she makes in her ninth chapter: 'All this [vision of Christ's Passion] was shewed by three [ways]: that is to say, by bodily sight, and by word formed in my understanding, and by ghostly sight. But the ghostly sight I cannot nor may not shew it as openly nor as fully as I would.' By 'understanding' Julian often means imagination, as she shows when she says, 'One time mine understanding was led down into the sea-ground, and there I saw hills and dales green, seeming as it were moss-be-grown, with wrack and gravel. Then I understood thus: that if a man or woman were under the broad water, if he might have sight of God so as God is with a man continually, he should be safe in body and soul, and take no harm; and overpassing, he should have more solace and comfort than all this world can tell.'

God, then, is to be found in all things, just as Traherne found him. For Julian, God is first immanent, informing and upholding all created being, and only afterwards transcendent, that is to say, above all things. Her relationship with God is therefore an intensely personal one – 'he [God] will be seen and he will be sought: he will be abided and he will be trusted' and again, '. . . the continual seeking of the soul pleaseth God full greatly . . . The seeking, with faith, hope, and charity, pleaseth our Lord, and the finding pleaseth the soul and fulfilleth it with joy.'

As I have said, Julian, when she speaks of her understanding often means her imaginative faculty. She knows nothing of the careful philosophical distinctions of a John of the Cross; yet she is as fond of enumeration, cataloguing and categorizing as any other fourteenth- or sixteenth-century mystic. Her writing, however, differs from that of Walter Hilton or the author of *The Cloud* in that where their teaching and message are essentially discursive (though filled with images for purposes of illustration and analogy), Julian's are of their very nature pictorial and often vividly and tangibly physical. She is, in many ways, more like a painter than a writer; she sees pictures and communicates them by means of language. But where many visionary painters have often created an entirely imaginary, sometimes apocalyptic world to express their visions, Julian's descriptions of hers are essentially realistic, and they are realistic because they are based on the actual sufferings and Passion of Christ. Thus she describes the Crucifixion with an extraordinary vigour and sensuousness: 'For that same time that our Lord and blessed Saviour died upon the Rood, it was a dry, hard wind, and wondrous cold, as to my sight, and what time the precious blood was bled out of the sweet body that might pass therefrom, yet there dwelled a moisture in the sweet flesh of Christ, as it was shewed. Bloodlessness and pain dried within; and blowing of wind and cold coming from without met together in the sweet body of Christ . . . And though this pain was bitter and sharp, it was full long lasting, as to my sight, and painfully dried up all the lively spirits of Christ's flesh . . . And when I said it seemed to me as if he had been seven nights dead, it meaneth that the sweet body was so discoloured, so dry, so clogged, so deathly, and so piteous, as [if] he had been seven nights dead, continually dying.'

Such a description as this, which is much more detailed than any of the accounts of the Crucifixion in the Gospels, is reminiscent in its realism and compassion of many fifteenth-century paintings of the same subject. In its emphasis on suffering and on Christ's manhood, it also adumbrates David Gascoyne's *Miserere* sequence of poems. Descriptions like this one, however, are by no means the whole, or even perhaps the most vital part, of the *Revelations*. As I have suggested, Julian's teaching (that teaching which both grows out of and supports her 'shewings') is formal and categorical. Thus she says, when speaking of her own approach to her vision – 'There are two workings that may be seen in this Vision: the one is seeking, the other is beholding. The seeking is common – that every soul may have with his grace . . . It is God's will that we have three things in our seeking :— The first is that we seek wilfully and busily . . . gladly and merrily without unskilful heaviness and vain sorrow. The second is that we abide him steadfastly for his love, without grudging and striving against him, to our life's end . . . The third is that we trust in him mightily of full sure faith, for it is his will. We know that he shall appear suddenly and blissfully to all that be his lovers.'

In this passage, Julian makes clear that the experience of mystical union with God is a special vocation, a gratuitous gift. And yet, so great is her generosity and humility, she is prepared to affirm that anyone who really longs for such an experience will be granted it. There is no sense of election or arbitrary choice in her teaching; like all orthodox Western mystics she asserts the necessity of reciprocity, of man *seeking* God, in the union of God and man.

Continuing her listing and categorizing, but never doing so in a cold, abstract way, Julian, later in her *Revelations*, speaks of three essentials for the complete submission of the mind and heart to God. These essentials or conditions are 'contrition, compassion and longing after God'. And the emphasis here is always on activity, an activity based on trust, humility and charity. So, with a daringly adroit handling of mediaeval scholastic theology she says in Chapter fifty-four, after reflecting on the presence of God in the soul which is in a state of grace, 'And I saw no difference betwixt God and our Substance : but as it were all God; and yet mine understanding took that our Substance is in God : that is to say, that God is God, and our Substance is a creature in God.' Julian is careful in this last sentence to qualify her bold statement and thus free herself from any charge of pantheism.

Above all, the *Revelations* are a demonstration, a personal avowal of the power of divine love and mercy. As Julian says, '. . . love suffereth never to be without pity', thus foreshadowing Bernanos's cry, in his novel *Joy*, 'Can anything go beyond pity?' And again, she declares, 'Marvellous and solemn is the place where the Lord dwelleth, and therefore he willeth that we readily answer to his gracious touching, more rejoicing in his whole love than sorrowing in our often fallings.' Like the author of *The Cloud*, Julian insists that 'perfect meekness' springs from love not simply from contrition. And in the above passage she uses, as so many other mystics have done, the sense of touch to denote the union of God with man.

But perhaps the boldest and most beautiful of Julian's celebrations of divine love is shown in her chapters on the *motherhood* of God. She writes, 'To the property of Motherhood belongeth kind love, wisdom and knowing . . . thus he [Christ] is our mother in kind by the working of Grace in the lower part for love of the higher part. And he willeth that we know this: for he will have all our love fastened to him. And in this I saw that all our duty that we owe, by God's bidding, to Fatherhood and Motherhood, for [reason of] God's Fatherhood and Motherhood is fulfilled in true loving of God; which blessed love Christ worketh in us. And this was shewed in all [the Revelations] and especially in the high plenteous words where he saith: "It is I that thou lovest." '

Julian makes this belief even more vivid when she compares Christ's love with that of an ordinary human mother: 'The mother may give her child suck [of] her milk, but our precious Mother, Jesus, he may feed us with himself, and doeth it, full courteously and full tenderly, with the Blessed Sacrament that is precious food of very life . . . The mother may lay the child tenderly to her breast, but our tender Mother, Jesus, he may homely lead us into his blessed breast, by his sweet open side, and shew therein part of the Godhead and the joys of heaven . . .' Intimate and 'homely' as Julian's approach to God is, it is always also 'courteous' and reverent. Something of the knightly courtesy which we find in so much mediaeval secular poetry is strikingly evident in her whole treatment of the spiritual life. Her Lord is her 'darling' but he is also 'dearworthy', 'blessed', and 'almighty'. This attitude, whose motive power is true charity, is expressed with absolute conviction and simplicity at the beginning of Chapter eighty-three of the *Revelations:* 'I had in part,' says Julian, 'touching, sight, and feeling in three properties of God, in which the strength and effect of all the Revelation standeth . . . The properties are these: Life, Love, and Light. In life is marvellous homeliness, and in love is gentle courtesy, and in light is endless kindhood.' For her, nothing is incommunicable, nothing too elusive to be pinned down in bright images.

Conrad Pepler, in an examination of the writings of Julian of Norwich and a number of other fourteenth-century English mystics, has made some interesting remarks about the element of poetic experience in their work: '. . . all these writers,' he says, 'were poets of some degree and even when they are attempting to describe the "heights" beyond words and beyond any human form – even beyond the conceptual affirmations of human reason itself – they express themselves with a freedom of imagery and right use of word and phrase that show willy-nilly their imaginative spirit. They have not, in fact, denied their own nature, nor reached a speechless state of identification with the purity of God in which all senses and sensible images are rejected. Their true anchor is the humanity of Christ, which of course extends itself in the liturgy of the Church centred round the Mass. In this way we can see that the essential mystical experience, this "feeling" of the work of the Holy Ghost, although it be in the high point of the soul, is shared in some way by the whole man through his interior senses.'

These words seem of particular relevance to the writing of Julian. The sense of wholeness which is so apparent in her work springs from an undivided personality, a nature which is fulfilling itself not denying itself. The sufferings which she depicts so vividly are an essential part of this wholeness; far from diminishing her, they completed her. She accepted suffering *as* suffering, there is not a vestige of masochism in her work, nor is there any flinching away from pain. 'The problem of pain' would have meant nothing to her simply because she saw, in the Incarnation and Passion of Christ, both the explanation and apotheosis of pain. And she recognized this not by dialectic or logic but by intuition and affinity. It is this affinity, this sympathy, in the Greek sense, that takes every trace of complacency out of her affirmation that 'we shall say all with one voice: "Lord, blessed mayst thou be, for it is thus: it is well; and now see we verily that all-thing is done as it was then ordained before that anything was made." ' '

# 5. THE FRUITFUL WATERS

## A study of the Life of Teresa of Avila

---

*. . . He who wishes to see a Vision, a perfect Whole,*
*Must see it in its Minute Particulars, Organized.*
BLAKE – Jerusalem

IN CHAPTER NINE of her autobiography, Teresa of Avila tells us that her imagination was weak and that she had great difficulty in conjuring up images. She says, 'I had so little aptitude for picturing things in my mind that, if I did not actually see a thing, I could make no use at all of my imagination in the way that others do who can induce recollection by calling up mental images.' This is an innocent, humble remark but it is not a true one. Of all the articulate mystics Teresa has, perhaps, the greatest skill in finding analogies and selecting metaphors. She is never at a loss for a comparison or a simile. Her whole approach to the spiritual life is a repudiation of the abstract. It seems strange, then, that someone who in other ways had self-knowledge to such a rare degree, should have had so little awareness of the strength of her own creative imagination. But perhaps this particular lack of awareness is simply another aspect of Teresa's enchanting unselfconsciousness. Self-knowledge she possessed, certainly, but not that twisted, narrow and superficial self-knowledge which is only a euphemism for introspection and selfconsciousness.

Teresa's *Life* was written at the suggestion of a spiritual director but, as we read it, we quickly realize that she *enjoyed* writing it and, indeed, was compelled to write it not by an external order but by an inner compulsion. It is the story of her life and more particularly of her journey towards union with God. In the book Teresa describes, by means of images and in great detail, the most difficult thing any writer can attempt – namely, contact with God in the mystical experience. The *Life* also contains accounts of her childhood and youth and all the practical difficulties which attended her foundation of many convents for the Order of Discalced Carmelites. But it is the personal, spiritual part of the book which is its heart and its *raison d'être*.

This autobiography is quite without solemnity or sententiousness.

It is candid, humorous, loving. It attracts by its charm and honesty as well as by the splendour of the vision which it embodies. It casts a spell that no merely secular document could cast so potently. The *Life* is also, in a way, a lonely story. It is lonely because, surrounded by friends and admirers as Teresa was, she knew that the discovery of God first meant a struggle within herself, a conquest of her passions, a battle which no one could fight for her. She had a number of confessors and spiritual advisers throughout her life, it is true, but there were times when she could find no one who really understood her or who was strict enough with her. She suffered from this lack and she says of it, '. . . I found no other guide – no confessor I mean – who understood me, though I sought one for the next twenty years. This did me great harm, for I very often fell back and might have been utterly lost, and a guide would at least have helped me to avoid the frequent risks I ran of offending God.'

In Teresa of Avila we find all the austerity and all the fervour which are so characteristic of the religious spirit of sixteenth-century Spain – that spirit which informs the passionate, uplifted ascetics of El Greco's paintings who seem rather to embody a vision than themselves to be struggling to attain one. Like St John of the Cross, Teresa depicts the way of purgation, the dark nights of the senses and the spirit. Yet where St John is analytical, she draws together, where he explains, she presents an experience. Her psychology is quite as subtle as his even if, being expressed in entirely personal terms, it sounds more like simple common sense.

But what is original in Teresa is her warmth, magnanimity and joy. If her visions ennobled her, they also made her more human, more compassionate. She wishes to reveal everything, not out of pride but out of humility. And she finds her humility in the tenderness of her friendship with God. She talks constantly of her sinful state, of her unworthiness, yet she never falls into despair. She can talk to God intimately without ever losing the sense of His majesty and glory – 'How true it is that You suffer those who will not suffer You to be with them! What a good friend You are, O my Lord, to comfort and endure them, and wait for them to rise to Your condition, and yet in the meantime to be patient of the state they are in!'

As I have suggested already, Teresa had a powerful and delicate imagination, even though she disclaimed that power. This is what brings her in line with the poets. When she describes a spiritual state, she never uses the cool, conceptual language of philosophy. On the contrary, she always finds analogies for these states in concrete things. And, far from feeling the poverty of concrete imagery, she positively rejoices in it. She knows that the complete union of the soul with God is ineffable but, with an exquisite temerity, she attempts at least to penetrate that mystery. But she is most prolific of images in her descriptions of the various stages of prayer which culminate in that union. An examination of some of this imagery will reveal not only its appropriateness but also its simplicity. In discussing the 'prayer of quiet', for example, Teresa says, 'The will must quietly and wisely understand that we cannot deal violently with God; and that our efforts are like great logs of wood indiscriminately piled on, which will only put out the spark,' and again, 'A few straws laid on with humility – and they will be less than straws if it is we who lay them on – are more effectual here, and will be of more use in kindling the fire than any number of faggots made of what seems to us the most learned argument, which will put it out in a moment.' Still speaking of the same kind of prayer, she turns to a different image but a no less vivid or simple one, 'A child that has grown up and whose body has formed does not shrink and become small again. But this may, by the Lord's will, happen to the soul.' Always the language is homely, the images familiar.

To obtain some idea of the directness, simplicity and wholeness of Teresa's approach to prayer, we should recall what she says when describing a later stage of it – 'How what is called union takes place and what it is, I cannot tell. It is explained in *mystical theology*, but I cannot use the proper terms; I cannot understand what *mind* is, or how it differs from *soul* or *spirit*. They all seem one to me, though the soul sometimes leaps out of itself like a burning fire that has become one whole flame and increases with great force. The flame leaps very high above the fire. Nevertheless it is not a different thing, but the same flame which is in the fire.' Like Aquinas, Teresa loathes anything that savours of Manichaeism, anything that suggests a fundamental severance between the body and the soul.

In all her descriptions of the mystical approach to God, she manifests a deep generosity, an all-embracing charity; she does not wish to hug her visions to herself or to escape into a private world of self-made peace. She wants illumination for others as well as for herself. With further striking examples of exact imagery, she demonstrates her complete understanding of other people's difficulties – 'The soul perceives man's blindness to the nature of pleasure, and his failure to realize that even in this life it purchases trials and disquiet. What rest-lessness! What discontent! What useless labour! Not only is the soul aware of the cobwebs that cover it, but the sunlight is so bright that it sees every little speck of dust besides, even the most minute. However hard it may have laboured to perfect itself, therefore, once the sun really strikes it, it views itself as most unclean. It is like the water in a glass, which seems quite clear when the sun is not shining on it, but, if it does, is seen to be full of tiny specks. This comparison is quite literal.'

But it is not only in the handling of various and separated similes or metaphors that Teresa displays her greatest skill in depicting the total life of prayer. It is her sustained and brilliant conception of the Four Waters, or the four stages towards mystical union with God, which perhaps most vividly demonstrates the fertility of her invention and the comprehensive nature of her imagination. The soul is seen as a garden and the Four Waters are the four ways in which it is purified, nourished and brought to fruition. Teresa describes these Waters thus: 'Now let us see how this garden is to be watered, so that we may understand what we have to do, and what labour it will cost us, also whether the gain will outweigh the effort, or how long it will take. It seems to me that the garden may be watered in four different ways. Either the water must be drawn from a well, which is very laborious; or by a water-wheel and buckets, worked by a windlass – I have some-times drawn it in this way, which is less laborious than the other, and brings up more water – or from a stream or a spring, which waters the ground much better, for the soil then retains more moisture and needs watering less often, which entails far less work for the gardener; or by heavy rain, when the Lord waters it Himself without any labour of ours; and this is an incomparably better method than all the rest.'

Teresa goes on to examine each of the Waters in elaborate detail. 'Beginners in prayer,' she says, 'are those who draw the water up out of the well.' These beginners must 'pay no attention to what they see or hear' but 'meditate on the life of Christ'. There is much activity in this stage and, clearly, the imagination plays its part in formulating images and so keeping the mind intent on the idea of Christ. But there are numerous 'torments' and 'temptations' too, Teresa declares. Yet God helps the gardener and Teresa continues, most skilfully enlarging her central image, 'He shows us a great favour when He grants us a desire to dig in his garden.' Full of her characteristically sensible psychology, she urges beginners in prayer not to be discouraged by 'aridities', 'disturbances' or 'distractions'. She never, however, advocates a quietist attitude; she may say 'if the well yields no water we can put none in', but she also adds, 'It is true too that we must not be careless, and fail to see when there is some there.'

In her explication of the purpose of the First Water, Teresa omits nothing; she exhorts the beginner not necessarily to use 'set prayers' but to approach God with 'such words as express its desires and its needs'. She also stresses the paramount necessity of humility and the humble and grateful acceptance of 'favours' from God. And though she emphasizes activity, she also forbids the soul to attempt, simply through its own efforts, 'to pass on and raise his spirit to taste of pleasures that are denied him'. If he does this, she implies, he will lose his state of calm and recollection and so fail to reach the next stage towards union with God which is sometimes called 'the prayer of quiet'. The soul, then, is not to strain for union with God or to demand union with him as a right. But if God does grant this union, Teresa says, 'we know it immediately'. As with Augustine's experience at Ostia (Teresa, incidentally, often refers to Augustine), there will be no 'dark riddle of a similitude' but a contact direct, immediate and unmistakable.

In her discourse on the Four Waters, Teresa never abandons her imagery. Whether she is talking of the most elementary distractions and temptations or speaking of the sublime majesty of God, she adheres always to language, never doubting its efficacy in making her meaning clear. Yet she never tries to oversimplify complex things, never attempts to by-pass difficulties either in the life of prayer itself or in the effort to describe that life. Her writings shed a radiant and unique light but they illuminate only what is unwaveringly orthodox. Sin, penance, self-mastery, the need for grace, the power of the sacraments, the wisdom of spiritual guides – the reality of these things is stressed again and again in her spiritual writing. Like the wise author of *The Cloud of Unknowing*, and like John of the Cross with his piercing intellect, she understands human nature in all its frailty and all its aspirations; but she understands these things because she first understands herself. Her humour springs from this very understanding and it denotes not only a remarkably well-balanced character but also a witty and engaging one. People who do not know her work well tend to think of Teresa of Avila either as an advocate of stern penances or else as a slightly hysterical person whose physical sickness was the cause of her 'visions' and levitations. She suffered certainly and suffered very deeply, but there is absolutely nothing hysterical or pathological about her spiritual life. Throughout her autobiography she repeatedly warns seekers after God to beware of visions, locutions and other physical phenomena. The warmth and intensity of her own temperament made her peculiarly susceptible to physical manifestations yet she herself so disliked and distrusted these manifestations that she begged her nuns to hold her down when she felt her body might rise from the ground, and she did this simply because she detested any attention being drawn to herself.

I have stressed the wisdom of Teresa's advice, advice which becomes more urgent and detailed as her exposition of the Four Waters proceeds. She constantly makes remarks such as the following – 'It is very important at the beginning, when we embark on prayer, not to be frightened by our own thoughts' and 'There is another very common temptation, and that is, when one begins to enjoy the calm and fruit of prayer, to wish everyone else to be very spiritual too.' She never forgets that 'constant, mutual charity' which both leads to complete oneness with God and is also fully realized in it. When she examines the Second Water, Teresa explains that though 'the memory and imagination . . . help the will to make itself more and more capable of enjoying this great blessing' they are also sometimes 'a great hindrance to it'. These faculties are not in themselves a hindrance but only so because, since the Fall, they have become unruly and hard to govern.

Teresa is not a philosopher, she makes no stern and uncompromising definitions. When she uses words like 'memory', 'understanding' and 'intellect', they are not rigid counters but rather useful approximations. Thus when she says of this second stage of prayer that 'The intellect now works very gently and draws up a great deal more water than it drew from the well,' she does not appear to be making any clear distinction here between 'intellect' and 'memory'. She works by intuition and it is our own intuitive response she demands, not our cold calculations. So, in a bold and lively image, she explains that God now 'wants us to understand that He understands us, and to realize the effect of His presence' and that 'He seems to be filling up a void in it [the soul], which was scooped out by our sins.' There is great sweetness and consolation in this Second Water for now, Teresa says, 'the trees begin to grow heavy with blossom and afterwards with fruit, and . . . the carnations and other flowers begin to smell sweet'. Yet there is sometimes aridity too when 'the soul feels itself to be anything but a garden' and when 'everything appears to be dry, and there is no water to keep things green'.

There is nothing cloying or sentimental about this garden imagery;

the images are alive and active and they are formulated and put to work by a luminous intelligence and a bracing wit. Teresa resembles the poet in that, like him, she demonstrates best both the fertility and organizing power of her imagination in her manipulation of imagery.

This Second Water is what some other mystical writers have called 'the prayer of quiet' and it is, explains Teresa, 'a little spark of true love for Him which the Lord begins to kindle in the soul.' In this stage, she continues, 'all that the soul has to do . . . is merely to be calm and make no noise'. And it is in this Second Water that the intellect begins to be difficult and disorderly. Great concentration and serenity are now required, the kind of concentration which the poet feels as an almost active force within him before the poem is written. The intellect must now be, for a little, in abeyance, for, as Teresa declares, 'once it begins to compose speeches and draw up arguments, especially if these are clever, it will soon imagine that it is doing important work'. But the intellect is only fitfully in abeyance although it is the will, according to Teresa, which, in this second stage, is liable to make 'a better thanksgiving'. This is also the time of great trials and temptations; courage is demanded and also humility. And we must be grateful for and secure in the 'favours' God grants us when we reach this stage. 'A certain security,' says Teresa, 'combined with humility and fear for our salvation, immediately expels servile fear from the soul, and puts in its place a much stronger growth, which springs from faith. Then we see that an entirely disinterested love of God is arising in us, and we desire spells of solitude, the better to enjoy this new blessing.'

This might well be a description of the poet's state of mind and, indeed, much of Teresa's psychology of prayer is equally applicable to the psychology of making poems. One must not, however, carry the comparison between the person of prayer and the poet too far since there are many decided differences. Where the man of prayer lays himself open to the movements and will of God, the poet *prepares* himself to make the poem or, more precisely, to be the channel through which the poem will arrive. There is more activity in the poet than in the mystic, although some passivity is obviously also essential to the poet. With the true mystic, who has passed beyond the ascetic training of the 'beginner' in prayer, the activity which he experiences may be said to be the direct action of God.

In the Third Water the soul moves into a state that is passive and peaceful but without in any way being merely quietist. Teresa describes it thus – 'the faculties of the soul are asleep, not entirely lost nor yet entirely conscious of how they are working. The pleasure, sweetness, and delight are incomparably more than in the previous state, for the water of grace has risen to the soul's neck, and it is powerless, knowing neither how to advance nor to retreat; what it wants is to enjoy its very great glory.' She follows this audacious image with another equally daring one – 'It is like the man with the funeral candle in his hand, on the point of dying the death he desires.'

It is noteworthy that, in describing this stage, Teresa refers to the soul's great desire to speak of its joy, and in making this point tells how one such soul (almost certainly herself) was moved to speak in the forms of conventional verse: 'I know someone who, although no poet, yet suddenly composed some stanzas, full of feeling, which well expressed her pain. They were not the work of her intellect. But for the deeper enjoyment of that blessing which gave her such sweet pain, she complained of it to God.'

There is pain but it is felt as 'sweet'. There is also less sense of *struggle* than in the Second Water; as Teresa puts it – 'There is the will, alone and abiding in great peace, while the understanding and the memory, on the other hand, are so free that they can attend to business or do works of charity.' There is no escape, no discord. But there is still suffering and this suffering is usually caused, even in the third stage, by the unruly movements of the imagination – 'The memory necessarily remains free, together with the imagination, but when they are left alone, it is marvellous to see what havoc they can make, and how they throw everything into disorder.' In discussing this Third Water, Teresa makes clear that it is the human will, 'the greater part' of the soul, which is at peace both with itself and with God; but, she says, 'the memory and the imagination make such war on it [the will] that it cannot prevail against them', while 'the intellect gives the soul no help whatever in dealing with the imagination'. She is as adamant as St John of the Cross in stressing the dangers and delusions of the imagination yet, at the same time, she never doubts its power to express, with the utmost subtlety and fidelity, not only the stages towards union with God but also that very union itself. Like Augustine, she teaches that images must, in complete mystical union, be in abeyance but, like him again, she only relinquishes temporarily the uses of the imagination, she does not repudiate them. And she herself leans on the imagination with complete confidence when she transcribes her own direct contact with God.

The Fourth Water, or complete union with God, is a gratuitous gift. We attain it 'not through our merits, but only by the goodness of God'. We cannot take God by storm or force our wills upon him. Yet we must not be entirely passive in this stage. What we can do by our own efforts is to prepare ourselves for this sublime union and we can only do this by possessing that charity which 'beareth all things, believeth all things, hopeth all things, endureth all things'. This fourth stage, this ecstasy which is the central subject-matter of every mystical writer, has nothing to do with the senses, declares Teresa – 'there is no power left in the body – and the soul possesses none – by which this joy can be communicated'. But this conviction does not prevent her from attempting to describe her ecstasy, and her descriptions are vivid, graphic and immensely detailed. God, she explains, rests in the soul and the soul 'understands by not understanding'. There is no mere theory in Teresa's writing, no detached analysis; she is, on the contrary, presenting her own most intimate and elevated experiences. 'In this way,' she says, 'some hours may be – and are – spent in prayer. For once the two faculties have begun to grow drunk on the taste of this wine, they are very ready to give themselves up again in order to enjoy some more. Then they keep company with the will, and the three rejoice together.' The soul now 'conceives itself to be near God, and . . . is left with such a conviction that it cannot possibly help believing'.

There is nothing wild, nothing emotional about all this. Teresa questions and tests every flutter of feeling, every movement of the passions. Much of her *Life* is concerned with pointing out the dangers of false mysticism and of seeking out mystical experience not to find God but to obtain some private and sterile satisfaction. Much of the *Life* also deals with the wiles of the devil, the treatment of temptation, and the necessity of regarding 'visions', levitations and 'lights' with extreme suspicion. Teresa is careful to indicate that the soul should take no notice of these things, so that if they are from God they will do their work unimpeded, while if they are diabolic, they will have no power to harm. She is interested only in the end, not the means. The titillation of the senses is no part of her experience of God. However, as I have said, she was acutely sensitive and consequently often had to endure sensuous raptures; but she always endured them rather than enjoyed them. She did not, nevertheless, distrust the senses for Puritanical or Manichaean reasons. God had made them, so they must, of their intrinsic nature, be good. Only man's disobedience to God

since the Fall had made those senses, and consequently the imagination which acts on their findings, disorderly and untrustworthy.
Perhaps the greatest disservice that has ever been done to Teresa is
the statue of her by Bernini in the Church of Santa Maria della Vittoria
in Rome, which depicts her fainting away in what looks like a wholly
sensual ecstasy of profane love. She would herself have eschewed such
an analogy from secular love and her own homely, natural and precise
imagery for the four stages of contemplation is an indication of this.

The last of the Four Waters is noteworthy not only for the loftiness
and beauty of its sense of God but also for its gracious human qualities.
This stage brings with it, says Teresa, 'a very great tenderness and a
complete confidence in God'. But with these perfected human virtues
also goes the possibility of falling into sin again, since in this life no
man is wholly perfect or wholly secure. This very proneness to sin,
however, can be turned into a grace because those who do fall, Teresa
declares, 'must not faint unless they wish to be utterly lost. For tears
gain everything; and one kind of water attracts another.' This precision
of expression and this desire for clarity are shiningly apparent throughout her autobiography. If Teresa tells us she does not know the delicate
differences between imagination and memory or between intellect and
understanding, she never falters at describing the nuances of mood, the
nervous gestures of the human heart or the perilous balance of the
charged mind. She has the novelist's gift for noticing and explaining
motives and actions, and also the kind of observant sensibility which,
so many centuries later, was to manifest itself in the poems of Emily
Dickinson and the novels of Virginia Woolf. Like them, she writes
first straight from her own experience but she never probes so deep
into her own motives and thoughts as to be wholly absorbed in them.
She knows nothing of the closed doors of the sensitive heart or the
masochistic movements of introspection. Always she moves outwards
and it is from things that she has herself seen, tasted, heard and
touched that she takes her scintillating imagery.

She has another gift too and it is a gift that only the natural writer
possesses, something that cannot be learnt or acquired by the strenuous
application of reason alone. It is a gift for the pithy phrase, the surprising aphorism. Thus, throughout her *Life*, we find countless remarks
like the following, remarks which are notable for their brevity and
insight – 'discretion is necessary in everything', 'they [beginners in
prayer] ought also to observe a kind of Sunday, when they should rest
from their labours', 'the questions of sin and self-knowledge are the

bread which we must eat with even the most delicate dish on this road of prayer', 'great help can be obtained by consulting a learned man who is virtuous, even if he is not spiritual'. Exhortations and axioms like these throng Teresa's autobiography especially when she is describing her own early life and early stages of prayer. As she moves into her description of the Fourth Water, however, her eloquence becomes more intense, less reflective; the afterthoughts of experience give way to a passionate attempt to depict the penultimate stage of mysticism – 'the prayer of union', of union with God. 'Union,' says Teresa, 'seems to be the same at the beginning, the middle, and the end, and is altogether inward.' But beyond this there is an ultimate contact with God, something almost ineffable; Teresa calls it 'rapture' and speaks of it thus: '. . . rapture is, as a rule, irresistible. Before you can be warned by a thought or help yourself in any way, it comes as a quick and violent shock; you see and feel this, or this powerful eagle bearing you up on its wings.' This rapture is a favour granted directly by God; it induces 'a deep humility' and also a sense, even a bodily sense, of 'being lifted'. Ecstatic and wholly satisfying as this experience is, it is also attended by great suffering and solitude. Yet these things are themselves felt as a source of peace since they are a participation in the Incarnation of Christ and, indeed, as Teresa says, 'the way of the Cross'. From the presentation of these moments of illumination Teresa moves gently downwards, as it were, and proceeds to give lengthy descriptions of the 'assaults' of the devil, the dangers of 'delusions' and the vital necessity of a constant watchfulness on the part of the mystic. The imagination which, during union with God, was in total abeyance now comes into its own again. Teresa enlarges once more on the uses of the imagination and in the following lines adumbrates the message that was to be the informing power of Traherne's *Centuries of Meditations* – 'Until then it [the soul before it has reached an advanced stage of prayer] must, of course, seek the Creator through His creatures . . . But what I should like to make clear is that Christ's Humanity must not be reckoned among these bodily objects.' Anthropomorphism must be avoided at all costs.

As I have said, Teresa moves gently downwards to less celestial things after her description of the last Water but, so unified is her vision, so vehement and energetic her teaching, she moves upwards again in a later chapter. It is as if she can never entirely satisfy herself with one portrayal of mystical experience but must keep on trying to get nearer to the truth and to become more precise in depicting it.

Thus in Chapter twenty-eight she presents 'an imaginary vision' in words which are radiant with the kind of light we find all through the poems of Vaughan: 'It is not a dazzling radiance but a soft whiteness and infused radiance, which causes the eyes great delight and never tires them; nor are they tired by the brilliance which confronts them as they look on this divine beauty. The brightness and light that appear before the gaze are so different from those of earth that the sun's rays seem quite dim by comparison, and afterwards we never feel like opening our eyes again. It is as if we were to look at a very clear stream running over a crystal bed, in which the sun was reflected, and then to turn to a very muddy brook, with an earthy bottom, running beneath a cloudy sky . . . It is a light that never yields to darkness and, being always light, can never be clouded.'

Imagery is always the arbitrator, even among things almost inexpressible. Thus the whole of Teresa's *Life* is a kind of half-aware tribute to the potency of imagination. Her denial of the strength of her own imaginative faculty was, as I suggested at the beginning of this chapter, a needless denial. Teresa not only conveys her own mystical experience through the medium of imagery (the products of the imagination), but she also elevates the imagination to a very high place in human perception. It is not, therefore, surprising to find her using, in the Second Water, an image which Keats used when he was describing his theory of 'negative capability'. Teresa writes, 'It – I mean the will – should remain in the enjoyment of that grace, and recollected like the wise bee. For if no bees entered the hive and all flew about trying to bring one another in, there could not be much honey made.' Keats, employing the same image, declares, 'Let us not therefore go hurrying about and collecting honey, bee-like buzzing here and there impatiently for a knowledge of what is to be aimed at; but let us open our leaves like a flower and be passive and receptive.' The application of the simile is slightly different here; nevertheless, what Keats says of the 'wise passiveness' essential to the mature poet, Teresa applies to the dedicated person of prayer. Both writers are speaking of their own vocations yet both approach those vocations in precisely the same way. Without in any way straining the similarities one can, I think, see here some of the affinities between mysticism and poetry. And Teresa, though she went so much further, would also have endorsed Keats's fervent plea for 'the Holiness of the Heart's Affections and the Truth of Imagination'.

# 6. THE INNOCENT AUDACITY

## *An approach to St John of the Cross*

---

*Study me then, you who shall lovers be*
*At the next world, that is, at the next spring.*
JOHN DONNE – A Nocturnal upon St Lucy's Day

IF ONE DID not know their context, it would be easy to mistake many of the mystical poems of John of the Cross for the most passionate declarations of profane love. Influenced in content and imagery by the *Song of Songs*, and in form and rhythm both by sixteenth-century Spanish court poetry and by traditional folk verse, the poems assimilate several traditions, several attitudes. In one of St John's songs between the soul and the Bridegroom, the Bride cries,

> My Love's the mountain range,
> The vallies each with solitary grove,
> The islands far and strange,
> The streams with sounds that change,
> The whistling of the lovesick winds that rove.
>
> .        .        .
>
> Deep-cellared in the cavern
> Of my love's heart, I drank of him alive:
> Now, stumbling from the tavern,
> No thoughts of mine survive,
> And I have lost the flock I used to drive.

If the reader did not know St John's own commentaries on his *Spiritual Canticle*, it would not be difficult to assign such verse as this to the plane of physical love. The poem shocks because it is so intimate. This is as true of the original Spanish as of the English translation; the problems involved in conveying, without loss, the extraordinary intensity of the original poems into another quite different language are well stated by the American poet John Frederick Nims, who has himself recently produced a very vivid rendering of St John's poems: 'My venture,' he says, 'the windmill I am tilting at, is to give some inkling of the poetry. That means that I have chosen the rhythms and forms of the original instead of turning the content into a slack free verse favourable, perhaps, to thought and imagery, but at what fatal cost to their pulsing blood-rhythms! – rhythms very different from those brain rhythms that count beads on a wooden abacus. It means too that I have aimed at the kind of diction St John used: a diction direct and colloquial, sometimes rustic, sometimes solemn with echoes of the *Song of Songs* or the courtly pastoral. And, since "the sound", as Frost has said, "is the gold in the ore", it means I have tried to do something about sound values and special sound effects . . . Ernest Jones has described how Freud translated: "Instead of laboriously transcribing from the foreign language, idioms and all, he would read a passage, close the book, and consider how a German writer would have clothed the same thoughts – a method not very common among translators." But a highly sensible way: otherwise one merely turns the poor content out of its comfortable home into the dreary winter of no-language. The translator of poetry has a far more ticklish task: he has to consider not just what to say but how to say it in certain images, rhythms and sounds. What this amounts to is writing a poem of his own, using as much of the material of the original as he possibly can. His doom is that there will always be parts left over and gaps he will have to caulk with inferior oakum.'

This is an admirable statement of method and approach; and, for this study, I shall use some of the results of Mr Nims's careful labours. What is most noteworthy in his remarks about the difficulties of translating St John is the complete absence of any complaint about having to transfer to another tongue a *mystical* poetry clothed in the language of profane love. The truth is that in this particular matter no serious problem arises. It is not St John's content that is baffling but his form. If the translator keeps closely and humbly to the original, he will convey, through his translation, the same literary *mode* which St John employs. There is no danger of misunderstanding his metaphors or tampering with his message – problems which arise when one is attempting to translate a mystical intensity which depends on concepts rather than images, on abstractions rather than on concrete objects or relationships. Vaughan, for example, would be a difficult poet to translate because his intensity often resides in a verbal texture unrelated to ordinary human experience.

St John, then, that most austere and analytical of Christian mystics in his prose works, does not scorn human analogies in his poetic interpretation of divine things. The subject-matter of his poetry is the ecstasy of mystical contact with God; his expression of that experience uses the joy of human love, even though it transcends that love. St John himself never had any doubts about the religious aspect of making poems; he never felt that writing conflicted with his contemplative vocation. He trusted God but he also trusted language. He was a superb technician, a painstaking craftsman, and himself declared when asked if God directly inspired his poems, 'Sometimes God gave them to me, and other times I had to find them for myself.' It is, perhaps, the Puritan tradition, the passion to separate and demarcate, which are responsible for the inability of many writers of the last two centuries or so to believe in the efficacy and truthfulness of poetry as a medium for the expression of man's closest possible contact with God. With John of the Cross one senses no restless dissatisfaction with the limitations of language and imagery; he does not seem to have *descended* from his mystical experiences to the laborious task of describing them in verse. The poems are an essential part of the experience. And it is for this reason that his poetry has such a radiant unity.

Paradoxically perhaps, some of the most intense and sublime of his poems foreshadow not the exquisite clarity of Traherne or the light-pervaded stanzas of Vaughan, but the poems of Donne, and not so much Donne's divine poems as his love poetry. There is, for example, much in St John's mystical poems that recalls the following lines from Donne's *The Ecstasy*:

> And whilst our souls negotiate there,
> We like sepulchral statues lay;
> All day, the same our postures were,
> And we said nothing all the day.

This is startlingly like the last stanza of one of St John's rapturous songs:

> Lost to myself I stayed
> My face upon my lover having laid
> From all endeavour ceasing:
> And all my cares releasing
> Threw them amongst the lilies there to fade.

St John's prose books and, indeed, his own commentaries on his *Spiritual Canticle* give a very different picture of the man from that which his poems provide. It is the analyst, the dissector of the human soul, even the psychologist, not the poet, who informs *The Ascent of Mount Carmel*, *The Dark Night of the Soul*, and *The Living Flame of Love*. And yet, because the subject-matter of his prose and his verse is the same, it is only the approach which is different, together, of course, with an intensity which only poetry can attain. The prose writings are, in a sense, the foothills, while the poems are the mountain peaks.

In the prose, it is the note of admonishment, of exhortation which is the most notable element. Pedantry and dogmatism are just round the corner, one feels; and this is only fitting and prudent since, in all Western European mystical literature, St John's prose is the most profound and subtle explication of the soul's struggle and search for union with God. Compassion and severity are perfectly mingled and St John will have nothing to do with the sham or the second-rate. At times, the urgent advice which he gives in, for example, *The Ascent of Mount Carmel*, seems slightly at variance with his own poetic practice. Thus he declares, 'Be assured of this: the more the soul clings to images and sensible motives the less will its devotion and prayers descend upwards unto God. When God grants graces and works miracles, He does so, in general, through images not very well made, nor artistically painted or adorned, so that the faithful may attribute nothing to the work of the artist.'

This bare statement would seem to be a denial of even the possibility of poetry being a medium which can both enact and contain a mystical experience. If, one may well ask, St John really believed that sensible images were of little use in the attainment of direct union with God, why did he himself try to express that union in poetic terms? Since so clear-sighted a man cannot be accused of self-deception, the only answer to this dilemma, I think, is to remember that in his prose St John is always speaking as a priest, a teacher, a director of souls; he is clearing the ground for the entire journey towards God. His thought and message are cautious, forward-looking, wary of the smallest sign of danger. His poems, on the other hand, are personal not didactic, a drawing together not an analysis. They are, as it were, the overflow of a vision, the expression of a consummation; they spring from an absolute certainty of the validity of his own mystical experience, just as all true poetry, whether secular or sacred, is an implicit affirmation of the reality and value of the various experiences from which it came. In his poems St John is not concerned to teach but to assert, not to warn but to invite.

If the personal element in his great prose works is largely concealed, it is, nevertheless, still present. A man, after all, can only teach what he himself knows, and in supernatural matters this knowledge must be more than an accumulation of facts; it must be both an appropriation and a distribution of experience. Thus the sense of deprivation and obscurity which is so important a part of St John's teaching (but a part which has, perhaps, been over-emphasized in modern times) are experiences which he knew from personal suffering. This obscurity, these darknesses also appear in his poems but, since poetry leaps over analysis and explanation, the darkness is close to the light, and intuition bridges the gulf between desolation and ecstasy. The very essence of lyric poetry is, after all, compression and intensity; it does not concern itself with the plains, only with the high points. And we have a perfect proof of this in the lengthy commentaries St John feels disposed to give of those lyric moments which subsist by the delicate balance of music with image. The lyric hints, the commentary explains and elaborates. Thus the following five lines from *The Spiritual Canticle* are a purely poetic way of suggesting the wiles of the devil:

> Catch us the foxes,
> For our vineyard hath flourished;
> While of roses
> We make a nosegay,
> And let no one appear on the hill.

On these comparatively lucid lines, St John feels obliged to reflect at some length: 'The evil spirits,' he says, 'now molest the soul in two ways. They vehemently excite the desires, and employ them with other imaginations to assail the peaceful and flourishing kingdom of the soul.' This prose comment is not an explanation on a *literary* level; the real illumination is all in the poem. The poem imparts the mystical experience, hands it over to others who have never had, or even wanted to have, a direct contact with God. The commentary, on the other hand, is designed for those who wish to follow St John's own journey, with all its snares and all its sweetness. Or, to put it another way, the poems arrive, the commentaries only approximate.

In the two streams into which the Western mystical tradition has divided, John of the Cross is usually said to represent the rejection, not the affirmation, of images. For myself, I would be inclined to say that his work embodies both traditions. In his prose, we are proffered the possibility of direct union with God by means of the rejection of images, in his poems, by the way of affirmation. The strict asceticism of St John's life, the stern directions of his teaching flower into what one can only call the sensuous spirituality of his poems. The poems absorb his careful and always orthodox theology and transform that theology into images taken from the intimacy of sexual love. What Dante said of God – namely, that he was 'an intellectual light full of love' – might well be applied to *The Spiritual Canticle* and the other poems. The intellect provides concepts, ideas, definitions, and the poetry transmutes these things into imagery, but without in any way diminishing the intellectual meanings. Gerald Brenan has expressed this whole complex process very well when he says of St John's poems, 'It is true that love for created things plays only a subsidiary part in the action, but that is because it is describing a more advanced stage. Such love serves merely to raise the mind of the chief character towards their Source. But love for this source is the dynamic of the poem . . . The distinctive thing about this class of poets [Brenan is here comparing St John with Coleridge and Rimbaud] is that they write from so deep a level, about things so essential to their inner nature, with so little dilution of secondary material that (1) their rhythms have an unusual penetrative power; (2) their imagery is symbolic; and (3) they exhaust themselves . . . And although the two greatest of his prose works describe the Night, with its hushed suspense and its sharp stabs of longing, it is chiefly the coming of Day that the lyrics celebrate. The poet, emerging from the dim states that precede the ecstasy of composition, finds in the marvellous illumination of that ecstasy his best subject-matter. The poems are the explosions of a man whose ordinary condition had up till then been, if not *noche oscura*, then twilight.' In other words, Brenan sees St John's poems not simply as a re-presentation of his vision but as an integral part of that vision. The flame that burns in the vision also burns in the poems which follow, and burns without diminution. One is reminded of a remark one of his friends made to Yeats – 'Belief makes a mind abundant.' Belief, or faith, not only makes St John's mind abundant, it also enriches his poetry. And belief is founded on truth not on dogma alone, since dogma is only a vehicle of truth. In his less directly personal poems, St John allows his imagination to play on the dogmas which his faith affirms, and in doing so he produces an almost metaphysical poetry. Thus in Romance XI, which is concerned with the relationship beween the three persons of the Blessed Trinity, he writes,

He who in naught resembles You
Shall find of Me no trace or sign,
Life of My Life! for only through
Your own can I rejoice in Mine.

Here the thought is intricate, the language almost entirely abstract.
Paradoxically, when St John is trying to describe the ineffable experience of union with God, he makes use of a rich assortment of sensuous
images; but when he is trying to explain a Mystery of Faith he uses a
much more abstract terminology. This is an important difference of
usage and it seems to imply that the most sensuous resources of
language must be ransacked and plundered to depict a close relationship (and 'relationship' here is the key word) of man with God,
whereas only more limited, more abstract words can be used when St
John is trying to formulate an article of faith in poetic terms. Thus,
when he is most personal, he is most sensuous, while when he is most
objective, his poetry is most abstract.

These facts alone, I believe, tell us a good deal about the nature of
poetry and the nature of mysticism. In the first place, poetry wishes to
communicate and so to form a relationship; but, prior to this, the poet
has himself formed a relationship with the subject which is the content
of his verse. *Mystical* experience, which implies the highest kind of
relationship a human being can have – namely, contact with God –
would seem, then, when the question of communication arises, to be
best suited to poetry whose very basis and being are some kind of
direct, intuitive, supra-rational relationship. St John himself certainly
seems to make an implicit affirmation of this when he uses poetry to
express the loftiest moments of his mystical experiences, while
reserving prose for the explanations and preliminaries of those
experiences. What an American critic, Mr Cleanth Brooks, says of
poetry as a means of communication seems to have a very particular
application in the case of the mystical poems of St John of the Cross.
He writes, '. . . our examination has carried us farther and farther
into the poem itself in a process of exploration. As we have made this
exploration, it has become more and more clear that the poem is not
only the linguistic vehicle which conveys the thing communicated most
"poetically", but that it is also the sole linguistic vehicle which conveys
the things communicated accurately. In fact, if we are to speak exactly,
the poem itself is the *only* medium that communicates the particular
"what" that is communicated.' In the case of St John, this 'what' is his

own mystical contact with God, an experience which he entrusts to the perilous particularity of poetic language.

In St John's poems, then, there is no sense of the poet using this particular form, music and imagery for lack of something better. Warnings, exhortations, reservations are thrust aside and the poems stand – assured, unique, unambiguous. They are assured because they are, in a very real sense, self-contained; they find an absolute anchorage in imagery and so are not swept hither and thither in the necessary guesswork of conceptual thought. Experience is the only arbiter and when experience has found its perfect image, the dialectic is over, not perhaps in the poet's mind but quite certainly in the poem he has just made.

If the dialectic is over, the questioning is not, but in poetry, even in the greatest, questions are always rhetorical ones. They are means of exploring, hinting, suggesting, they do not really want answers, certainly not direct ones. So, in one of the stanzas of his *Canticle* St John writes,

> Why, after wounding
> This heart, hast Thou not healed it?
> And why, after stealing it,
> Hast Thou abandoned it,
> And not carried away the stolen prey?

These are not questions in the ordinary sense at all; they are a cry from the heart, a description of a particular condition of the soul, not a request for knowledge or even for reassurance.

It is not, then, that St John's prose is at odds with his poetry, but rather that the poetry transcends the prose. In the poems, we have the mystical experience in a pure form, in the prose it is always diluted, analysed, cautious. Like Eliot's 'first voice of poetry', the poems represent 'the poet talking to himself'; the prose, like 'the second voice', is a voice 'addressing an audience, whether large or small'. Indeed, what Eliot says about the first voice of poetry is highly relevant to the poems of St John: 'He [the poet] is oppressed by a burden which he must bring to birth in order to obtain relief. Or, to change the figure of speech, he is haunted by a demon, a demon against which he feels powerless, because in its first manifestation it has no face, no name, nothing.' Now, if we replace the word 'demon' here with the word 'God', we surely have a very accurate description of precisely what St John is doing in his mystical poems.

From the testimony of St John's poetry, it would seem that mystics, when they try, in verse, to express their direct contact with God, often go further than their rational, prose-inclined minds would permit. In the same way, poets such as Rilke and Hart Crane, who were neither Christian nor by any means certain what vision it was that their poetry seemed to be reaching towards, often hinted in their poetry at some transcendent experience that their prose drew back from. Poetry, in effect, seems to induce an audacity that prose alone can never attain. Every written poem embodies an act of faith in the validity of that poem; truth to experience is the only test. Thus the mystic, by simply attempting to express his vision in poetic language, is asserting implicitly that such language is a fit medium to contain that vision. Uncertainty only arises *before* the poem is written; after it is written, the battle is over. And further, in both mystical and secular poetry, literary judgment follows, it does not precede, the reader's assurance of the poet's sincerity. If there is even a hint of the 'phoney', there is no need to examine technique, imagery or rhythm; the poem has already fallen apart. But where honesty is proved, then purely literary considerations can move in. If the poem in question does not stand up to such examination, it is, of course, a failure as literature; but it is also a failure as the expression of a mystical experience since even the loftiest of mystical apprehensions demand the perfection of artistic technique if they are to be expressed fully. This is a fact that is often forgotten by those who judge 'religious' verse simply by the sincerity of its content. A clumsy, ill-made mystical poem is, in a sense, a denial of truth, even though no moral blame can be attached to its writer. On the other hand, it is a culpable blindness on the part of the reader if he praises a poem for its good intentions and wilfully ignores its technical weaknesses.

The generous audacity of St John's poems, the directness of their approach to God are, perhaps, explained by the fact that they represent a consummation. When the soul has moved through the Purgative and Illuminative Ways, when it has been cleansed in the Dark Night of Sense and Spirit, when, in fact, it has attained humility, charity and self-forgetfulness – then, in the Unitive Way, it will find not a loss of human things but a new knowledge of them. Nature will not be thwarted but perfected. The Incarnation is the beginning and end of the Christian mystical experience; it represents a gathering together not an act of discarding. And it is the Incarnation which explains and justifies St John's analogues of profane love.

Some students and writers of the history of mystical experience have been inclined to misunderstand the austerity of St John's teaching; they have tended to interpret such lines as the following from *The Ascent of Mount Carmel* as more in accord with Eastern mysticism than with Western Christianity:

> Strive not to desire anything but rather nothing.
> Do those things which bring thee into contempt,
> and desire that others also may do them.

Such words as these can only be understood properly if they are seen in the context of Christ's Crucifixion and Resurrection. They connote a sacrifice which is made in order that a greater good may be achieved, not an abandonment of self into some sort of pantheism. If St John's teaching is austere, it is also joyous, and to obtain a perfectly balanced picture of his conception of mystical experience we must set beside the lines I have just quoted, the following reflections from his *Spiritual Canticle*: 'It is the property of love to place him who loves on an equality with the object of his love. Hence the soul, because of its perfect love, is called the bride of the Son of God, which signifies equality with Him. In this equality and friendship all things are common.' Thus, far from advocating a vague species of pantheism, St John sees, at the very height of mystical contact, an experience which is a relationship, a love which is both received and given. And so his poetry too is a poetry of reciprocity. In it, St John is speaking both to himself and to God. His lyricism enacts and perpetuates the love which his prose can only adumbrate.

# 7. THE LYRIC INTERVENTION

## Herbert and Vaughan

---

THE WORLD OF Herbert is a dramatic world. This is a fact that has been too often neglected, partly because of the quiet tone of Herbert's verse (a quiet which can deceive those who look for drama only in the theatre or the market-place), and partly because his drama resides in the continually changing relationship between one man and God. It is a two-sided drama not one of many voices. The tension of Herbert's poetry is felt in this conflict: the poet desires peace but knows he must struggle for it, and when peace is attained it can only be possessed by effort, striving and vigilance.

Many of his poems open with dramatic commands to God or equally dramatic praise of him:

> I struck the board, and cry'd, No more.
> I will abroad.
> > (*The Collar*)

> How fresh, O Lord, how sweet and clean
> Are thy returns!
> > (*The Flower*)

> My God, I heard this day,
> That none doth build a stately habitation,
> But he that means to dwell therein.
> > (*Man*)

> When my devotions could not pierce
> Thy silent ears;
> Then was my heart broken, as was my verse.
> > (*Denial*)

Such opening lines as these are striking both for the intimate directness of their language and for the warmth of their feeling. They are
prayers expressed in poetry – taut, bare, unflinching.

Herbert has often been compared with Vaughan – and suffered
through the comparison. People tend to forget that it was in fact
Herbert's example which influenced Vaughan's early religious verse
though, of course, Herbert's work was a point of departure for
Vaughan and not a dominating influence. Herbert has often been called
homely and human where Vaughan is rapt and remote. His vision has
almost been domesticated where Vaughan's has been left free, unique,
shining. In this study, I wish to consider Vaughan and Herbert not so
much to compare them as to isolate the especial quality of each, the
individual visions of two deeply religious men.

Herbert's dominating theme is one that has become familiar to us
through Francis Thompson's *Hound of Heaven*; it is the theme of flight
from and return to God. This theme includes an intense awareness of
sin and an equally intense desire for penitence, forgiveness and satisfaction. The symbols of the Prodigal Son and of the Lost Sheep are central
to Herbert's religious spirit. Yet there is nothing of mere abnegation
or false humility in his verse. Man is on speaking terms with God for
when Herbert addresses him he is almost always approaching God the
Son, the God-Man:

> In heaven at his manor I him sought:
> They told me there that he was lately gone
> About some land which he had dearly bought
> Long since on earth, to take possession.
> I straight return'd, and knowing his great birth,
> Sought him accordingly in great resorts;
> In cities, theatres, gardens, parks, and courts:
> At length I heard a ragged noise and mirth
> Of thieves and murderers: there I him espied,
> Who straight, *Your suit is granted*, said, and died.
>                                           (*Redemption*)

This, like so much of Herbert's work, is essentially dramatic in
spirit and it is interesting to note that even in an age which, despite
sectarian differences, accepted Christian teaching in general, Herbert
brought his religious symbols to life by placing them in a dramatic
setting and giving them a dynamic quality of their own. He used, in

fact, the method and approach that Christian writers and painters today, such as Bernanos, Rouault and Stanley Spencer, have employed. He wished to impart his own experiences, not to attempt to convert anyone else. I think this fact is relevant to the difficulty, for a Christian, of creating a specifically religious art in an age like our own, when not only are Christian doctrines not understood or widely accepted, but where the Christian symbols themselves have ceased to have much meaning. As Eliot has said, a religious poet does not write in order to convince anyone but simply to convey the feeling and nature of his own religious experience. The experience must be personal, unique and direct so that 'the willing suspension of disbelief' which Coleridge wrote of *will* be willing and not reluctant. As Keats has said, we distrust poetry that has 'a palpable design upon us'.

Herbert's world, then, was a dramatic world, a world of struggle, conflict and tension; but it was also a place of peace. He wrote of prayer,

> A kind of tune, which all things hear and fear;
> Softness, and peace, and joy, and love, and bliss,
> Exalted Manna, gladness of the best,
> Heaven in ordinary, man well drest,
> The milky way, the bird of Paradise,
> Church-bells beyond the stars heard, the soul's blood
> The land of spices; something understood.

Herbert employs many images to describe the nature and power of prayer but, at the end of his poem, he can say with a lovely simplicity that it is 'something understood'. And this implies a two-fold understanding – both God's acceptance of the prayer and man's realization of precisely what he is doing and offering.

These lines on prayer prompt some consideration of Herbert's religious experience. Unlike Vaughan, he did not write chiefly of the great heights of praise and devotion, of the almost ineffable union of man with God; like the fourteenth-century English mystics, he explored and depicted all the stages of approach to God, from the articulate, discursive prayer of the beginner to the wordless prayer of the man far advanced in the spiritual life. Like John of the Cross, he has much to say about affliction or the purgative way, an affliction which, several centuries later, Simone Weil was to make the very centre of her religious life. Herbert says in his poem called *Affliction*,

> Yet, though thou troublest me, I must be meek;
> In weakness must be stout.
> Well, I will change the service and go seek
> Some other master out.
> Ah my dear God! though I am clean forgot
> Let me not love thee, if I love thee not.

The tender intimacy and boldness of such a relationship with God are reminiscent of Julian of Norwich when she called Christ her 'dearworthy Lord' or her 'darling'. It is a tenderness that appears again in what is perhaps Herbert's most famous poem, *Love*:

> . . . let my shame
> Go where it doth deserve.
> And know you not, says Love, who bore the blame?
> My dear, then I will serve.
> You must sit down, says Love, and taste my meat:
> So I did sit and eat.

The sacrament of the Holy Eucharist, that sacrament in which Christ is known and experienced again in his incarnate form under the appearances of bread and wine, is at the heart of Herbert's prayer:

> Love is that liquor sweet and most divine
> Which my God feels as blood; but I as wine.

But to discover and isolate the highest peaks of Herbert's experience of God, we have to examine whole poems and extract the relevant passages from them, rather than set aside whole poems which are entirely devoted to attempts to express the nearly inexpressible and to embody a complete vision. There are in fact few such poems; for, as I have already suggested, Herbert's relationship with God is a reciprocal, dramatic one, constantly changing in mood and tempo. What I want to do now is to illustrate the moments of sublime rest which that relationship also included. In *Affliction* he writes,

> I took thy sweetened pill, till I came where
> I could not go away, nor persevere.
>
> Yet lest perchance I should too happy be
> In my unhappiness,
> Turning my purge to food, thou throwest me
> Into more sicknesses.
> Thus doth thy power cross-bias me, not making
> Thine own gift good, yet me from my ways taking.

Here is the pain not felt as pain, the demands of the senses temporarily laid aside – but still the struggle and the humble perseverance.

But in *The Temper*, Herbert makes a clear, unambiguous statement of the experience of a man entirely caught up in God:

> How should I praise thee, Lord! how should my rhymes
> Gladly engrave thy love in steel
> If what my soul doth feel sometimes,
> My soul might ever feel.

Words, it seems, are almost failing the poet yet he still feels impelled to communicate what he has learnt of God. He knows that perfection, though real and valid, is also fleeting, and so he resigns himself to complete acceptance:

> Whether I fly with angels, fall with dust,
> Thy hands made both, and I am there:
> Thy power and love, my love and trust
> Make one place everywhere.

These lines remind us of the words which Julian of Norwich heard God speak in her vision of him – 'Behold I lift never my hands off my work.'

In *The Pulley*, Herbert sees man's very condition of unrest as a state which God has ordained in order to make him see the futility of all else and turn at last to God alone:

> Yet let him keep the rest
> But keep them with repining restlessness:
> Let him be rich and weary, that at least,
> If goodness lead him not, yet weariness
> May toss him to my breast.

As always with Herbert, the words are concrete, energetic and exact. In *The Temper* again, Herbert employs many different images to express his wrestle with and final succumbing to God – the engraver's steel, the roosting bird, a stringed instrument, and the dust from which man is fashioned.

> Wilt thou meet arms with man, that thou dost stretch
> A crumb of dust from heav'n to hell?
> Will great God measure with a wretch?
> Shall he thy statue spell?

From a nervous and delicate manipulation of imagery Herbert moves to a condition not of defeat but of acceptance. Almost every poem is a record of a relationship of reciprocity between God and himself. Sometimes he inserts a dexterous aphorism into a description of hard-won peace, as in the final stanza of *Vanity*:

> What hath not man sought out and found,
> But his dear God? who yet his glorious law
> Embosoms in us, mellowing the ground
> With showers and frosts, with love and awe,
> So that we need not say, Where's this command?
> Poor man, thou searchest round
> To find out *death*, but missest life at hand.

Herbert himself never missed 'life at hand'. For him, the life of prayer was one with natural life and natural pleasures. There is no Puritanical fear of the senses in his work. In a poem called *Aaron* he writes of the difficulties and temptations of being a priest with:

> Profaneness in my head,
> Defects and darkness in my breast,
> A noise of passions ringing me for dead
> Unto a place where is no rest.

But he consoles himself with a paraphrase of St Paul's 'I live, now not I, but Christ liveth in me':

> Christ is my only head,
> My alone only heart and breast,
> My only music, striking me even dead;
> That to the old man I may rest,
> And be in him new drest.

Finally, in a poem called *The Forerunners*, in which Herbert adapts the image of harbingers sent ahead of a royal progress in order to requisition lodgings by chalking on doors, he explicitly examines the purpose and value of language and symbol. It is a deeply auto-biographical poem, a confident assertion that even in a man's most intimate relations with God,

> Beauty and beauteous words should go together.

There is a kind of gentle paradox in a poem such as this which, while using every resource of language and imagery, questions that usage:

Farewell sweet phrases, lovely metaphors.
But will ye leave me thus? when ye before
Of stews and brothels only knew the doors,
Then did I wash you with my tears, and more,
    Brought you to Church well drest and clad:
My God must have my best, ev'n all I had.
                    *          *          *

Henry Vaughan, who was born twenty-eight years after Herbert, had,
despite the influence on him of the older poet's forms and metres, a
totally different approach to the writing of religious or visionary verse.
Where Herbert argued or conversed, he looked and marvelled; his
verse is the verse of a man who never ceased to be astonished, to
exclaim, to give thanks. There is no ratiocination in his poems, and
little sense of struggle. It is a poetry of awe in which the majesty of
God is stressed more than the humanity of Christ. Like Traherne,
Vaughan inhabited a world transformed by his own blinding visions,
a world supernaturalized almost. He takes his images from natural,
elemental things – light, air, roots, water – and he is perhaps one of
the very few English poets whose verse gives one an unmistakable
sense of poetry at the *source* even while the forms he uses are often of
the utmost complexity and intricacy. Hopkins is another such poet;
and it may be that form, which in literature is the counterpart of order
in the natural world, is more instinctive, more fundamental, more, in
fact, beyond reason than many modern critics, who confine the creative
process to the area of reason, will allow. Form is not imposed on chaos
or apparent disorder but *discovered* in it, and it is more often discovered
by intuition than reason alone. If there is an intensity, a bareness in
Vaughan which we seldom find in Herbert, this does not mean that
there are no shadows or darknesses in his verse; the shadows in
Vaughan are cast by his own sense of unworthiness when confronted
by a transcendent vision. They have little in common with the struggles
of the beginner in the life of prayer:

          . . . oft have I prest
          Heaven with a lazy breath, but fruitless this
          Pierc'd not; Love only can with quick access
                    Unlock the way,
                    When all else stray
          The smoke, and Exhalations of the breast.

Vaughan is, perhaps, more than anything else, the poet of inno-

cence; his sense of sin, or at least the way he writes about it, is general
and theoretical rather than particular and concrete as it is with Herbert.
And *because* he appears to be innocent, sin holds no fears for him; it is
only those who have once fallen into a trap or a temptation who are
terrified of falling again. This innocence, however, is accompanied by
a complete maturity, an absolute refusal to shun anything however
terrible. In the poem called *The Retreat*, which is a re-creation of a
child's sense of the presence of God in everything and above everything, Vaughan writes with a kind of tender regret for his own past:

> Happy those early days! when I
> Shin'd in my Angel-infancy.
> Before I understood this place
> Appointed for my second race,
> Or taught my soul to fancy aught
> But a white Celestial thought.

By not understanding, Vaughan here quite clearly means that he
longs not for a state of ignorance but for the innocent eye of the child
which sees all things as good in themselves. He is alluding to the
scriptural exhortation, 'Unless ye be as little children . . .', and, indeed,
he ends *The Retreat* with an explicit desire to move 'backward' into the
clear vision he had as a child:

> Some men a forward motion love,
> But I by backward steps would move,
> And when this dust falls to the urn
> In that state I came return.

Vaughan's verse is shot through with images of light or of whiteness
as a symbol of purity. In *The Morning Watch* he says,

> . . . The Pious soul by night
> Is like a clouded star, whose beams though said
>         To shed their light
>         Under some Cloud
>         Yet are above,
>         And shine, and move
> Beyond that misty shroud.

And in the same poem, Vaughan declares what prayer for him means:

> Prayer is
> The world in tune,
> A spirit-voice,
> And vocal joys
> Whose echo is heav'n's bliss.

This is slightly different, and also more fundamental, than Herbert's simple description of prayer as 'something understood'. But the difference is one of subjective attitude rather than objective formulation. Herbert needs to *understand* where Vaughan is content to contemplate, to wait patiently for those moments of vision when the world appears in 'a dexterous and starlight order'. Such a moment is perpetuated in the beautiful poem called simply *The World* which opens with these lines:

> I saw Eternity the other night
> Like a great Ring of pure and endless light,
>     All calm, as it was bright,
> And round beneath it, Time in hours, days, years
>     Driv'n by the spheres
> Like a vast shadow mov'd, In which the world
>     And all her train were hurl'd.

In these lines Vaughan has expressed a moment's clarity and awareness in entirely concrete, even in visual terms. But if light is the predominating image in his verse, darkness and night also have their place, and for Vaughan even they hold no terrors. He calls the night 'my soul's calm retreat' and even goes so far as to say that the ordinary natural light of the sun, 'this world's ill-guiding light', can make him 'err' than he does by night. In the poem *The Night*, from which these words come, Vaughan makes his most intimate avowal of a personal mystical union with God:

> There is in God (some say)
> A deep, but dazzling darkness; As men here
> Say it is late and dusky, because they
>     See not all clear.
> O for that night! where I in him
> Might live invisible and dim.

Vaughan's poem *Man* makes an interesting comparison with Herbert's *The Pulley* since the subject of both poems is the same –

man's necessary state of restlessness since the Fall. Vaughan's poem seems more theoretical, less personally involved than Herbert's. Here, one feels, is a man stating an idea and a belief rather than an experience of his own. The reason for this is, I think, that Vaughan usually writes of his own experiences at their most elevated moments, whereas Herbert's work is the record of a complete life-journey of one man. This is not in any way an adverse criticism of Vaughan, for the feeling of remoteness is an essential part of the strength of *Man*. It is interesting and also significant that when he writes most objectively Vaughan uses more homely, less elemental images, as, for example, the image of weaving in the final stanza of this poem:

> He knocks at all doors, strays and roams,
> Nay hath not so much wit as some stones have
> Which in the darkest nights point to their homes,
>  By some hid sense their Maker gave;
> Man is the shuttle, to whose winding quest
>  And passage through these looms
>  God order'd motion, but ordain'd no rest.

But this sort of poem is rare in Vaughan's *oeuvre*. Most of his verse appropriates the varieties, effects and sources of light to contain and express his vision of God:

> They are all gone into the world of light!
>  (from *Silex Scintillans*)

> Father of lights! what Sunny seed,
> What glance of day hast thou confin'd
> Into this bird? To all the breed
> This busy Ray thou hast assigned;
>  Their magnetism works all night,
>  And dreams of Paradise and light.
>  (*Cock-Crowing*)

> Though thy close commerce nought at all embars
> My present search, for Eagles eye not stars,
>  And still the lesser by the best
>  And highest good is blest.
>  (*The Star*)

Such metaphors could be paralleled over and over again in Vaughan's work. Like Herbert, he had an unshakable belief in the power of poetry to convey even the most apparently inexpressible experience of the presence of God. His glittering translucent poems communicate not only the authenticity but also the vividness and immediacy of such experiences. In the modern sense of metaphysics as the study of *being*, Vaughan is not a Metaphysical at all; he does not study being but embraces it. His poetry appears at that point where inquiry ends and affirmation begins. He stands passive before the transcendent but is intensely active in the *communication* of the transcendent and makes it immanent through the medium of poetry.

# 8. THE ACCESSIBLE ART

*A study of Thomas Traherne's* Centuries of Meditations

---

> . . . *The spirit afterwards, but first the touch.*
> CHARLOTTE MEW – Madeleine in Church

THE POETIC PROSE of Traherne's *Centuries of Meditations* is an example of the art of sharing, of participation. It is an art wholly accessible, in no way private. The subject of these reflections – the search for God in a mystical experience by means of an intense delight in the natural world – is entirely personal. Traherne exposes himself more completely than any other seventeenth-century writer, more completely even than Donne whose irony served as a shield between the intimacies of his confidences and the speculations of his readers. Traherne is an innocent writer in the only valuable sense that a writer can be innocent – that is to say, the sheer momentum of his experience carries him beyond any tendencies towards selfconsciousness. He never pauses to inquire whether his revelations may lay him open either to mockery or hostility. The mood of his work is joy and this joy exorcizes and renders general what would otherwise be personal and particular. His blithe ignorance of any cult of personality means that he can penetrate to parts of his own mind and heart that most writers would either disguise or else transmute into generalities. He knows nothing of the art of self-protection; we can, as a result, walk all round his work without any sense of audacity or intrusion.

We have become accustomed, in the poetry and prose of this century, to the literary appropriation of selfconsciousness. Nothing need be left unsaid, or so we imagine. In fact, our most selfconscious most self-revealing writers have adopted a method of selection quite as successful as that of less autobiographical writers. The wish to conceal is never far from the passion to uncover. The reason for this apparent contradiction is that selfconsciousness is usually a not quite complete fusion of two qualities – exhibitionism and apprehension. Nobody is prepared to take off his masks for long, or to let his readers choose his masks for him.

Traherne wears no masks, casts no concealing shadow. He is, in the deepest sense, a man possessed. What possesses him is a sense of God, and this he wishes to share and distribute. But his sharing is not done from any lofty height; he demands neither reverence nor awe, not because his work is not penetrated with these things but because we, his readers, are admitted to the heart of his experiences where reverence and awe have other names. Traherne's work becomes, in fact, our property, part of our life. This is more true of his prose than his verse. Eliot has indicated that literature may often be genuinely poetic even when it is not presented in the forms of conventional verse. Traherne's formal, disciplined poems lack the accessibility, the immediacy of his *Centuries of Meditations*. It is as if the poetic forms were a barrier to the content and we, his readers, can seldom penetrate that barrier. His art of sharing seems to have stopped short at his prose. The poems are often lovely artifacts, certainly, but they *are* artifacts – sealed off, separate, curiously unattainable. And the delight appears to have diminished, the joy to be diluted. We admire but we do not participate.

R. P. Blackmur, the American critic, has said that vision is 'the observation of the ideal', and this definition describes the attitude of both the maker and reader of visionary literature. With Traherne we are drawn into the vision. He is entirely innocent of those literary devices which keep the reader at arm's length or which define meticulously the distance the poet wishes to preserve between himself and his readers. 'You never enjoy the world aright till the sea itself floweth in your veins, till you are clothed with the heavens and crowned with the stars' – this exhortation to enjoyment is reiterated throughout the *Centuries;* the writer invites us not simply to enter his work but also to enter fully, without reservation, into the natural world. There must be no withdrawal, no withholding. This persuasive request is oddly reminiscent of D. H. Lawrence's demand that we should become one with the earth and with nature. There is a good example of this similarity in Lawrence's poem, *Saint Matthew:*

So I will be lifted up, Saviour,
But put me down again in time, Master,
Before my heart stops beating, and I become what I am not.
Put me down again on the earth, Jesus, on the brown soil
Where flowers sprout in the acrid humus, and fade into
    humus again.

So different in almost every other way, Traherne and Lawrence nevertheless share this central preoccupation – a desire for oneness, for union.
Where Lawrence sought it angrily and passionately, where he preached
it as a fiery message, Traherne asserts it by persuasion. Yet with both
men, there is the same simplicity of purpose, the same desire for honesty
and wholeness. However, where Lawrence's simplicity was a state
of belief fashioned out of torment, Traherne's appears to have been
a prevailing mood; his work is a still centre, whereas Lawrence's is
always a battle to get nearer the centre. Both, however, would have
firmly rejected Yeats's statement that 'the centre will not hold'.

The sensuous excellence of Lawrence's beast and flower poems is
closer to the mood of the *Centuries of Meditations*, I think, than any of
the literature of Traherne's own time; and Traherne would have
understood Lawrence perfectly when he said : 'One has to be so terribly
religious to be an artist.' Lawrence meant by this statement that the
artist must be dedicated, devoted and single-minded. But where
Lawrence had to *make* an ideal to which he could dedicate himself,
Traherne found his in the established Christian religion of his own
time. His writing was one with his faith and, indeed, so inextricably
are the two united that it is impossible to imagine Traherne feverishly
seeking out either a suitable subject-matter or fitting symbols. He
accepted Christian teaching without question and yet, so powerful and
exultant is his eloquence, his *Centuries of Meditations* are entirely
acceptable even to unbelievers. Traherne's art is not so much an art of
enticement as an art of invitation; we are *in* his work, compelled and
carried away by it, long before our minds need adjust themselves to
any 'willing suspension of disbelief'.

From what has been said so far, it might be thought that the
*Centuries* are a work of compulsive, natural genius where craftsmanship and ingenuity play little part. This is not the case at all. If we are
swept away by this poetic prose, it is not simply because we are over-
powered by the ebullience of the artist; we are intoxicated, yes, by the
vision, the radiance, the revelation, but we are intoxicated by the
brilliant simplicity of these things – and simplicity in literature is
seldom artless. In the *Centuries* Traherne shows a childlike delight in
the manipulation of imagery and in the resources of language, but he
is a child with learning. Like a child, too, he takes pleasure in form
and rhythm. He abhors confusion and seeks not to impose order but
to reveal it, both in the natural world and in the relationship between
God and man.

The key to the *Centuries* is contained in the following lines from them: 'For God hath made you able to create worlds in your own mind which are more precious unto him than those which He created.' This denotes an almost sublime trust in the human imagination. We are far from the categories both of the philosophers and of those religious writers who have systematized their studies of prayer and so fabricated a method of prayer. With Traherne, there is no cold formulation or categorizing; we are reminded of Keats's remark about poetry: 'If it do not come as easily as the leaves to a tree, it had better not come at all.' The *Centuries* appear to have grown, not to have been devised. And to say this is not to contradict the earlier statement about Traherne's literary craftsmanship; it is simply to assert that there is no contriving in his work, no adorning for the sake of adornment. The words flow, yet the flow is directed, and it is directed not by cool reason but by a loving care. There is order but no artifice.

In his bold statement that men can create worlds in their own minds which are more valuable to God than his own physical creations, Traherne is asserting the immediacy of human knowledge. What has vexed philosophers throughout the ages, does not concern Traherne at all. He by-passes ratiocination and he does this simply by believing implicitly in the efficacy of the imagination as an instrument of know-ledge. For him, imagination is something much more elevated than a power which shapes images out of the findings of the senses. We may say, I think, that what love was to Augustine and what intellect was to Aquinas, imagination was to Traherne. He gives, in fact, unmistakable utterance to what was to become the chief tenet in the aesthetics of poets like Keats and Coleridge. He is a precursor of the Romantics, but he lacks both their anxiety and their introspection.

The *Centuries* are the exploitation of a childlike sense of wonder, yet Traherne's raptures are always securely anchored both to Christian doctrine and to the demands of the intellect. In other words, there is a solid basis of thought beneath every flight of eloquence. There is nothing muddle-headed or incoherent about his ideas. In fact, the first thing that strikes the reader of the *Centuries* is their extraordinary clarity, a clarity which is produced by a sense of order, not by an undirected originality. And this very clarity is a source of freedom; Traherne is, perhaps, one of the most untrammelled writers of the seventeenth century, but his sense of liberty is produced by a desire for order, not for anarchy. Yet there is audacity in his writing too, and the supremacy which he accords to the imagination is an adumbration of Coleridge's theories of the Primary and Secondary Imagination. 'For we can unsuppose Heaven and Earth,' says Traherne, 'and annihilate the world in our imagination.' But he adds, '. . . the place where they stood will remain behind, and we cannot unsuppose or annihilate that.' Traherne's theory of knowledge (which is implicit in his work, not explicit) and his mystical teaching are, however, entirely orthodox and could be paralleled in the writings of Augustine, John of the Cross or Julian of Norwich. Of man's ability to know about the universe, he says: 'That things are finite, therefore, we learn by our senses. But infinity we know and feel by our souls: and feel it so naturally, as if it were the very essence and being of the soul. The truth of it is, it is individually in the soul: for God is there, and more *near* to us than we are to ourselves.'

Traherne's world is a Platonic one in the sense that it postulates a system of hierarchies and an aristocracy of the human spirit. Yet with him there is nothing of Plato's rigid categorizing or almost determinist placing of men in higher or lower states according to their intellectual equipment. For Traherne, as for all Christian mystics, God is not only substantially present in every human soul, but can also be known directly by love by every human being who really desires to know him. Traherne, then, sees the mystical experience not as a special vocation but as the only true aim of every human life. He never ignores sin, guilt or the evil in the world; rather, he accepts them and explains them: 'Your soul being naturally very dark, and deformed and empty when extended through infinite but empty space, the world serves you in beautifying and filling it with amiable ideas; for the perfecting of its stature in the eye of God. For the thorough understanding of which you must know, that God is a being whose power from all Eternity was prevented with Act [Aquinas defined God as 'the act of pure being'] . . . He knows all which He is able to know, all objects in all worlds being seen in His understanding . . . His essence also is the Sight of Things. For He is all eye and all ear. Being therefore perfect, and the mirror of all perfection, He hath commanded us to be perfect as He is perfect.'

In Traherne's teaching there are no categories, no compartments. There are divisions, yes, but they are only found where man is disobedient to God and refuses the happiness which is his birthright – 'to conceive aright and to enjoy the world, is to conceive the Holy Ghost, and to see His Love; which is the Mind of the Father'. Words, images, metaphors, objects are not, as with some mystical writers, stepping-stones or stages, something to be rejected one by one for a loftier vision. In Traherne's view the whole universe is permeated by God and so all things are sacred. He not only affirms images, but his own writing is itself an art of accumulation not of relegation or disposal. The more man enjoys 'the world aright' the closer he is to God : God is love and the world is upheld by this love – 'The whole world ministers to you as the theatre of your Love. It sustains you and all objects that you may continue to love them. Without which it were better for you to have no being. Life without objects is a sensible emptiness, and that is a greater misery than Death or Nothing.' And 'nothing' here seems to be equated with evil just as Augustine centuries earlier had equated it.

If Traherne's message stresses freedom and delight, if it eschews artificial systematization, it does not, however, elevate uniformity or canonize similarity. The universe is beautiful, but it is beautiful because it is diverse. Man's soul too has infinite potentialities, infinite pleasures. Thus, although to Traherne all things are holy and the whole of life consequently religious, he does not ignore the variety of man's enjoyments or the many different approaches to prayer and, therefore, to God. So he speaks in luminous detail of that meditation which has always been regarded by mystical writers as the first stage towards ultimate union with God. For Traherne, meditation is itself a sweet and pleasurable thing, though his sensible psychology is perfectly aware of the difficulty of meditating well: 'What is more easy and sweet than meditation? Yet in this hath God commended His Love, that by meditation it is enjoyed. As nothing is more easy than to think, so nothing is more difficult than to think well. The easiness of thinking we received from God, the difficulty of thinking well proceeded from ourselves . . . So that an evil habit and custom have made it difficult, not Nature. For by nature nothing is so difficult as to think amiss.' Evil is the assigning of things to the wrong places. In art it leads to dishonest analogy, in the moral sphere to the unfitting, unworthy, thought or act; '. . . we please God when we are most like Him,' says Traherne. 'We are most like Him when our minds are in frame. Our minds are in frame when our thoughts are like His.' Goodness is, in effect, truth, the humble recognition of what *is*. Thus at the heart of Traherne's simplicity there is a profound philosophy. Love is not simply acquiescence, it is also intelligence. Love floods the intellect with light, certainly, but it also *needs* the intellect to order, direct and contain it.

Traherne's passionate concern with the individuality of every created thing is similar to Hopkins's theory of 'inscape' and 'instress'. The being of each thing is unique whether it is the being of a stone, a star or a human soul. Man's inmost being, however, is stamped with the image of God, an image which can be blurred by disobedience but never totally destroyed. It is able, therefore, of its very nature, to participate in infinity. For Traherne, a human life is a sanctified form of self-realization; every desire, he believes, is made to be satisfied, and man is designed for happiness. He would, in fact, differ from Augustine in that where Augustine said the world was created for man's use, Traherne believed that it was intended for man's enjoyment. Yet he teaches no facile doctrine of hedonism; pleasure is not to be sought for its own sake but only as the satisfaction of desires which God has created within us. Traherne would agree with Walter Hilton when the latter said that God creates the love of Himself in us.

The *Centuries*, then, present a total picture of the universe and demonstrate how God is to be found in all things: 'It was His wisdom made you the Sun. It was His goodness made you need the sea. Be sensible of what you need, or enjoy neither. Consider how much you need them, for thence they derive their value.' In other words, Traherne is saying that our very need of things gives them their meaning and worth. He continues: 'To have blessings and to prize them is to be in Heaven; to have them and not to prize them is to be in Hell, I would say upon earth: To prize them and not to have them, is to be in Hell.' We too, then, must value all things as the manifestations of the creative power of God. But we must value them without covetousness, desire them without possessiveness. The *Centuries* are a whole-hearted, almost an obsessive, examination of the nature of love, and Traherne studies the power to love in all its forms, human and divine: 'When you love men, the world quickly becometh yours . . . You are as prone to love, as the sun is to shine . . . Consider therefore the extent of Love, its vigour and excellency. For certainly he that delights not in Love makes vain the universe, and is of necessity to himself the greatest burden.' But Traherne is quick to point out the misuses of love: 'By Love our Souls are married and solder'd to the creatures: and it is our Duty like God to be united to them all. We must love them infinitely, but in God, and for God; and God in them: namely all his excellencies manifested in them. When we dote upon the perfections and beauties of some one creature, we do not love that too much, but other things too little. Never was anything in this world loved too much, but many things have been loved in a false way: and all in too short a measure.' It is man's fallen nature that has cast a shadow over his ability to love deeply, purely and completely. In the *Fourth*, and last, *Century*, where Traherne is considering and describing mystical union with God, he says, 'Our friendship with God ought to be so pure and so clear, that nakedly and simply for His Divine Love, for His glorious works and blessed laws, the wisdom of His counsels, His ancient ways and attributes towards us, we should even in public endeavour to honor Him.' This is reminiscent of that 'naked intent unto God' in *The Cloud of Unknowing*. And in the same *Century*, Traherne discourses of the fall of man and of the change that event has produced in every human creature since: 'If you ask, what is become of us since the fall? because all things now lately named seem to pertain to the estate of innocency; truly now we have superadded treasures, Jesus Christ, and are restored to the same principles, upon higher obligations . . . For God is more delightful than He was in Eden. Then He was as delightful as was possible, but He had not that occasion, as by Sin was afforded, to superadd many more delights than before.' Here Traherne is referring to that 'felix culpa', that happy fault which was the cause of the Incarnation and so of God's closer union with us by means of his Son made man. Thus, through the *Centuries*, we can trace the direct, undevious line of the Western tradition of Christian mystical teaching. Its culmination and flowering are the birth, Passion and Resurrection of Christ.

Traherne's rapturous celebration of the physical world in the earlier *Centuries* is seen now to be a vital part of a fuller vision. Delight and pleasure are not cast out; on the contrary, they are glorified and thus intensified. What might have been an innocent hedonism or a guileless search for self-expression is shown now to be a necessary movement towards a deeper conception of love. To point the difference between Traherne's exultant delight in all creation and a rapture discovered by means of the senses only, it is interesting to quote a passage from André Gide's *Fruits of the Earth*. This book is an eloquent paean of praise to the sensuous beauty of the world, but it is an empty eloquence because the idea of God has been removed from creation and things are enjoyed and possessed with concupiscence and greed. In Traherne's word, they are loved 'falsely'. The straightforward, almost imagistic delight in the world in the following passage from Gide's book could be paralleled superficially in Traherne's *First Century* – 'Springs, so sweet in the evening, more delicious still at noon; icy waters of early

morning; breezes blowing from the sea; bays crowded with shipping;
warm, wave-lapped shores . . .' But in fact such ecstasy as this is
very different from Traherne's. It moves in an area of appetite and
voluptuousness; the eye is dazzled by desire and the hand trembles to
reach out and grasp. Gide continues,

> Satisfactions, I seek you;
> You are beautiful as summer's laughter.
> I know that not one of my desires
> But has its own answer ready.

Traherne also believed that every human desire was made to be
satisfied, but satisfied for the sake of God not for the sake of self.
Gide's vision, on the other hand, is a vision of pagan ecstasy in which
even the natural world is seen to exist most powerfully, to be most
alive, only when it is consumed by lust: 'The eagle is drunk with its
flight. The nightingale with summer nights. The plains tremble with
their heat. Nathaniel, let every one of your emotions be an intoxica-
tion to you.' The simple *being* of things is not enough in the pagan
myth; everything must be intoxicated and heightened and excess itself
is elevated into a virtue. Where Traherne sees order as a necessary
component of intensity and clarity, Gide sees anarchy as the only step
towards freedom. And Gide's is the more restricted view since it
necessitates so many omissions. The pagan dream, the voluptuary's
pleasure, limit a man, they do not fulfil him. The reason why they do
not fulfil him is that they put so much pressure on the senses that the
mind is diminished and disabled. And yet, in *Later Fruits of the Earth*,
Gide himself admits the limitations of merely sensual pleasures. He
says: 'But all the same, what in those days I called God – that confused
mass of notions, sentiments, appeals, which I now know existed only
through and in me – all of this seems to me now, when I think of it,
much more worthy of interest than the rest of the world and myself
and the whole of humanity.' His humility and honesty compel him to
make this admission although he has now moved from one extreme to
another. He is unable to see the world, humanity and himself as part
of God's creation. The rejected pagan view swiftly becomes the Puritan
view if no place has been found for the Incarnation. Traherne's world
view, on the other hand, omits nothing, neither God nor animal
pleasures. It is, in every sense, a *whole* view.

The *Centuries of Meditations* moves from a passionate declaration of
the presence of God in all things, through a careful analysis of nature

to a practical exposition of the way in which man may find God, fulfil his own nature and discover true happiness. The process is cyclical yet it is never coldly analytical. As I have suggested already, we are carried along by the sheer exuberance of Traherne's poetic prose, we partake of his own exhilaration and ecstasy. Yet his appeal is far from being merely emotional. There is thought in every sentence he utters. The vision which he shares with us is the vision of a whole man in whom mind, emotions and senses all have their place and their expression. In the *Fourth Century*, Traherne declares, 'That a man is beloved of God, should melt him all into esteem and holy veneration' and 'Like the sun we dart our rays before us, and occupy those spaces with light and contemplation which we move towards, but possess not with our bodies.' This uncompromising description of mystical union with God as the proper end of each man's life occurs near the end of the *Centuries*, but it comes as no surprise or cause for amazement. The reason why we, the readers, accept it so easily and gladly is that all the *Centuries* have been leading up to this declaration, have, in fact, been adumbrations of it. The book begins with a vision and ends with the same vision. In between are the areas of explanation which demarcate the path towards that vision and describe how it may be followed. The first and the last *Centuries* are like two mountain peaks. Between them is the valley, not an arid, barren valley, nor a counterpart of the 'dark night of the soul' of the more austere mystics, but a rich, fertile plain, a place of doing and making.

The *Third Century* is Traherne's spiritual autobiography, a frank, delightful document in which he reveals his own first movements towards God and his own desires and difficulties. In a passage such as the following, we are reminded of Wordsworth's exalted pantheism, but this is only a surface resemblance. Traherne's universe is permeated by personality, a place where man's nature confronts God's and where all creation cries out with the presence of God. Traherne writes: 'Sometimes I should be alone, and without employment, when suddenly my Soul would return to itself, and forgetting all things in the whole world which mine eyes had seen, would be carried away to the ends of the earth: and my thoughts would be deeply engaged with enquiries: How the Earth did end? . . . Whatever I could imagine was inconvenient, and my reason being posed was quickly wearied.' This passage bears a very striking resemblance to Augustine's description of his experience at Ostia; there is even a close verbal similarity, for Augustine writes, 'And we came to our own minds and went beyond them.' This is simply one more testimony to the unity of mystical experience. And Like Augustine also, Traherne owes much to St Paul; his childish questionings always come upon the same answer, the answer which St Paul had found centuries before – 'For all things shall work together for good to them that love God.'

But Traherne does not seek only his own felicity. He wishes to enjoy and to share his enjoyment. Like all true mystics, he wants to hand on to others the light and peace which his own experiences have revealed to him. So, in his last *Century* he says: 'The world is best enjoyed and most immediately while we converse blessedly and wisely with men. For whomsoever I love as myself, to him I give myself . . . Yea, in him I receive God, for God delighteth me for being his blessedness.' He also adds, 'To think the world therefore a general Bedlam, or place of madmen, and oneself a physician, is the most necessary point of present wisdom: an important imagination, and the way to happiness.' Again, it is by the sensitive insights of the imagination that man is implored to learn about loving God and loving men.

However childlike, carefree and original the *Centuries* appear on a first reading, they are nevertheless profoundly orthodox and always firmly attached to Scripture and to Christian dogma. It is *because* Traherne is so acquiescent to Christian teaching that he *can* be so original. He has discovered that 'service' which is 'perfect freedom'; he knows that anarchy always finally turns back upon the anarchist and that order is not the denial of freedom but its fulfilment.

It would be possible, in an examination of the *Centuries of Meditation*, to find counterparts and even close echoes of Julian of Norwich's vision of the whole world in a hazel-nut and of Teresa of Avila's spontaneous abandonment to God. But to discover and point out these things would only be to demonstrate yet again the unity of all mystical experience. Every mystic, however, also adds something of his own to our knowledge of mysticism. Traherne's personal contribution is one of an open-hearted accessibility and a joyously complete transcription of his own knowledge of God. He demonstrates 'the excellencies of human nature', 'its inclinations, propensities and desires', as well as man's 'power of admiring, loving and prizing, that seeing the beauty and goodness of God, he might be united to it for evermore'. He demonstrates too the weakness and fallibility of man and he finds that the only answer to man's needs and miseries is the infinite compassion of God – 'One deep and serious groan is more acceptable to God than the creation of a world.' But these needs and this compassion do not, in Traherne's view, make a division in man between his moral frailties and his exquisite imaginative faculty. He makes no dichotomy between man's moral and his artistic nature. His answer to all men's probings and questions sounds simple but it is an answer that could only spring from brilliant insights. The message he bears proceeds not only from joy and acceptance but also from his own sufferings and surrenders; it is perfectly summed up in the following lines from the *Third Century*: 'It needeth nothing but a sense of God to inherit all things . . . Do but clothe yourself with Divine resentments and the world shall be to you the valley of vision, and all the nations and kingdoms of the world shall appear in splendour and celestial glory.'

# 9. THE UNITY OF INCARNATION

## A study of Gerard Manley Hopkins

---

*So then it was necessary for the mediator between God and us to have a temporal mortality and an eternal beatitude; to have correspondence with mortals by the first, and to transfer them to eternity by the second.*
ST AUGUSTINE – The City of God

IN AN ESSAY called *Religion and the Muses*, David Jones has made a valuable and perceptive examination of modern religious art. He is concerned with the difficulty of creating an art that is Christian both in frame-work and in depth in an age which has largely lost not only faith in Christian teaching but also the sense of a Christian tradition. The Christian artist who feels that art is at the centre of his religion and, indeed, linked inextricably with it, is in a paradoxical position. What is central to him, is central to very few others; he must convince and enchant by force of his own personality rather than by the strength of a lively and lived tradition: and tradition means, among other things, a set of interconnected images, a sequence of metaphors linked naturally not artificially. When the natural life of such images dies, the artist, whether he is poet or painter, is left with a series of symbols which, while they bear vestiges of their old significances, are now separate and autonomous – and autonomy, in this context, is a kind of death. What tradition did once, only the individual artist can do now – that is, fashion a context in which those images may not only live again but be relevant again. This kind of relevance has nothing to do with preaching or trying to convert; it is an attempt to establish a relationship, a relationship built on something more solid and lasting than a momentary 'willing suspension of disbelief'. Religious art has, in the twentieth century, solved this problem in two distinct ways. It has either sought to revive moribund symbols by placing them in dramatic forms or contexts (the plays of Eliot, the paintings of Rouault), or it has moved inward, drawing upon all the resources of the artist's own personality to find meaning and purpose.

The poetry of our own time, whether secular or religious, is more inward-turned than the poetry of any previous century. There are

many reasons for this – the decline of religion, the cult of psycho-
analysis, among others. But all art, because it cannot honestly be
divided into compartments labelled 'secular' or 'sacred', moves with
the feeling and ideas of its time. It is therefore interesting to note that
even overtly religious poetry has moved in the same direction as other
poetry – that is, inwards to the core of the individual human personality – even though one of the reasons for this general movement
was, originally, the *decline* of religion. For the truth is that art springs
from a source deeper than any particular creed or sect, although on the
level of expression and communication, it must to a greater or lesser
degree also conform to the styles and preoccupations of its own time.
Even the great experimenters and innovators have, after all, taken
note of the fashions of their time even if only to deviate from them.

But there are also the poets who have stood outside the traditions
of their own time not simply because they wished to renew the language
or try out new literary techniques but because they were out of sympathy with what one can only call the spirit of the age; the problem
here is one of subject-matter not of treatment, of conviction not of
style. But few writers can thus stand outside their time without some
damage to their work. Most retreats are retreats into obscurity, even
though obscurity itself can sometimes yield fresh values as, for example,
in David Jones's ambitious poetic work, *The Anathemata*. But the
obscurity here is entirely objective, even linguistic; the difficulties in
*The Anathemata* do not arise from the complexities or conflicts of the
artist's personality but from the attempt to write a religious poem and
revive a tradition at one and the same time. The form and the content
of this poem cannot be separated; annotation assists but it does not
and cannot simplify. *The Anathemata* is not so much out of its time as
outside time itself.

David Jones, in his prose works, has never ceased to inquire into
the problems of religious art in modern times. Nor has he tried to give
any easy answers. He is himself both a painter and a poet so that he
speaks from a practical experience of two arts. In *Religion and the
Muses* he says, 'Those arts which demand the minimum of collabora-
tion, which depend least for their existence on material – which remain
more in the region of "the idea" would *seem* to stand more chance. It
will seem more possible to write a good poem than build a good
cathedral – although, of course, all these things are, in the end,
inextricably related. There is no escape from incarnation. It's like a
shunting train.'

'There is no escape from incarnation' might well be an epigraph to all the work of Gerard Manley Hopkins. So much has been written about his theories of 'inscape' and 'instress' and about the apparent conflict in him between poet and priest, that few critics have remembered that to write vital religious verse *at all* in the late nineteenth century was itself a problem. The lag-end of an age which was divided into insensitive materialism on the one hand and emotional pietism on the other was not a propitious time for the revival of religious literature since it is harder to purify degraded symbols than to revive dead ones.

Hopkins, who is so often thought of as a twentieth-century poet (he was, in every sense of the word, a *modern* poet), is an example of the religious writer who first turns to the exploration of his own personality to test the validity of religious experience. And modern religious verse, unlike medieval religious verse, is a poetry of religious *experience* not of religion itself. This is also true of the plastic arts today. The men who carved the statues on the walls of Chartres Cathedral were depicting the relationship between God and man in historical and scriptural terms. Dogma was sufficiently alive in their minds to be itself dramatic; it needed no individual colouring of personality or personal conflict to bring it to life. The creative power of the Chartres craftsmen sprang from their ability to play variations on traditional themes or, indeed, on the theme of tradition itself.

With Hopkins it is quite a different matter; the tradition of Catholicism which he inherited at his conversion was re-presented in his own poetry in entirely personal terms; yet it was completely orthodox in the theological sense. As I have said, he first turned inward, and perhaps for that reason alone is regarded as a master of modernity. But he did much more than this; he also turned outward and saw God's signature written on all creation, creation upheld by the love of God:

> Glory be to God for dappled things

> and . . . Christ plays in ten thousand places,
> Lovely in limbs and lovely in eyes not his
> To the Father through the features of men's faces.

What is really new in Hopkins is not so much his ingenious and fastidious experiments with language and rhythm, as his double vision of the relations between God and man – God both substantially present in the centre of each man's soul, and God also pervading the whole universe. His poetry is therefore elemental rather than analogical; his unique vision reconnects the separated Christian symbols by putting them to work, as it were, in the context of all creation – of nature, astronomy, the seas, the tides, the earth, the air.

This extraordinary blending of acute selfconsciousness with an intense awareness and observation of objects and likenesses in the physical world is achieved in and through an obsession with technique. For it cannot be stated too often that the most sublime reaches of a poet's work are only arrived at through discipline and through a never-ceasing effort to make language appear new. As Blake said, 'Technical excellence is the only vehicle of genius.'

Like all visionary writers, Hopkins had to learn himself before he could learn fully about God and the universe. The marvel of his poetry is that it describes all the stages in the struggle from obscurity to clarity; it does not simply celebrate the great moments of pure vision, as Vaughan's verse does, or the reconciling power of compassion which we find in Péguy. Nor does it arrive at truth through the medium of dreams and allegory as Edwin Muir's verse does. It is, in the strictest sense of the word, a poetry of *Incarnation*, and therefore has a wholeness and a dynamic power which silence all questions about the problems of religious art.

The profundity of Hopkins's perception would have only a moderate value and conviction if his whole conception of poetry did not demand and include that contact with God which only the mystics know – a contact which reaches through and beyond the senses – and also that vision which must 'enjoy the world aright' *before* it can understand or be united with God. The sense of hierarchy is innate in Hopkins's work, and it is the very struggle between different modes of being (plants, animals, man, God) which gives his poetry both its structure and its tension. But the vision is never impersonal; 'inscape' for Hopkins meant the unique individuality of every living thing, while 'instress' was the power, namely that of God, which keeps that individuality in being.

What is startling, and even shocking, in Hopkins's verse is not so much the audacity with language or the uninhibited play of imagery as the wholeness, the integration of the vision which these things embody. His images are never approximate counters or substitutes for some statement which for ever remains out of reach. They are the vision itself, both the subject and shape of the verse. It is rather ironic that a poet who has so often been praised or condemned for the idiosyncrasy of his style (as if style were an embellishment not an

embodiment) should reveal, when his work is examined with concentration and without prejudice, that this style is entirely merged
with what the poet has to say, and could say in no other way. The
contemporary obsession with 'concrete imagery' becomes almost
irrelevant when we find in, for example, the sonnet, 'No worst, there
is none', an adherence not to concrete things for their own sake but
for their supreme power of conveying and giving life to inner states
of mind and conditions of the soul:

> My cries heave, herds-long; huddle in a main, a chief
> Woe, world sorrow; on an age-old anvil wince and sing –
> Then lull, then leave off. Fury had shrieked 'No ling-
> ering! Let me be fell: force I must be brief!
> O the mind, mind has mountains; cliffs of fall
> Frightful, sheer, no-man-fathomed. Hold them cheap
> May who ne'er hung there.

The equating here of unscaleable mountains with a condition of
despair and desolation tells us infinitely more about both the mind
*and* despair than any careful arrangement of abstractions could. The
mood is personal, the application entirely general; the dark night of
one particular man is disclosed and shared by means of an image from
the physical world. Even in his most desperately personal conflicts,
Hopkins first moves inwards and then outwards. For him, this difficult
objectivity is effected by means of imagery; the mind is cleared, the
senses satisfied.

Hopkins is perhaps the only 'modern' English poet who shows no
sign of that separation of thought and feeling which Eliot called
'dissociation of sensibility' and which he traced back to the seventeenth
century. It may well be that it is the religious nature of Hopkins's
verse that permits this unity. Tormented and battling as much of his
work is, the battle always takes place on solid ground and in a world
of order. It is a world where disruption only occurs where there is a
lack of innocence. It is not surprising, therefore, that so many of
Hopkins's poems are concerned with innocence and childhood. He
shares this love of and delight in innocence with Traherne, Péguy and
Bernanos. In *Spring* he writes,

> What is all this justice and all this joy?
> A strain of the earth's sweet being in the beginning
> In Eden garden. – Have, get, before it cloy,

> Before it cloud, Christ, lord, and sour with sinning,
> Innocent mind and Mayday in girl and boy,
> Most, O maid's child, thy choice and worthy the winning.

And again, in *The Bugler's First Communion*, Hopkins praises the
freshness and simplicity of the young soldier:

> Frowning and forefending angel-warder
> Squander the hell-rook ranks sally to molest him;
>     March, kind comrade, abreast him;
> Dress his days to a dexterous and starlight order.

Like Vaughan, Hopkins constantly pursues this 'dexterous and
starlight order' and his moments of clearest vision are closely allied
with his delight in the simplicity and innocence of childhood:

> Margaret, are you grieving
> Over Goldengrove unleaving?
> Leaves, like the things of man, you
> With your fresh thoughts care for, can you?

This is a kind of foreshadowing, a pre-echo as it were, of the children
in Eliot's rose garden – 'hidden excitedly, containing laughter'. It is
this passionate interest in the 'free and open disposition' rather than
the terrible sufferings of the later sonnets which herald, for Hopkins,
the awareness and reality of union with God.

As I have suggested already, Hopkins's poetry is a poetry of Incarnation. His oneness with God is oneness with Christ, both as God and
man. His great devotion to Mary, the Mother of God, is therefore an
essential element in his verse:

> So God was god of old:
> A mother came to mould
> Those limbs like ours which are
> What must make our daystar
> Much dearer to mankind;
> Whose glory bare would blind
> Or less would win man's mind.
> . Through her we may see him
> Made sweeter, not made dim,
> And her hand leaves his light
> Sifted to suit our sight.
>         (*The Blessed Virgin Compared to the
>         Air We Breathe*)

'Made sweeter, not made dim' and 'sifted to suit our sight' are important keys to Hopkins's own religious and mystical experience. The moments of pure illumination in his verse are almost always concerned with Christ, God the Son, the Incarnate God:

> . . . There he bides in bliss
> Now, and seeing somewhere some man do all that man can do,
> For love he leans forth, needs his neck must fall on, kiss,
> And cry 'O Christ-done deed! So God-made-flesh does too:
> Were I come o'er again' cries Christ 'it should be this.'

What Hopkins's most strenuous searches are trying to recover is, in effect, that state of innocence in which the human soul is a window for the concentrated light and reflection of God. The sufferings which he describes in the so-called 'terrible' sonnets are dark nights in which the soul becomes obscured both by its individual infidelities to God and also by the fallen condition of all mankind. Each vision of God is a recovery, a winning-back of some lost state. Like all deeply religious men, Hopkins never forgets the necessity and ennobling power of suffering. The Jesuit discipline and the practice of the *Ignatian Exercises* alone would have been sufficient to imprint this attitude towards suffering firmly on his mind.

Yet there is no masochism in Hopkins's agonies; he recognizes that suffering is part of the condition of man, a condition that has been made sweet and acceptable by Christ's Passion and death. He recognizes too, as Bernanos does, that suffering is often undergone vicariously, that it is never wasted even at its darkest moments. His work is shot through with a joyous acceptance and with that patience or 'waiting on God' which is the mark of the true mystic:

> We hear our hearts grate on themselves: it kills
> To bruise them dearer. Yet the rebellious wills
> Of us we do bid God bend to him even so.

In this sonnet there is nothing passive. God is sought with a personal, willing love and with a childlike confidence:

> . . . He is patient. Patience fills
> His crisp combs, and that comes those ways we know.

The poet knows too that he must be patient with himself and not demand from himself an inhuman courage and sacrifice:

> Soul, self; come, poor Jackself, I do advise
> You, jaded, let be; call off thoughts awhile
> Elsewhere; leave comfort root-room; let joy size
> At God knows when to God knows what . . .

One of the prerequisites of mystical experience is abandonment to God, an abandonment which is the only true source of peace. And, for the Christian mystic, peace is not so much a state as a person, is, in fact, Christ himself. Several of Hopkins's poems are explicit requests for this 'peace that surpasses all understanding':

> O surely, reaving Peace, my Lord should leave in lieu
> Some good! And so he does leave Patience exquisite,
> That plumes to peace hereafter. And when Peace here does house
> He comes with work to do, he does not come to coo,
>   He comes to brood and sit.
>
>                                         (*Peace*)

>           And I have asked to be
>             Where no storms come,
>     Where the green swell is in the havens dumb,
>       And out of the swing of the sea.
>
>                                 (*Heaven-Haven*)

Poets and mystics who have experienced some close, personal but supra-rational awareness of God have always carried away from such moments of illumination an increased subtlety, a profoundly original understanding of human experience and of the apparent contradictions even in the physical universe. This kind of understanding is one of those gifts which Catholics refer to as 'the gifts of the Holy Ghost'. On a *natural* level all true poets have this understanding. When, however, such natural intuition is permeated by grace in a poet of more than ordinary talent, his whole work is flooded by perceptiveness and by a sensitiveness to truth in all its forms. In Hopkins's poem, *The Wreck of the Deutschland*, there is a remarkable example of this kind of power carried to the point where prayer and poetry meet. The poem's subject is the shipwreck of some Franciscan nuns in 1875, but that subject is only a jumping-off ground for a complete vision of creation held in the hands of God. The poem is a celebration of the glory of human and divine life, of both the physical and the spiritual world. It is also pervaded with a humble and intelligent charity; all things are seen in the light of God.

The first eleven stanzas of the poem are an astonishingly well-sustained lyrical expression of Hopkins's own knowledge and love of God; in the last lines of the first stanza, there is an unmistakable description of a *mystical* experience:

> Thou mastering me
> God! giver of breath and bread;
> World's strand, sway of the sea;
> Lord of living and dead;
> Thou hast bound bones and veins in me, fastened me flesh,
> And after it almost unmade, what with dread,
> Thy doing: and dost thou touch me afresh?
> Over again I feel thy finger and find thee.

This 'touch' of God, expressed in entirely concrete terms, is language familiar to readers of mystical literature throughout the centuries. The poem continues with an account of the 'terror' and 'stress' of the poet when confronted by God; this terror is the terror of awe not of craven fear. But the poet moves away from this sense of almost unbearable awe to the comfort and simplicity of the Holy Eucharist (the Incarnation theme is beginning to emerge):

> I whirled out wings that spell
> And fled with a fling of the heart to the heart of the Host.

All is activity and the soul 'flings' itself into the mercy of Christ. Hopkins then acknowledges both his weakness and his strength. He is 'soft sift in an hour glass' and also 'steady as a water in a well'. The water can easily be stirred but is controlled and kept in balance by grace. What steadfastness he has, Hopkins asserts, springs from his priestly calling; he is one who can offer 'a pressure, a principle, Christ's gift'. Whatever he himself possesses is to be handed on to others.

The fifth stanza is the beginning of Hopkins's hymn to creation:

> I kiss my hand
> To the stars, lovely-asunder
> Starlight, wafting him out of it; and
> Glow, glory in thunder.

Like Eliot's last two *Quartets*, this part of the poem expresses a vision which embraces all creation. God is here seen as both immanent and transcendent, and Hopkins makes quite clear his belief that God can be found *in* natural things; his is the way of the affirmation of images:

Since, tho' he is under the world's splendour and wonder,
His mystery must be instressed, stressed;
For I greet him the days I meet him, and bless when I understand.

There is a pun here on the word 'stressed'. Hopkins is using it both in the sense of the individuality of every existing thing and also in the sense that God *needs* us to stress him, to speak to him and for him. In other words, he *wants* our love and our willing surrender in order that he may fulfil his own plans for us.

*The Wreck of the Deutschland* goes on to state that this love is not received from and exchanged with some lofty being far removed from men but that it begins and 'dates from'

His going in Galilee;
Warm-laid grave of a womb-life grey;
Manger, maiden's knee;
The dense and the driven Passion, and frightful sweat.

This love, that 'rides time like riding a river', entails suffering and submission, both ours and Christ's. It should, however, be noted that Hopkins is not here denying valid mystical experience to all those visionaries who lived before the coming of Christ; on the contrary, he states quite definitely,

Though felt before, though in high flood yet –

From this exalted presentation of the Incarnation, Hopkins moves to a celebration of the Blessed Trinity:

Be adored among men,
God, three-numberèd form.

.          .          .

Beyond saying sweet, past telling of tongue,
Thou art lightning and love, I found it, a winter and warm.

Even when speaking of a God who is pure spirit, Hopkins is able to introduce so simple and familiar a metaphor as that of one of the seasons. The proof of the success of such an image is the unquestioning delight with which we accept it. Once again, Hopkins illuminates and gives life to the abstract by presenting it in completely concrete terms. He may say that God and experience of God are 'past telling of tongue' but this does not prevent him from trying to tell these things and, what is more, from succeeding in doing so.

In all our reading of Hopkins, we should remember his deep sympathy with the thirteenth-century Franciscan philosopher, Duns Scotus. Duns Scotus was an important influence since his theology included the belief that God the Son would have become man even if Adam had not fallen from grace. This belief was not held by Aquinas and it is sometimes regarded as rather unorthodox. Unorthodox or not, this unusual attitude towards the Incarnation had a powerful effect on Hopkins's poetry in that it enabled him to see the Incarnation as more than simply the means of man's redemption. For him, such a doctrine glorified the material world and was, perhaps, largely responsible for the lovely, carefree poems of praise such as *Pied Beauty, God's Grandeur, The Starlight Night, The Windhover,* and *Hurrahing in Harvest.*

*The Wreck of the Deutschland* continues with a vigorous description of the voyage and wreck of the ship in which the Franciscan nuns were sailing. It is a powerful evocation of the strength of the elements, the elements which men struggle with and from the very struggle find peace. Hopkins's world is a dynamic world; all is moving, vital, urgent. The poem goes on to give a portrait of the leader of the group of nuns, and this portrait presents Hopkins with an opportunity to examine the meaning of the life of prayer:

> . . . Then further it finds
> The appealing of the Passion is tenderer in prayer apart.

And in the following lines he depicts the struggle to find words which will embody the experience of union with Christ. Here there is no sense of a vision recaptured in memory, but rather an attempt to portray it at its very moment of accomplishment and consummation:

> But how shall I . . . make me room there:
> Reach me a . . . Fancy, come faster –
> Strike you the sight of it? look at it loom there,
> Thing that she . . . there then! the Master,
> *Ipse,* the only one, Christ, King, Head.

After this, God is shown not simply as 'master of the tides' and 'of the year's fall' but also as 'ground of Being and granite of it', immanent and transcendent. 'Past all,' says Hopkins, we can 'grasp God, throned behind Death.'

The God of *The Wreck of the Deutschland* is a being who can be refused, wrestled with or surrendered to. There is nothing passive about man's approach to him. He is terrible but also merciful and to be

found not simply through our sorrow for sin but also through our
insatiable desire for beauty:

> With a mercy that outrides
> The all of water, an ark
> For the listener; for the lingerer with a love glides
>     Lower than death and the dark;
> A vein for the visiting of the past-prayer, pent in prison,
> The-last-breath penitent spirits – the uttermost mark
>     Our passion-plungèd giant risen,
> The Christ of the Father compassionate, fetched in the
>     storm of his strides.

This is the Christ of Palm Sunday and of the Resurrection, not the
gentle, effeminate creature, the travesty of divinity which so many
modern 'religious' statues and pictures portray. He is a person whom
the poet knows through the confrontation of personalities.

In a sermon which he preached in November 1879, Hopkins gave a
detailed and impassioned portrait of Jesus Christ. After speaking of
him as a warrior and a hero, he refers to his genius: 'I come to his
mind. He was the greatest genius that ever lived. You know what
genius is, brethren – beauty and perfection in the mind.' This idea is
crucial to an examination of the relationship between art and religion,
between poetry and mystical experience. In Hopkins's view, human
genius implied a likeness to God similar to that of human sanctity. For
him it *was* an aspect of sanctity. His sermon continues, 'For perfection
in the bodily frame distinguishes a man among other men his fellows:
so may the mind be distinguished for its beauty above other minds and
that is genius. Then when this genius is duly taught and trained, that
is wisdom; for without training genius is imperfect and again wisdom
is imperfect without genius.' It is interesting to note the stress laid
here on training, on asceticism as essential both for the man of prayer
and for the artist. The phrase 'wisdom is imperfect without genius' is
important too and makes a perfect answer to those who think that
nobility of subject-matter and intention alone can be responsible for the
creation of a work of art. 'But Christ,' Hopkins goes on, '. . . advanced
in wisdom and in favour with God and men: now this wisdom, in
which he excelled all men, had to be founded on an unrivalled genius.
Christ then was the greatest genius that ever lived. You must not say,
Christ needed no such thing as genius; his wisdom came from heaven,
for he was God. To say so is to speak like the heretic Apollinaris, who

said that Christ had indeed a human body but no soul, he needed no mind and soul, for his godhead, the Word of God, that stood for mind and soul in him. No, but Christ was perfect man and must have mind as well as body and that mind was, no question, of the rarest excellence and beauty; it was beauty; it was genius. As Christ lived and breathed and moved in a true and not a phantom human body and in that laboured, suffered, was crucified, died, and was buried; as he merited by acts of his human will; so he reasoned and planned and invented by acts of his own human genius, genius made perfect by wisdom of its own, not the divine wisdom only.'

This sermon shows clearly that Hopkins believed Christ to be a supreme example of natural, *human* genius. The poet's whole being was directed, with a kind of innocent passion, towards Jesus Christ, God and man. Such a devotion is a characteristic of the Jesuit priest, but in Hopkins it was a poetic as well as a spiritual fervour. *The Windhover*, for example, is expressly dedicated 'To Christ our Lord', and in it Hopkins likens Christ to a great soaring, plunging bird – 'kingdom of daylight's dauphin, dapple-dawn-drawn Falcon' – and the whole poem is full of movement and energy. Yet, within this energy, the poet can make contact with God, can over again 'feel Thy finger and find Thee'. The image of Christ as a falcon is the very source of the poet's ecstasy:

> . . . My heart in hiding
> Stirred for a bird, – the achieve of, the mastery of the thing.

The bold play with language here, the use of 'achieve' as a noun, the audacity which can conjure power even from a vague word like 'thing' – all this is evidence of a blend in Hopkins of artistic and ascetic discipline. He provides us, in fact, in his own life with a perfect example of the similarities between spiritual 'ascesis' and poetic craftsmanship. For the poet's training corresponds in many ways with the training of the priest – the self-mastery, the ability to discard what is inessential, the patient waiting during the times when poems cannot be written, the terrible 'dark night of the senses' in which everything seems plunged in meaninglessness and obscurity. In the life and character of Hopkins we see the two disciplines interconnected. His achievement is to have endured and mastered both the priest's and the poet's sufferings, so that the two ways of life did not conflict with one another but complemented one another. It is a shallow judgment which blames Hopkins's priestly vocation for the unhappiness of much of his life. The tension in his poetry is caused by something much more profound than a conflict between passion and celibacy or between profane and sacred love. For the truth is that there is tension at the heart of all great poetry, but this tension is the source of life not of impotence or death. The poems which satisfy most are not those which simply give a sense of reconciliation and order, but those which show life and order as the fruits of conflict; and we need to *feel* this tension even in the most triumphant and reconciled poems. Poetry is not rationalization but revelation and what is healing in it, both for the poet and his readers, is the ability to depict conflict at its most vulnerable point; with Hopkins, this point is the wrestling of man with God – but also the surrender of man to God.

In the poem called *Henry Purcell*, Hopkins gives an account of the ecstasy which Purcell's music opened to him, an ecstasy in no essential way different in kind from Hopkins's experience of God at Mass or in his own prayers. The aesthetic experience of listening to Purcell's music is seen as a direct approach to knowledge of God. In his epigraph to the poem Hopkins explains clearly just why this particular music was so important to him: '. . . whereas other musicians have given utterance to the moods of man's mind, he has, beyond that, uttered in notes the very make and species of man as created both in him and in all men generally.' We are back once again with the theme of Incarnation and also with the long-held belief of all Western Christian mystics that Christ, God made man, is at the heart of mystical experience. Purcell's music is for Hopkins, then, a window through which 'the very make and species of man' shine. Christian doctrine has always insisted on man's likeness to God so we are quite justified in interpreting Hopkins's epigraph as the belief that music too can contain and reflect the being of God. We are reminded also of the wonderful carving on one of the outer walls of Chartres which depicts God possessing the idea of man in his mind even before he created men.

In *Henry Purcell*, Hopkins declares that it is 'the forged feature' that delights him and he clearly means that, through Purcell's music, he can encounter the essence and soul of Purcell himself:

> Not mood in him nor meaning, proud fire or sacred fear,
> Or love or pity or all that sweet notes not his might nursle:
> It is the forgèd feature finds me; it is the rehearsal
> Of own, of abrupt self there so thrusts on, so throngs the ear.

It is in such words as these that Hopkins demonstrates his really original contribution to English poetry, and it is a contribution not so much of prosody or versification as of *subject-matter*. No other poet, religious or secular, has ever before used poetry as a means whereby men may encounter one another's inmost beings unprotected by masks or veils. In Shakespeare, Milton, Donne and Herbert, poetry often reaches a point where such encounters seem possible or even achieved (one thinks particularly of Leontes's discovery that his wife, Hermione, is alive at the close of *The Winter's Tale*), but what seems to me entirely new in Hopkins is the expression *within* his poems not only of the possible meetings of personalities at a very deep level, but also of the emotions and ideas which accompany such meetings. Hopkins presents a kind of existentialism in action, so that what might have been simply a metaphysical abstraction is a warm, human experience. And in his descriptions of his own relationship with God, he writes with the same ardent, vigorous language.

It is surely significant that a number of Hopkins's poems are about particular people – the bugler, the soldier, Harry Ploughman, Purcell, Felix Randal. He was consumed by the true Christian charity which sees God in all things and all things in God. In the poem, *Brothers*, he gives a moving account of how affected he himself was by the love which a schoolboy showed towards his brother. The subject of the poem is the vicarious anxiety which the boy Henry suffers as he watches his brother John act in a play. John was 'brass-bold' and Henry need not have feared for him. That he did feel for and indeed wholly identify himself with his brother is what moves Hopkins almost to tears:

> Ah Nature, framed in fault,
> There's comfort then, there's salt;
> Nature, bad, base, and blind,
> Dearly thou canst be kind;
> There dearly then, dearly
> I'll cry thou canst be kind.

It is the grace of such a *natural* expression of love that moves Hopkins so deeply. There is nothing sentimental about the poem; Nature is seen as 'base' and 'bad'. What is remarkable, Hopkins is saying, is that out of baseness and evil such sweetness and selflessness can spring. *Brothers* is, in fact, a very fine expression of Hopkins's attitude to Nature and to all things in the natural world.

The same graciousness of natural love is celebrated in *At the Wedding March*; this poem reminds us of the imagery of secular love which

John of the Cross incorporated into his *Spiritual Canticle*. Hopkins writes,

> Each be other's comfort kind:
> Deep, deeper than divined,
> Divine charity, dear charity,
> Fast you ever, fast bind.

God is love and so *all* manifestations of love are reflections and adumbrations of that love. In *The Caged Skylark* Hopkins makes a triumphant affirmation of his belief that it is as *whole* men, body and soul, with the soul 'the form of the body', that we can be most at one with Christ:

> Man's spirit will be fleshbound when found at best,
> But uncumbered: meadow-down is not distressed
> For a rainbow footing it, nor he for his bones risen.

This joyful vision of the created world, in which all things are seen to be good when they keep their appointed places in a universal hierarchy, is a vision which pervades all Hopkins's poems, even the darkest, most tormented ones. Like Eliot and like Edwin Muir, he sees man as an august creature who is free to choose good or evil. If he chooses evil, he is responsible not only for imperilling his own soul but also for introducing a little more disorder into the whole universe – 'No man is an island . . . each is a part of the main.' Hopkins's own union with God is a union with absolute beauty, a union which he desires all men to share, but to share by freely choosing it:

> . . . deliver it, early now, long before death.
> Give beauty back, beauty, beauty, beauty, back to God,
> beauty's self and beauty's giver.

# 10. THE POWER OF COMPASSION

*A note on the poetry of Charles Péguy*

---

*That simplicity of the soul, that sweet surrender to the Divine Majesty –
which in him is a momentary inspiration, a grace and like to the spark of
genius – we consecrate our lives to find or to recover if we have known it,
for it is a gift of childhood which more often than not does not outlive
childhood.*
GEORGES BERNANOS – The Fearless Heart

PÉGUY WAS NOT simply a religious man who found poetry the best
medium to express and embody a private vision. For him, the poetry
*was* part of the religious experience. As some men move from one
stage of prayer to another, Péguy moved from the meditation of ideas
to the sensuous expression of them in language. And this was no
retrogressive step. Words were absolutes and ultimates for him. No
one who has written religious poetry has ever, perhaps, been on such
humanly intimate terms with God. With the great religious poets of
the past one is usually aware of the gulf between God and man: poetry
cries across that gulf. For Péguy, there is no barrier, no gulf, therefore
no equivalent, in the completed poems, of the too often artificial stages
of prayer. Yet, as Gide has rightly pointed out, the abundant use which
Péguy makes of repetition is 'like the probing of a man in prayer':

> Now you, my daughter night, my daughter of the great
>     cloak, my daughter of the silver cloak,
> You are the only one who sometimes overcomes that rebel
>     and can bend that stiff neck of his,
> It is then, O night, that you appear.
> And what you have done once,
> You do every time.
> What you have done one day
> You do every day.
> As you came down one evening,
> So you come down every evening.
> What you did for my son who was made man,
> O great and charitable one, you do for all men his brothers,

You bury them in silence and shadow
And in the salutary oblivion
Of the mortal unrest
Of day.

These long, loose lines, these numerous repetitions are something much more profound than a peaceful compromise between poetry and prose. They have at once the intensity and clarity of poetry yet also a strong, *undemanding* rhythm, a rhythm that swiftly adapts itself to changes of mood or thought. What we derive, in more regular verse-forms, from the *expected* pleasure of rhyme or stanza, we here find in the *unexpected* yet always acceptable repetition of certain key-phrases and ideas. This is poetry of celebration, yes, but it never becomes mere rhetoric; it neither becomes inflated into the grandiose nor deflated into the prosaic. And a repetition is never simply a repetition, it is always a development, a step forward, has, in fact, a powerful cumulative effect.

No one would guess from the ease and sweetness of Péguy's verse that he was a tormented man. Yet throughout his life he suffered from the two afflictions most calculated to make a poet *manqué* – almost complete lack of recognition and an unresolvable inward conflict. He was too tough for lack of recognition to affect him profoundly, while the way he dealt with his inner torment is surely unique. Just as in his private life he would permit of no makeshift to reconcile him outwardly to the Catholic Church after his return to it, so, in his poetry, he was never satisfied with fake solutions or facile reconciliations. Nor did he make his torment his poetry as many fine religious poets have done (Baudelaire and Hopkins, for example), and if his work was an escape then it was an escape into hope and praise. Few poets, perhaps none, have written so eloquently of the theological virtue of Hope:

> . . . But contrariwise to all that comes down and the numberless
>    rains and numberless bad days,
> At once, instantly, almost before, they go and make running
>    water of it,
> Quick, clear, soft water,
> Lovely transparent water,
> Pure water, springing and trickling through those meadows
> On the banks of the Meuse.
> Lovely Lorraine water, a soul of lovely water and the very
>    source of hope.

Péguy, then, was an optimist but it was not an easy optimism. There was nothing of Browning's 'All's right with the world' about it. His optimism was based on confidence and trust, trust, above all, in the Incarnation of Christ. But perhaps Péguy only reached this attitude in and through his poetry. His disillusionment with socialism, largely on account of the Dreyfus Case, his theory of *mystique* and *politique* or idealism and expediency, were resolved rather than confirmed in his poetry. And the inner torment which he endured (largely caused by a civil marriage which his wife would not allow him to put right when he returned to the Catholic Church) was not, as with men like Claudel or Baudelaire, the torment of suppressed or thwarted passion. It is, indeed, remarkable that a man who knew so little in his own life of the anguish of the flesh, should have felt such compassion for others and have expressed it so lucidly in his verse. He speaks, in one of his poems, of 'the taste for man' which Christ acquired through the Incarnation. Péguy, although a retiring man and a difficult friend, kept this taste all his life. The *persona* he presented to the outside world may have seemed grim and even harsh at times, but this mask was forced on him by the utter lack of sympathy which his work received in his own life-time. Few people read his poetry and prose but this did not deter him from going on with it.

It is, I think, the French element in Péguy's mind and personality which prevents his simplicity from ever slipping into sentimentality. Also, he came of a tough peasant stock and never lost his love of the soil, especially of French soil. From his youth he had a passionate admiration for Joan of Arc and wrote an immense, but quite unactable, dramatic work about her. This he revised later and, in fact, all his verse springs from this central inspiration. Joan of Arc was a symbol of all that he most admired – courage, hope, innocence, tenacity, trust and self-sacrifice. He said that freedom was 'a system of courage' and he found this exemplified in her martyrdom. How very different from Marx's definition of freedom as 'the recognition of necessity'.

However, what interests me most in Péguy's work is not his thought or philosophy but the visionary quality of his poetry. It is quite unlike most other visionary poetry. It is not concerned with the blinding moment of vision that obsessed a poet like Vaughan, or with the austere ecstasies which we find in St John of the Cross. The closest equivalent in English literature and that not a very near one, is, I think, to be found in George Herbert and Thomas Traherne. Certainly, much of Péguy's work corroborates Herbert's lines:

You must sit down, says Love, and taste my meat:
So I did sit and eat,

or Traherne's remark in *Centuries of Meditations*, 'You never enjoy
the world aright till the sea itself floweth in your veins, till you are
clothed with the heavens and crowned with the stars.'

Péguy's visionary poetry is in accordance with all Western traditional mystical experience and literature; that is to say, it is founded
on charity. A vision is something to be shared with other men, and
men are neither disembodied spirits nor spirits trapped within the
prison of the flesh. What Péguy expressed was not man wrestling with
God in darkness but God leaning down to man. As I have said, the
struggle towards expression, which in poetry is the equivalent of the
early stages of prayer for the mystic, is not apparent in Péguy's work.
His is the poetry of childlike acceptance, but it is an acceptance based
on free choice:

All the submissions in the world
Are not worth the springing forth
The beautiful straight thrust of a single invocation
Of a free love.

Yet there is Grace also and Péguy never forgets this. He might,
indeed, almost be called the poet of Grace. He recognized the intervention of Grace in men's lives and in poetry. He knew, too, as all
visionaries have known, that union with God is itself a God-given
thing. As I said at the beginning of this chapter, few poets have been
on such intimately *human* terms with God as Péguy was. He was able
to sustain this delicate relationship because he never saw the flesh and
the spirit as opposites, he never forgot the Incarnation. In his verse
there is no darkness, no straining for apt imagery to express something
ineffable, nothing, in fact, of Eliot's 'intolerable wrestle with words
and meanings'. If there was a struggle, then it was resolved, in the
poet's own mind, before the poetry started. Péguy's world was not
only a 'world of light' but also a 'world of love'.

# 11. THE SECULAR ANGELS

## A study of Rilke

AT A SUPERFICIAL glance there seems to be little in common between Rilke and most of the other poets and mystics who have been discussed in this book. The majority of them, if they have not been orthodox Christians, have usually employed many of the Christian symbols even though they have sometimes wrenched them into odd and surprising shapes. Such writers have often expressed their personal visions in terms of Christian symbolism and at the same time have re-formulated or re-interpreted those symbols for their own ends.

Rilke, however, does not fit into this category; indeed, he does not fit into any category at all. Among the writers and mystics I am considering in this book, he stands quite alone. There are many reasons for this isolation but one overriding one. It is this: Rilke's poetry was for him a way of life. It was visionary, philosophical, emotional, sensuous and abstract, all at the same time. His poetry *was* his life, not simply in the sense that he was a supremely dedicated artist, but also because it was the only medium in which reality, for him, existed. Words did not formulate a previously articulated philosophy or vision of life; on the contrary, the vision, the ideas, only had existence in the medium of words. Desperate and painful as Rilke's poetic struggles often were, he never for a moment doubted the power of poetry. In his view, nothing was inexpressible. If reality was not to be found in words and images, then reality was at fault not language.

From this august conception of poetry spring all the contradictions in Rilke's life and thought – the struggle for an autonomous existence, the narcissism that sometimes overshadowed his most apparently objective inquiries, the opposition between subject and object, the mutilation of accepted beliefs in order to refashion an entirely personal world-picture. These were the problems which Rilke made for himself by leaning so heavily upon language, not only as a vehicle of truth but also as the only valid *approach* to truth.

Both on the level of day-to-day living, that world of 'telegrams and anger' as E. M. Forster has called it, and on the level of metaphysics and philosophy, Rilke's beliefs are untenable; one could not live by them and remain sane. Yet, within his poetical and, indeed, his prose work, they are not only tenable but acceptable. This is not to say that what is false in human affairs can be true in literature but rather that Rilke's intensity of vision and his power in the manipulation of images have proffered us an aspect of truth, an insight into truth, that we could attain in no other way; for poetry moves by intuition not by dialectic.

Rilke was a poet who was by no means totally turned inwards upon himself; if he had been, his work would have had only a limited, perhaps only a pathological interest. Poetry which depends solely upon the interior searchings and discoveries of the poet must, of its nature, sooner or later, reach a dead end. But Rilke's sort of subjectivity led him beyond introspection and self-analysis; he looked at the outer world in ecstasy but felt that he could only comprehend the being and individuality of animate and inanimate things by bringing them under the light of his imagination and by transforming them into shining symbols.

Mr Holthusen, in his valuable little study of Rilke, has pointed out that Rilke, who died in 1927, lived in a society where the traditional Christian beliefs were no longer widely accepted and where doubt and uncertainty were more prevalent than faith. He sees the *Duino Elegies* as attempts to find 'bearings' in such a society. Rilke is not the only major twentieth-century poet to find himself in this predicament. Eliot, before his conversion to the Anglican Church, depicted a world of chaos and openly declared,

> These fragments I have shored against my ruin.

In other words, he felt the need at least to attempt to build some kind of world, to erect a set of provisional beliefs. Yeats too, while he eschewed all accepted orthodoxy, created, by means of his verse, a philosophy which, for him, explained the meaning of human existence. Rilke's world-picture, though entirely different in content, was, in purpose, more like Yeats's than Eliot's; it was created not so much as a gesture against the uncertainty of an uneasy universe but rather as itself an ordered, autonomous world compared with which the 'real' world seemed to Rilke only a shadow.

Rilke led a sheltered, withdrawn life. His deep affection for his mother was partly responsible for his inability to form equal or reciprocal relationships with other women. His marriage was an unhappy one and he preferred a distance (that 'distance' which Simone Weil regarded as so essential to true friendship) of respect and admiration to exist between himself and those whom he loved. He formed a number of mother-child, patron-poet relationships with various sympathetic and sensitive aristocratic women such as the endlessly kind Princess Marie von Thurn und Taxis who helped him so much in his last years. He seems to have been one of those men who need to hold things off, to keep at arm's length, their most valued possessions, as if to draw those things nearer would blur their significance or injure their purity. At first sight, this attitude appears to be totally opposed to Rilke's passionate need to draw all things into his own mind before he could affirm their reality. In fact, his relations with women, his fastidious fear of approaching, of getting too involved, were an essential part of his apparently subjective attitude towards all things. It may well be that he was so afraid of being overwhelmed by things and by people, so sensitive to the possibility of being swamped and submerged, that he could only know things by re-imagining them, by bringing them under the power of his imagination. His whole world-scheme was, in a sense, a denial of the reality of things in themselves when not observed by the creative imagination, so that Rilke abstracted (though he would never have used such a word) those qualities and attributes he needed from objects, ideas and people and then re-created them. It is an amazing paradox that a man who loved to be possessed in the poetic sense, feared possession on the ordinary human level. He was extremely active in the construction of his poems yet remarkably passive in his relations with people – in so far as observing and standing aside can be regarded as passive attitudes. No facile doctrine of 'compensation' can, I think, solve this mystery.

The clue, however, to many of the paradoxes in Rilke is the undoubted fact that poetry was to him a religion. Where many great Christian poets have regarded their gifts as God-given, as things to be used rightly and honestly and returned, in humility, to God, Rilke's poetry was itself a religious faith with its own creed, dogmas, demands and hierarchies. It made as great and exhausting demands on him as the life of prayer and discipline makes on the monk. But where the man of prayer trains himself and prepares himself for union with God in the mystical experience, Rilke laid hands, as it were, on his own visions, proclaimed them in the ecstasies of his poetry and suffered, much as the religious man suffers, when the great moments of vision withdrew and the darkness returned.

Some critics have thought that the 'angels' which appear in, and are indeed the protagonists of, the *Duino Elegies*, are 'pseudonyms' for God and it does seem to me that this is the most profound interpretation of the strange powerful beings whom Rilke invokes. In the *Second Elegy* he writes:

> . . . the gods
> may press more strongly upon us. But that is the gods' affair.
> If only we too could discover some pure, contained
> narrow human, own little strip of orchard
> in between river and rock! For our heart transcends us
> just as it did those others. And we can no longer
> gaze after it into figures that soothe it, or godlike
> bodies, wherein it achieves a grander restraint.

And in the Annunciation poem in *The Life of the Virgin Mary*, he says,

> No, not his entering; but he so inclined,
> the angel, a youth's face to hers, that it combined
> with the gaze with which she looked up, and the two
> struck together, as though all outside suddenly were empty.

This description is remarkably like those descriptions which many orthodox Christian mystics have employed to express their sense of union with God. And indeed what on the surface appears, in Rilke, like an extreme form of narcissism is in fact the expression of an intense awareness of God, of a Being who cannot be circumscribed by language but who at least can be hinted at in poetry.

On this matter, Thomas Merton, the Cistercian monk, has, in his journal called *The Sign of Jonas*, made some illuminating remarks: 'I am abashed by the real solitude of Rilke which I admire, knowing however that it is not for me because I am not like that. But his is a solitude I understand objectively, perhaps not by connaturality at all but it moves me tremendously. You see, to begin with, he did not *want* it or go looking for it. It found him. Tremendous how he finds himself in the solitude of Christ (David) in the psalms, all of a sudden, there on p. 53 of Malte Laurids Brigge . . .

'Anyway, here is something Rilke himself wrote down . . . "For a while yet I can write all this down and express it. But there will come a day when my hand will be far from me and when I bid it write it will write words I do not mean. The time of that other interpretation will dawn when not one word will remain upon another and all meaning will dissolve like clouds and fall down like rain. Despite my fear I am yet like one standing before something great . . . This time I shall be written. I am the impression that will change." '

As Merton indicates, Rilke longed to be possessed, in the most literal sense. But though he is surely right to point out the discipline and austerity of Rilke's approach to truth, he is wrong, I think, in thinking that he did not sometimes try to seize and possess it, to bring the vision down and to appropriate it for his own ends. There is, in fact, a very great danger in too closely aligning Rilke's visionary experience with that of the Christian mystic, for where the Christian confronts God in the darkness of faith and accepted dogma, Rilke tried to create his own faith and his own dogmas; what he did share with the true mystic, however, was a fundamental and pervasive humility before the ineffable. Mr Holthusen has said of him, 'Rilke, then, appears . . . as the patron-saint of the loneliness of modern man; not as an advocate of a spurious retreat into other-worldliness, but as the authentic opposite of the mass-mind and of the civilization of machines and ideologies.' And elsewhere he writes, 'He hurls his standard far into the hostile field of the unexpressed and apparently inexpressible – and safely recaptures it.'

As I have said, one must not try to strain the similarities between Rilke and the orthodox Christian mystics or to twist his personality and genius into a shape that will fit neatly and comfortably into any accepted hagiology. He was not like Simone Weil in that he accepted the beliefs of Christianity yet refused to become a member of the Christian Church. On the contrary, he often denied specific dogmas while still employing Christian symbols; Christianity was a set of images which, like everything he observed and contemplated, might usefully and fruitfully be drawn into his own world-picture. And Rilke's angels, those potent beings who soar through the *Duino Elegies*, are secular angels not sacred ones. Stephen Spender has written of them, 'The angels are gigantic figures (borrowed perhaps from El Greco) in which outward reality fuses with inward significance . . . The angel, then, is a projection of the task which began originally with Rilke piecing his soul together out of experiences whose continuity he entered so passionately into. These experiences gradually demanded that he should bring to birth the invisibility of their existences with his own. The angel was the transformation of the task into a faith that there were forces in the world connecting the seen with the unseen, and making of the fusion language.'

That last sentence is a perfect summing-up of Rilke's attitude towards his insights and his poetry. Spender is right to insist on the poet's faith and trust not only in the intangible but also in the power of language to embody the apparently inexpressible. An examination of the activities of the angels in the *Elegies* will illuminate this passionate faith and also gives a precision and clarity to what sounds vague when stated baldly in prose. It should again be stressed that in these elegies Rilke is not simply abstracting what he wants from a known world, but actually *creating* a world. Without blasphemy, one can say of these poems, 'In the beginning was the Word.'

In the *First Elegy* he writes,

> Each single angel is terrible.
> And so I repress myself, and swallow the call-note
> of depth-dark sobbing. Alas, who is there
> we can make use of? Not angels, not men.

The poet feels himself confronted by an impossible task where all that has true meaning, namely the angels, is infinitely withdrawn from him. He examines the night, the stars, the Hero, and then the lovers. He wishes to lose himself in these things but is unable to. And so, towards its close, the *First Elegy* becomes an inquiry into the nature of *religious* experience:

> Hearken, my heart as only
> saints have done: till it seemed the gigantic call
> must lift them aloft; yet they went impossibly
> on with their kneeling, in undistracted attention:
> so inherently hearers. Not that you could endure
> the voice of God – far from it. But hark to the suspiration,
> the uninterrupted news that grows out of silence.

Nothing could be more sensitive and accurate than this description of the mystic's 'waiting on God'. But the poet cannot lose himself in such an experience, though he recognizes that

one's gently weaned from terrestrial things as one mildly
outgrows the breasts of a mother. But we, that have need of
such mighty secrets, we, for whom sorrow's so often
source of blessedest progress, could we exist without them?

The *Second Elegy* continues this inquiry into the possibility of self-
annihilation in God; but the examination is still on the level of the
senses and the emotions:

> For we, when we feel, evaporate.

And again, using now the image of Attic stelae, Rilke declares,

> Oh, think of the hands,
> How they rest without pressure, though power is there in
>     the torsos.
> The wisdom of those self-masters was this: hitherto it's us;
> ours is to touch one another like this; the gods
> may press more strongly upon us. But that is the gods'
>     affair.

Rilke sees something perpetual and fruitful in a work of art; it is
autonomous yet not sealed off from those who rejoice in it. Joy is one
of the keynotes of the elegies and these poems, so subtle, so profound,
are a hymn to creation as Rilke sees it, as well as a record of the poet's
struggle to achieve union with the power that underlies creation. The
elegies are then, in some sense, a denial of Rilke's constant assertion
of the inwardness of reality, and of his insistence that it only has
meaning when transformed and re-created by the poetic imagination.
In the *Elegies*, Rilke's conception of inwardness appears very like
Hopkins's theory of instress and inscape. But the difference between
Hopkins and Rilke is that, whereas Hopkins formulated his theory
*outside* his poetry, Rilke found his in the very act of writing. He obeyed
Eliot's requirement that a poet's theory should grow out of his
practice, though it is certainly true that, at times, Rilke's theories were
at odds with his practice.

In the *Third Elegy*, Rilke considers love, birth and childhood. He
insists that men love more than the one woman they are making love
to at a given moment; 'the innumerable fermentation', 'the dry river-
bed of former mothers' – 'This,' says Rilke, 'got the start of you,
maid.' And, characteristically, in his instructions to the girl about how
she should treat her lover, he passionately demands,

> . . . give him those counterbalancing nights . . .
> Withhold him . . .

Distance must be respected even in the most intimate relationship.
The *Fourth Elegy* scrutinizes more closely the fertile life of trees
and of nature and the sadness and ecstasy of childhood and of partings.
The angels reappear:

> Angel and doll! Then there's at last a play.
> Then there unites what we continually
> part by our mere existence.
>
> .        .        .
>
>         Over and above us,
> then, there's the angel playing.

Angels guard the child but even they cannot hold back death:

>                 death,
> the whole of death, – even before life's begun,
> to hold it all so gently, and not murmur:
> this is beyond description.

The child contains death fearlessly even before he has begun to
understand it.

In the *Fifth Elegy*, Rilke introduces his clowns and acrobats, those
creatures who

> . . . come down on the threadbare
> carpet, thinned by their everlasting
> upspringing, this carpet forlornly
> lost in the cosmos.

Like his angels, Rilke's acrobats are free beings who possess

> the great initial
> letter of Thereness.

It is the brooding intensity, the surrender and pliancy of these
clowns that give the poet an image of *being* at its purest and most
active. One is reminded of Aquinas's splendid definition of God as 'the
act of pure being'. In this elegy Rilke demonstrates his supreme power
over the use of verbs; he moulds them and shapes them as a sculptor
shapes clay. 'Galloping', 'tingling', 'chasing', 'veering' – these, and
many others, are employed to suggest a sense of controlled but

vehement energy. In this elegy too, Rilke invokes the angels to preserve this sense of strength and movement by converting it into the stillness of art:

> Angel! oh, take it, pluck it, that small-flowered herb of healing!
> Shape a vase to preserve it. Set it among those joys
> not yet open to us.

Such a passionate prayer is like that of the mystic who, held in the human bonds of desire and excitement, implores the silent ecstasy of union with God. This poem is crammed with secular symbols – with circus performers, lovers, fruits, urns – but they are only a means towards an end, an end which will both disclose and explain the unity of all things. It moves, too, precipately, as the poet's imagination leaps from one image to another; he permits his mind perfect freedom in the assurance that such unselfconsciousness, such lack of contrivance, will lead to a complete world-picture, a totally integrated vision of life. If the poet asks questions, then they are rhetorical questions containing in their very articulation the answers and the solutions:

> Angel: suppose there's a place we know nothing about, and there
> on some indescribable carpet, lovers showed all that here
> they're for ever unable to manage – their daring
> lofty figures of heart-flight . . .

Rilke is here postulating a world beyond the immediate one which the senses bear witness to. As I have suggested already, he believed in something resembling the Berkeleian view of the universe – that nothing existed until the mind had apprehended it. Similarly, he felt that he actually created a transcendent, spiritual world by invoking and capturing it in his verse. But the tension in these great elegies lies in the implicit yet unacknowledged belief that reality exists autonomously in an area of experience that only poetry can penetrate.

The *Sixth Elegy* presents a brief, concentrated merging of Rilke's prevailing symbols – the fig-tree, the Hero, the child, the mother. As the elegies proceed, the excitement becomes more nervous, the mind more darting. It is almost as if his words and images moved so fast that Rilke could scarcely capture them. The tumultuous words slow down, however, at the end of this elegy and Rilke comments again upon one of his major preoccupations – his dissatisfaction with the transitoriness of sensual things:

> For whenever the Hero stormed through the halts of love,
> Each heart beating for him could only lift him beyond it:
> turning away, he'd stand at the end of the smiles, another.

It is this 'beyond' that haunts Rilke, this vague awareness of a life and a power beneath and above the momentary delights of the senses. His poetry is, in a sense, a poetry of repudiation, of merely provisionary pleasures. Every poem is an act of discarding, not to destroy but, as Saint-Exupéry has put it, 'to pare down to perfection'. Rilke has expressed more vividly and fully than any other modern writer, the strange admixture of power and frustration which is perhaps the very source of poetry. He describes that desire for *more* senses, *more* thoughts, more *time*, which every poet feels when experience seems to be galloping ahead of his ability to communicate it. Rilke is unique in that he captures in his verse this acute awareness of things moving out of his reach. It is almost as if he were trying to tame his talent while still delighting in its uncontrollability.

The *Seventh Elegy* is gentler, more meditative than the *Sixth;* it is like the slow movement in a symphony. The metaphors follow one another relentlessly but not so rapidly as in the preceding poem. Stars are introduced as something timeless which can only be apprehended in death. And childhood, with its lack of a sense of time, is praised and affirmed:

> You children, I'd say, a single
> thing comprehended here's as good as a thousand.

Towards the end of this poem, Rilke expresses quite unambiguously his deeply felt philosophy of life:

> . . . the most visible joy
> can only reveal itself to us when we've transformed it, within.
> Nowhere, beloved, can world exist but within.

And, like the mystic struggling to contain his vision, the poet crys,

> Angel, gaze for it's *we* –
> O mightiness, tell them that we were capable of it – my breath's
> too short for this celebration.
>
> .          .          .
>
> Chartres was great – and music
> towered still higher and passed beyond us. Why, even
> a girl in love, alone, at her window at night . . .

did she not reach to your knee? – Don't think that I'm wooing!
Angel, even if I were, you'd never come! For my call
is always full of outgoing; against such a powerful
current you cannot advance.

But Rilke, unlike the mystic, feels that his own 'outgoing' is part of
the visionary experience, so that even the angel appears temporarily
to be vanquished.

The *Eighth Elegy* is entirely metaphysical in character. It asks the
kind of questions that are usually asked in prose by philosophers. Rilke
sees man trapped both by circumstance and by his very ability to know
his own limitations. The child and the animal are, on the other hand, free:

> . . . the free animal
> has its decease perpetually behind it
> and God in front, and when it moves, it moves
> into eternity, like running springs.

But we, says Rilke, as men, never have 'pure space before us'. The
visible world blocks our view and also acts as a mirror:

> . . . we perceive there
> only a mirroring of the free and open
> dimmed by our breath.

The animal is 'unintrospective' and, being free, 'sees everything . . .
for ever healed'. And yet, Rilke continues, even the beast carries 'the
weight and care of a great sadness' like 'a kind of memory'. He goes
on to praise the unborn creature, the being who, still in the womb,
'can still leap within'. He compares the half-assurance of a bird with

> . . . those Etruscan souls, escaped
> from a dead man enclosed within a space
> on which his resting figure forms a lid.

The elegy ends with a lovely and eloquent lament for man who,
delivered from the womb, grows every day more aware of all things
passing, himself included:

> we live our lives for ever taking leave.

The movement of the *Elegies* is immensely varied and supple; Rilke
has created a vehicle which, even in the heavy syllables of German, is
pliant enough for the highest flights of eloquence yet equally capable
of carrying the gnomic line or the philosophical reflection. Its cadences

move now to violence, now to gentleness. It leaps adeptly from one image to another, from one idea to another. There is no other modern poetry which gives so strong a sense of the poet both being carried away by his verse yet also of never quite losing his hold on it. It is easier to find a counterpart for the *Elegies* in music than in any other kind of verse. Like symphonic music, they repeat, improvise, return to the same themes, elaborate them and then, with an amazing simplicity, move into a single, bare, unfaltering phrase. Rilke has the elegance of a Mozart but also the sense of struggle of a Beethoven.

The *Ninth Elegy* is a painful, heart-rending consideration of time, of the fleeting moment. But the note sounded is a much deeper, more reverberating one than that of mere nostalgia. Rilke says,

> Us the most fleeting of all. Just once
> everything, only for once. Once and no more. And we, too,
> once. And never again. But this
> having been once, though only once,
> having been once on earth – can it ever be cancelled?

In other words, every moment, simply because it has once existed, can never finally disappear or be valueless. And yet, Rilke continues,

> we keep pressing on and trying to perform it,
> trying to contain it within our simple hands,
> in the more and more crowded gaze, in the speechless heart.
> Trying to become it.

However, he soon discards this impotent desire for possession and acknowledges that time cannot be detained in this way. Only two things can halt time and perpetuate it – suffering ('the hardness of life', 'the long experience of love' – the pain and surrender of the saint, in fact) and the act of *naming* things. It is surprising that Rilke was not more interested in the Christian sacrament of baptism, that sacrament which both confers a character and gives a name, for he writes,

> For the wanderer does not bring from mountain to valley
> a handful of earth, of for all untellable earth, but only
> a word he has won, pure, the yellow and blue
> gentian. Are we, perhaps *here* for saying: House,
> Bridge, Fountain, Gate, Jug, Fruit-tree, Window –
> possibly: Pillar, Tower? . . . but for *saying*, remember,
> oh, for such saying as never the things themselves
> hoped so intensely to be.

The finding and giving of names does much more than endow the namer with power over the things he has named : it also gives meaning and life to the things themselves. Similarly, in one of the *Sonnets to Orpheus* which is about the mythical unicorn, Rilke says that men

> . . . fed it, not with corn,
> but only with the possibility
> of being.

They imagined it and therefore it sprang to life. But the treatment of being and existence is more subtle in the *Elegies* for in them Rilke considers the whole universe, not simply the myths that man has conjured up to explain it.

The *Ninth Elegy* is about eternity as well as time. 'Here,' declares the poet, 'is the time for the Tellable' even though 'things we can live with are falling away.' The Angel represents timelessness and lives outside the dimension of here and now; yet man can do something which the Angel, of his very nature, is unable to do – he can speak of *things*, of fleeting particulars, of objects that begin to crumble even while they are being observed. The Angel, on the other hand, lives in eternity, in a cosmos where man is 'only a novice'. And so Rilke exhorts man to do what only he can do :

> . . . So show him
> some simple thing, refashioned by age after age
> till it lives in our hands and eyes as a part of ourselveᴊ.
>
> .      .      .
>
> Show him how happy a thing can be, how guileless and ours.

And he goes on to praise all those things which 'live on departure' and which are rescued 'through something in us, the most fleeting of all'.

Rilke ends this elegy with a vision of earth transformed, through us, into something invisible; he explains to the Earth that 'Beyond all names I am yours, and have been for ages', while Death, 'that friendly Death', is Earth's 'holiest inspiration'. Death is inspired and holy because by means of it man is at last wholly lost and contained both in the dust from which he came and in that world of the Untellable from which the Angel is the only messenger. Precisely *what* Rilke believed about immortality is hard to judge from the *Elegies*; it does seem fairly certain, however, that he expected a life after death and that such a life would be a fulfilment of personality rather than an extinction of it.

The *Tenth Elegy* begins by describing the poet's emergence from the 'terrifying vision'. After the rapture comes the recording of it and Rilke wishes to 'burst into jubilant praise to assenting Angels'. But, unlike the mystic who is too caught up in God's purposes to care whether or not the sign of his vision is written upon him, Rilke hopes that the 'new-found splendour' will appear on his 'streaming face'. Yet he shares with the religious visionary the knowledge of pain and of the 'Nights of Affliction', and embraces them gladly. The poet descends, like a man who has spent nights of prayer alone on a mountain-top, and he returns to earth cleansed, accepting and wiser. He has learnt the uses of suffering and explains,

> . . . We wasters of sorrows!
> How we stare away into sad endurance beyond them,
> trying to foresee their end! Whereas they are nothing else
> than our winter foliage, our sombre evergreen, *one*
> of the seasons of our interior year.

These lines are a kind of exorcism of the earlier cry of grief,

> we live our lives for ever taking leave.

The poet knows that he must now wander in the city of men, in 'the streets of the City of Pain'. He views the city with a sagacious disenchantment, reflecting 'how an Angel would trample it down without trace'. But there is the fair-ground also, the transitory home of clown, juggler and acrobat, those beings who do not try to stay the passage of time but whose whole lives conform to restlessness, rootlessness and wandering; and, by recognizing and accepting the tyranny of time, they are liberated from its restlessness. Beyond the almost tragic frivolity of the clowns are the lovers and the children. The lover loves 'gravely' while the girl is perhaps 'just a lament'. Such gentle distress can only be comprehended by 'the youthfully dead', by those who are too young either to be tarnished or disillusioned. The poet now enters a world of 'Lamentations', a world which might be cold and abstract had not Rilke something of Dante's power to make concrete the most tenuous thoughts and moods. The next lines of this elegy depict a world of fully realized and completely concrete ideas and perceptions. Here there are 'tall tear trees', 'fields of flowering sadness' and 'pasturing herds of grief'. 'And,' says the poet,

> at times
> a startled bird, flying straight through their field of vision,
> scrawls the far-stretching screed of its lonely cry.

Almost, this might be a Purgatorio, a place of waiting and suffering. The *Tenth Elegy* contains the most masterly handling of abstract ideas; Rilke has reached, delicately and surely, that state where reason has not been rejected but surpassed, where imagination creates an autonomous world not simply an analogical one or a counterpart of what we call the 'real' world. He gathers together all the themes, creatures and objects which have been celebrated in the earlier elegies but now sees them transformed into astronomy, as stars peerless and distant:

> There
> look: the *Rider*, the *Staff*, and that fuller constellation
> they call *Fruitgarland*. Then, further towards the Pole:
> *Cradle, Way, The Burning Book, Doll, Window.*
> But up in the southern sky, pure as within the palm
> of a consecrated hand, the clearly-resplendent *M*,
> standing for Mothers . . .

This last startling image which compares the moon with the Host held by the priest during Mass is linked with Rilke's conception of the role and power of the Mother; there may also perhaps even be a half-conscious allusion to the mother of Christ. The part played by the mother here also reminds us of Julian of Norwich's daring declaration of the Motherhead of God; in *Revelations of Divine Love* she says, 'the deep wisdom of the Trinity is our Mother'.

The glory of this earthly vision does not, however, distract the poet from his recognition of the necessity and ennobling power of pain. 'The elder Lament' brings him to 'the source of Joy' and she explains to him 'with awe' that joy 'among men it's a carrying stream'. From this point he must travel alone to 'the mountains of Primal Pain' and never submit to the temptation to turn back. The elegy concludes on one of those notes of utter calm and simplicity which are just as unique a part of Rilke's greatness as his tempestuous and crowded visions. The lines are like a hand pointing not to reprove but to guide:

> And we, who have always thought
> of happiness climbing, would feel
> the emotion that almost startles
> when happiness falls.

This is very like an admission, however tentative, that there is a greater experience to come which only death can reveal. And these

lines have also something of the entirely human and finite sense of
peace which Milton described thus, at the end of *Paradise Lost*:

> They, hand in hand, with wandering steps and slow
> Through Eden took their solitary way.

From this examination of Rilke's greatest work, we can see that it
would be a grave error of judgment to align him too closely or too
eagerly with the great orthodox Christian mystics; on the other hand,
there is so much in feeling, thought and expression in the *Duino Elegies*
that sounds like echoes of Christian mystical experience, that one can,
I think, justly claim not only that Rilke knew personally both the
darkness and the ecstasy of the search for and surrender to God (even
though he often expressed it in very different terms), but also that
such experience and the transcribing of it released him from his own
intense subjectivity. The great flights of eloquence in the elegies are
journeys from the self not *into* the self; they are, in effect, a kind of
denial of many of the things which Rilke said in his letters and his
prose works. It was honesty, not self-deception, that led him to
distrust everything that he could not experience and affirm in his own
mind. His poetry released him from the bonds this honesty imposed
upon him so that he often wrote more profoundly than his conscious,
rational mind knew. This is one of the paradoxes of the poetic faculty;
poets often do not know what they really think until they see what
they write. Like the mystics, they are channels for truths and perceptions that are received rather than sought out.

Critics have sometimes rebuked Rilke for the way in which he
altered, or appropriated, the parables and events of the New Testament, and they have cited his *Prodigal Son* and *Life of Mary* as cases
in point. But it is a shallow judgment to suppose that because he
interpreted these things in his own way, he was therefore either profoundly at odds with Christianity or else took up a frivolous attitude
towards it. He distrusted dogma, certainly, and yet most of his life's
work was an attempt to erect a system of ideas which would both
explain the universe and also make it tolerable. Where the Christian
mystic lives by the ordinary rules of the Christian life and waits
humbly upon God for the great moment of union and illumination,
Rilke built up a series of provisional, even pragmatic, beliefs as he
went along. The important thing is that he was not afraid to abandon
these beliefs when his poetic vision revealed to him a different world,
perhaps a more painful one, certainly one more sublime.

# 12. A WORLD OF CONTRADICTIONS

## A study of Simone Weil

---

*Suffering does not last but* having suffered *lasts for ever.*
LEON BLOY

SIMONE WEIL, WHO died in England in 1943 and who had lived in the United States as well as in France, seems to have been one of those people who pursue their own destruction and who, therefore, in an age of uncertainty like our own, become something of a symbol. Yet it would be false and misleading to regard her simply as a symptom or a summing-up of her own age, for she was a person not a type, an eccentric not a conformist. Her life in a sense exemplified the distress and anxiety of her times, yet it was still *her* life and she lived out her own predicament, not anyone else's.

The most important thing to remember about Simone Weil is that she was Jewish. In the many books and articles which have been written about her, I do not think that this fact has been sufficiently emphasized. She was a Jewess uprooted from her own religion, so that in a double sense she was a wanderer: she had the instinctive Jewish need to wander and she also felt lost because she *was* uprooted, both from her own past and her own race. It was no chance matter that one of her books was concerned with man's 'need for roots'. Péguy said that Jews were either 'merchants or prophets' and that one of their major characteristics was always to be 'elsewhere'. Simone Weil certainly had something of the prophet or seer in her temperament but this was qualified by an extraordinarily fine intellect. In many ways, she regarded the intellect as man's highest faculty and it is not surprising that when in *Waiting on God* she wrote about humility, she suggested that thoughts of one's own stupidity were more likely to induce humility than reflections on one's wickedness.

Simone Weil was a Jewess who hated Judaism. The religion of the Old Testament seemed to her a bloodthirsty and barbaric thing. Yet one of the contradictions in her nature (and she was full of contradictions) was that, like many orthodox Jews, she was obsessed with the idea of sacrifice; the scapegoat was something much more vivid than a mere symbol to her. Firmly established in her mind too was the idea of election or choice. Most of the books and essays which have been written about her, particularly those by Fr. Perrin and Gustave Thibon, are concerned with why she would not be baptized until she felt that God had personally and unmistakably indicated to her that she should be. Myself, I believe that this particular aspect of 'waiting on God' was part of her Jewish inheritance; it went much deeper than arrogance or egotism and was, perhaps, something beyond her conscious control.

And this is the all-important fact to bear in mind in any examination of Simone Weil's life and thought – that, precise and luminous as her intellect was and assured as she herself was of its paramount efficacy, she was by no means always guided by it; her mind often moved more by intuition than by rational argument. It is here that Simone Weil enters the world of the poet and the mystic, who have this in common – that their experience, while it does not deny the rational faculty, transcends the rational faculty. It is true that Simone Weil was not a poet in the strictly literal sense but, in those parts of her writing where images took over, she approximated to poetry. On the other hand, there appears to be very little doubt that she had had mystical experience. In the following passage in *Waiting on God*, she gives an account of it: 'In my arguments about the insolubility of the problem of God I had never foreseen the possibility of that, of a real contact, person to person, here below, between a human being and God. I had vaguely heard tell of things of this kind, but I had never believed in them. In the *Fioretti* the accounts of apparitions rather put me off if anything, like the miracles in the Gospel. Moreover, in this sudden possession of me by Christ, neither my senses nor my imagination had any part; I only felt in the midst of my suffering the presence of a love, like that which one can read in the smile of a beloved face.'

One of the many interesting things about this experience and Simone Weil's reaction to it is that, although she was never baptized into the Catholic Church, her attitude towards this particular experience was very close to that of the orthodox Western Christian tradition. But there *were* points where Simone Weil diverged from this orthodoxy; she was obsessed, for example, with the idea of syncretism, with that system of religious thought which endeavours to integrate the dogmas and traditions of many creeds and to make a whole from them. She loved Greece and its religion and philosophy with an almost fanatical passion; the contemplative religions of the East were also extremely sympathetic to her temperament.

I have said already that Simone Weil appeared to be in pursuit of her own destruction. This is, however, only half the truth. Her utter disregard for her health and personal well-being, the determination with which she sought the kind of life which would bring not only discomfort but illness, her love of the poor and the oppressed – these things were, at one and the same time, a pursuit both of perfection and of destruction. But it would be wrong to suppose that she was a masochist. She did not love pain and suffering for their own sake but because she felt they united her with Christ whom she worshipped both as God and man. Her whole doctrine of 'affliction' (and by affliction she meant bodily, mental and social dereliction) is based on the idea of participation in the passion of Christ. In this she resembled many of the great saints and mystics of the past, and especially Augustine and Teresa of Avila with whom she shared a fineness of intellect combined with strong emotion and the need to seek out appropriate images to express her experiences.

Like so many people who have been the recipients of some form of mystical experience, Simone Weil *questioned* her experience; she was eager to know its meaning and purpose. She shared with Teresa and John of the Cross that distaste for the sham that is so often the purest indication of a genuine and humble apprehension of the presence of God. Thus, she followed her brief account of her own mystical experience with these qualifying comments: 'I had never read any mystical works because I had never felt any call to read them. In reading as in other things I have always striven to practise obedience. There is nothing more favourable to intellectual progress, for as far as possible I only read what I am hungry for, at the moment when I have an appetite for it, and then I do not read, I *eat*. God in his mercy had prevented me from reading the mystics, so that it should be evident to me that I had not invented this absolutely unexpected contact.

'Yet I still refused, not my love but my intelligence. For it seemed to me certain, and I still think so today, that one can never wrestle enough with God if one does so out of pure regard for the truth . . . After this I came to feel that Plato was a mystic, that all the Iliad is bathed in Christian light, and that Dionysus and Osiris are in a certain sense Christ himself; and my love was thereby redoubled.

'I never wondered whether Jesus was or was not the incarnation of

God; but in fact I was incapable of thinking of him without thinking
of God.'

These passages raise several important points. Firstly, the equating
of Christ with Dionysus and Osiris not only displays Simone Weil's
passionate desire for some form of syncretism, but also shows that her
whole approach to experience was closer to the poet's than to the
mystic's. The emphasis she lays on the necessity of the play of the
intelligence even in the midst of the most apparently inexplicable
experience is one indication of this. The other is her painstaking search
for symbols, for equivalents. Christ is Christ, yes, but he is also seen
by her as Dionysus and Osiris. Time is set aside, history is, for the
moment, in abeyance, and indeed, for the poet, symbols are always
timeless since they can be brought to life over and over again in the
blinding clarity of an individual vision.

The idea also of man's wrestling with God is a poetic as well as a
religious conception; it is an image which tries to give bodily expression to a sense of spiritual torment and striving. Hopkins also used
this image when he wrote,

> . . . that night, that year
> Of now done darkness I wretch lay wrestling
> with (my God!) my God.

His source was certainly the Old Testament account of Jacob's
struggle with the Angel. It is here, I think, that we are at the very
heart of Simone Weil's message and the extraordinary paradox of her
life. She devoted an entire book to the subject of 'waiting on God' yet
in her expression of the search for Christ and for the life of prayer, she
was always active, exploring, feverish for fact. Even stillness and
attentiveness were matters for intellectual examination; there is, in
fact, in her entire work, little of that total abandonment to God which
is so shiningly evident in every Christian mystic who preceded her.

The restless demands of the intellect, the search for suitable imagery
– these are the things which place Simone Weil among the poets (in
the broadest sense) rather than in the company of the pure mystics.
For, as Bremond has indicated in *Prayer and Poetry*, the poet's very
vocation is in some way to spoil experience by the need to find language
which will embody it. In this sense, every communication of religious
experience necessarily taints the initial insight. And words, however
lovely, always have the seed of betrayal within them. The awareness
of this was constantly in Simone Weil's mind; she trusted in words

even while she knew how treacherous they could be. She loved the silence that falls between one utterance and another, but she also knew that the silence was itself intensified by the speech which preceded and followed it. She said, in some passages discussing her own meditation on the words of the Pater Noster: 'At times the very words tear my thoughts from my body and transport it to a place outside space where there is neither perspective nor point of view. The infinity of the ordinary expanses of perception is replaced by an infinity to the second and sometimes the third degree. At the same time, filling every part of this infinity of infinity, there is silence, a silence which is not an absence of sound but which is the object of a positive sensation, more positive than that of sound. Noises, if there are any, only reach me after crossing this silence.'

The urgency and eagerness of this sort of writing are very obvious; Simone Weil's intellect could never be wholly pacified but must forever be examining, appraising and drawing conclusions. Her intense seeking out of personal and often physical suffering was, I believe, partly a half-conscious attempt to abandon the demands of her intelligence. She *knew* that she was dazzled by the brilliance of her own intellect and so she sought darkness and oblivion in outward affliction, in the anonymous lives of factory workers and peasants, in the rejection not only of material pleasure but also of material necessities. Her way of life led to sickness, though it was something much deeper than sickness only that she was searching for. What she was seeking is revealed in the following words: 'It is not that I feel within me a capacity for intellectual creation. But I feel obligations which are related to such a creation. It is not my fault. Nobody but myself can appreciate these obligations. The conditions of intellectual or artistic creation are so intimate and secret that no one can penetrate into them from the outside. I know that artists excuse their bad actions in this way. But it has to do with something very different in my case.' The note of protest here, the half-aware eschewing of authority, the wish for an autonomous world created by the mind *for* the mind, are more consonant with the attitude of the poet or artist than with that of the dedicated person of prayer.

It does seem, then, that the conflict in Simone Weil's life was something much more subtle than the force of Christian teaching invading a very Jewish mind, or even than the wish for assurance and truth at odds with an appetite for uncertainties. There is something *manqué* about all Simone Weil's work and I think the explanation for this is that she was both a writer *manqué* and a mystic *manqué*. What one senses most powerfully in her work is a profound duality, a duality which she herself was perfectly conscious of when she wrote, 'If still persevering in our love, we fall to the point where the soul cannot keep back the cry "My God, why has thou forsaken me?" if we remain at this point without ceasing to love, we end by touching something which is not affliction, which is not joy; something which is the central essence, necessary and pure; something not of the senses, common to joy and sorrow; something which is the very love of God.

'We know then that joy is the sweetness of contact with the love of God, that affliction is the wound of this same contact when it is painful, and that only the contact matters, not the manner of it.'

These words, which could so easily be paralleled in the writings of Julian of Norwich or Teresa of Avila, describe an experience which is valid, honest, pure and indisputable; and yet the attitude of Simone Weil towards the experience, her desire for a perilous balance of opposites, her acceptance which has in it the note of despair (like hunting horns heard far off) as well as resignation, reveal that even in apparent serenity she could find anguish and uncertainty. For the truth is that when the saints and mystics have cried out to God in a language that sounds like despair, there has always been a profound and humble acceptance at the heart of their suffering – something very different from anxiety or doubt. What Simone Weil did was to assign to the moment of prayer the kind of anxiety which, in human experience, is only proper to the artist – the anguish of the poet, whenever words seem to fail his experience. It is as if Eliot's 'intolerable wrestle with words and meanings' were transferred to the life of prayer, the communication of man with God. This, I am sure, was the conflict which prevented Simone Weil's request for baptism. It was not humility that she lacked but rather that she possessed the wrong kind of humility – a humility which is proper to the poet when he moves in the world of language and symbols, but wrong for the mystic who knows that pride and humility can work in the intellect as well as in the will: and who, therefore, acknowledges that both intellect and will must be placed in God's hands and resigned to his purposes.

These reflections are, to a certain extent, corroborated in the brief biography which Gustave Thibon wrote about his friend. He is expressly concerned with the central conflict in Simone Weil's nature and attempts to reconcile her humility with her apparent aloofness, her intelligence with her passion, and, most subtle of all, her desire for detachment with her inability to be detached from detachment itself. For her, he says, 'genius meant . . . the opening of the intelligence of man to the wisdom of God'. He goes on to examine the contradictions in her character and says, 'On the one hand there was a longing for absolute self-effacement, an unlimited opening to reality even under its harshest forms, and, on the other, a terrible self-will at the very heart of the self-stripping; the inflexible desire that this stripping should be her own work and should be accomplished in her own way, the consuming temptation to verify from within, to test everything and experience everything for herself.'

'To verify everything from within' – this admirably sums up Simone Weil's attitude to philosophy, art and religious experience. As we have seen, there have for many centuries been in the West two streams of mystical literature – that which embodies the affirmation of images (exemplified by writers like Traherne), and that which approves the rejection of images, the way of which the prose of St John of the Cross is the supreme example. But Simone Weil's experiences and writings do not fit completely into either of these categories; she *wished* to reject images and yet could never quite manage to relinquish them. As she said, 'Perhaps . . . it may be given me, at least for a few moments, to receive the reward attached to work on the land and to none other, the feeling that the earth, the sun, the landscape really exist and are something more than mere scenery.' There is, surely, more than a suggestion of pantheism in this sort of speculation.

In spite of her penetrating intellect and her uncompromising honesty, there does seem to have been an element of self-deception in Simone Weil's thought; so often she seems to cling to the *means* when it is the end that she really desires. In this she resembles the poet who, when the poem is written, the end achieved, is no longer interested but only desires the means towards yet another end, another completed work. M. Thibon touches on this dilemma when he compares Simone Weil with Rimbaud: 'Someone has described Rimbaud as "a mystic in the wild state". Such a judgment can only be applied in a very indirect manner to Simone Weil. I have, however, often wondered how far certain very subtle values of Western civilization had penetrated to the deepest levels of her nature. What she lacked was that suppleness with regard to destiny . . . that spontaneous and actual sense of proportion which makes it possible to see everything in its right relationship . . .' This lack M. Thibon ascribes, rightly I am sure, to her Jewish blood and temperament. 'Is there,' he asks, 'anything more

Jewish than the perpetual tension and uneasiness, the urge to examine and test the great realities?' The Jews, for centuries, have been notable for their artistic and creative qualities and perhaps it is not too far-fetched to suggest that there is some connection between a race which needed to wander and which could never find a resting-place and the artist's own personal, and never satisfied, quest for a perfect work of art. Gustave Thibon quotes some highly relevant reflections on this matter from a letter which Simone Weil wrote to him about his own writing: 'You have already experienced the dark night, but it is my belief that a great deal of it still remains for you to pass through before giving your true measure; for you are far from having attained in expression, and hence in thought, to the degree of utter stripping, nakedness and piercing force which is indispensable to the style which belongs to you.' Here, she puts the language of mysticism at the service of literature and it seems clear that, divided as she was in so many other ways, she was convinced of the unity of prayer and poetic experience. Thomas Merton has written, in his diary *The Sign of Jonas*, of the difficulty of living the life of prayer with the equipment of the artist. I think that Simone Weil always had this difficulty in mind. The reason why she seems to have been unable to resolve it was that while affirming intellectually the possible union of prayer and poetry, she could not herself live out this possibility. Her great respect for the intellect tended to make her underrate the power of the imagination.

M. Thibon makes some profound remarks about this problem when he discusses the nature of her genius. It was, he says, 'of a philosophic and religious order', and was therefore founded on the intellect. Yet the play of the imagination and of the senses seldom ceased with her, even when she refused to recognize it. M. Thibon suggests that many of Simone Weil's writings should be taken on the level of 'myths' – in other words, as analogies and images which are valid as adumbrations or glimmerings of experiences which soar *above* the intellect though they do not deny it.

In Simone Weil we are presented with an unquestionably complex character. Hers was a world of contradictions in which there was room both for the ideal human beauty of Greece and for the most austere ascetical practices of northern Europe. Such ideas, such opposites were accepted by her even while they could never be reconciled to each other. Philosophic and speculative as her cast of mind was, there is no system or method in her thought: there are footnotes and fore-shadowings only. She longed to surrender herself completely yet lacked the ultimate confidence which hands over everything, even contradictions, into God's care.

At the beginning of this chapter I suggested that Simone Weil was, in many ways, a symbol of the troubled times in which she lived. In a world of war, starvation, suffering and anxiety, she tried to give a meaning to these things by bearing them in her own life and reflecting them in her writings. She was too clear-sighted to see any easy remedies, while the nature of her own gifts prevented her finally from seeing the deep-rooted connection between a sense of guilt and a sense of God.

# 13. THE VISION OF JOY

## A study of Georges Bernanos

IF A MAN could take his shadow and accept it not merely as a sign of himself written by the sun but as an essential part of himself, he might begin to understand something of the mystery of prayer and poetry, suffering and surrender, religion and imagery. This is what Georges Bernanos, the recently dead French novelist, has tried to do. He is not a poet, except at those moments where his novels reach the limits of prose and cry for a barer and simpler statement; nor is he a mystic in the sense that he is trying to depict his own religious experiences directly. But that he has something of the mystic in him is evident both from the subjects he selects and the way in which he treats them. In his novel *Joy*, he is concerned with the terrifying experiences of a young visionary. Here, the visionary is seen as something very like a victim, a bearer-away of the sufferings which other men refuse. She confronts evil, even accepts it, yet she does not let it overwhelm her. In one of the later chapters of this novel, Bernanos describes Chantal's surrender to God: 'For at present, the idea, the certainty of her impotence had become the dazzling centre of her joy, the core of the flaming star. It was by that very impotence that she felt herself united to the still invisible Master, it was that humiliated portion of her soul that had plunged into the abyss of suavity. Slowly, with infinite precaution, she amorously completed the consumption of that scattered light; she concentrated its rays at a single point of her being as though she hoped to pierce the last obstacle and through the breach to lose herself in God. For another little moment the waters were still. Then the flamboyant wave began gently, insidiously to recede, scattering its foam everywhere. The pain appeared again like the black tooth of a reef between two columns of spray, but now stripped of all other feelings, reduced to its essence, smooth and bare indeed like a rock worn away by the waves. By this sign Chantal knew that the last stage had been passed, her humble sacrifice accepted, and that the anguish of the past hours, the doubts and even her remorse, had now been engulfed in the prodigious compassion of God. – She dared not move, nor even lower her wide-open eyes, fixed on the same point of the wall, a little below her crucifix. She felt plainly the fatigue of her knees, her back, the weight of the nape of her neck, that sort of hardening of the eyeballs that paralysed her gaze. And yet her suffering no longer belonged to her, she could no longer contain it; it was like an effusion, outside her own shattered, annihilated flesh, of the precious blood of another heart. "I possess nothing now," she thought with a joy still naïve but yet august and solemn, and that she wanted to hug to her breast as though it had been the sublime fruit of her extraordinary union. "If it were His will I could die." '

This needs a close examination; first, there are the familiar images of mystical writing – the waters, the rocks, the lights, the blood, the attributes and activities of profane love. Second, there is the sense of concentration, the desire not to move or be moved, not even to flicker an eyelash. Then there is the sense of consummation, not of the flesh but expressed in terms of the flesh. Finally, there is felt the limpness and poverty of language, yet still the necessity to speak. We are reminded of Wittgenstein's final painful succumbing to silence because words only meant nonsense. We are reminded, too, of all things brought to a standstill, that subjective yet valid peace which Augustine knew when he spoke with his mother at Ostia – that solemn sense of order and tranquillity which the poet has an inkling of when he has completed a poem which he knows to be good. We recall Bremond's remark about poets having to rationalize their experiences, to ask questions and to find answers, so that the finished poem falls perilously but certainly somewhere between the questions and the answers.

Bernanos has, in fact, in the form of a perfectly conventional novel, described the exaltation and the agony which many mystics, of various centuries and countries, have also striven to describe. But with him there is this vital difference – they have been depicting their own feelings and thoughts, whereas he has projected what must certainly have been part of his own experience into the life of an imaginary character. And here we reach the difficult and much-disputed question of the place of imagination in mystical experience; and I mean here not imagination as a source of deception but as an instrument of knowledge itself. Imagination is the very ground of the life of the poet – 'the shaping spirit of imagination', Coleridge called it. But with the mystics it has always been slightly suspect. Even the author of *The Cloud of Unknowing* gave it a comparatively low place, among the experiences of the senses, in his exploration of the higher reaches of prayer. And yet, released from its adherence to sensual things, may not the imagination itself be an approach to prayer, even a means to it? Many writers on the spiritual life have admitted the uses of the imaginative faculty in preparing the mind for ultimate union with God; but I mean something much more profound and far-reaching than this – in short, the possibility of the participation of the purified imagination in the very act of surrender to God. For there seem to be moments when the poet is *given* some intuition of truth through the channel of the imagination and through *no other channel*. This, certainly, seems to be implicit in Bernanos's attitude to prayer, as well as in Péguy's, and, to move further back in time, in Traherne's and Herbert's. May it not be that mystical writers, fearful of the traps and charms of the imagination, have tried to omit it from their systems while still using it to *formulate* their systems? It may be argued that to grant validity to imagination in one sphere of experience is not necessarily to do so in others; but if the imagination can be employed both in the early stages of prayer and also in the *expression* of the highest forms of mystical experience, it is difficult to deny it a good deal of importance in the total approach to God. Imagination, certainly, may sometimes be a perilous intruder in the mystic's experience, but it is, without doubt, the *only* faculty that proffers the method and materials to re-create that experience. Coleridge understood this perfectly when, in Chapter thirteen of his *Biographia Literaria*, he defined the function of the Primary and the Secondary Imagination: 'The imagination, then, I consider either as primary or secondary. The primary imagination I hold to be the living power and prime agent of all human perception, and as a repetition in the finite mind of the eternal act of creation in the infinite I AM. The secondary imagination I consider as an echo of the former, co-existing in the conscious will, yet still identical with the primary in the kind of its agency, and differing only in *degree*, and in the mode of its operation. It dissolves, diffuses, dissipates, in order to re-create: or where the process is rendered impossible, yet still at all events it struggles to idealize and to unify. It is essentially vital, even as all objects (*as* objects) are essentially fixed and dead.'

This passage raises many abstruse questions, questions of a fundamentally philosophical character. What is relevant in it to a study of

Bernanos's approach to the mystical experience is the stress that is laid
on the power of the imagination. The author of *The Cloud*, Teresa of
Avila and John of the Cross would certainly not agree in assigning so
lofty a place to man's imaginative faculty; Teresa, in particular, was
only too well aware of the potential dangers of this faculty, but this
was certainly partly because she had a very strong imagination herself
and therefore knew its perils by personal experience. On the other
hand, even so austere and ascetic a man as John of the Cross encouraged
his readers and spiritual charges to seek out hills or mountainous places
when they wished to pray, because he regarded such scenery as con-
ducive to prayer ('I have lifted up my eyes unto the hills.'). However,
it would be to make a complete travesty of his work to suggest that
his attitude towards the imagination was anything remotely like that
of Coleridge. Indeed, he said, in *The Ascent of Mount Carmel*, 'The two
powers of imagination and fancy serve for meditation, which is a
discursive act by means of imagery, forms, and figures, wrought in
the senses . . . All these imaginations and apprehensions are to be
emptied out of the soul, which must remain in darkness so far as it
concerns the senses, in order that we may attain to the divine union,
because they bear no proportion to the proximate means of union with
God.' We should not forget, however, that in his *Spiritual Canticle*,
St John employs the almost erotic imagery of the *Song of Songs* to
convey the experience of complete union with God:

> Let us rejoice, O my Beloved!
> Let us go forth to see ourselves in Thy beauty.
> To the mountain and the hill,
> Where the pure water flows:
> Let us enter into the heart of the thicket.

While he certainly believed that the imagination is a positive
impediment to true mystical union, we have seen from his own verse
that he was perfectly prepared to entrust to the imagination the task
of expressing that union. His poetry is not a denial of his convictions
but it *is* the liberator and exonerator of his imagination. In a word,
even John of the Cross was not prepared to say that mystical experience
was totally inexpressible, but rather that poetry might provide glimpses
or echoes of it. The imagery he employed for this purpose was warmly
sensuous and often nakedly physical.

Bernanos was, then, in the orthodox Western tradition when he
described Chantal's union with God in amorous terms. He was in the

same tradition when he spoke of her suffering: 'Thus Chantal thought that her peace was still intact, her joy untarnished, when already the mysterious wound had opened from which flowed a more human, a more carnal charity, revealing God in man . . .' The suffering essential for the visionary is here indicated, and also the necessity for a complete participation in Christ's Incarnation. It is also noticeable in this book that when Bernanos attempts to describe Chantal's experience of prayer, his language becomes extremely intense, tends, indeed, almost towards the condition of poetry or, at least, towards the condition of the prose poem.

The title of this novel, *Joy*, is well-chosen and does, I believe, give an insight into Bernanos's prevailing subject-matter – joy attained not through ignorance but through innocence and suffering. He is a writer who has sometimes been misunderstood and critics have tended to see him simply as an explorer of the darkest parts of man's nature, as, perhaps, a more exalted Mauriac. And it is true that Bernanos has written of evil more subtly and more profoundly than any other twentieth-century novelist. But this acute sense of evil is only the reverse side of an exquisite sense of innocence. All his heroes and heroines possess knowledge, if not experience, of evil, and Bernanos makes it clear that his characters could never attain sanctity without such knowledge. Chantal, in *Joy*, and the young priest in *Diary of a Country Priest*, appear to be victims, but they are not, in the usual sense, victims at all. They are not passive; their surrenders are adamant and active, essentially matters of choice. Suffering has clarified their intuitions and insights ('Can any understanding of evil,' asks Bernanos, 'equal insight into pain? Is there anything that can go beyond pity?'); and, if they are not always children in years, they all have a childlike humility and understanding – the kind of audacious trust and faith that possessed Traherne and Péguy. In *Diary of a Country Priest*, the holy, uncouth Curé de Torcy speaks of this blazing innocence thus, 'Childhood and old age should be the two greatest trials of mankind. But that very sense of powerlessness is the mainspring of a child's joy . . . The shabbiest tuppeny doll will rejoice a baby's heart for half the year, but your mature gentleman'll go yawning his head off at a five-hundred-franc gadget. And why? Because he has lost the soul of childhood. Well, God has entrusted the Church to keep that soul alive, to safeguard our candour and freshness.'

It is worth noting that Bernanos's saints, for that is what Chantal and the young country priest are, are often misunderstood by the men

and women they live with. Chantal is regarded by her family as a
totally inexperienced and perhaps backward girl, while the young
priest is thought by his parish to be either a fool or a drunkard. This
is because their sufferings, their 'dark nights' are entirely interior
events; their battlefields are their own souls. Only a similar innocence
and inwardness (something very different from self-absorption or mere
introspection) can recognize such simplicity and so Chantal's and the
priest's closest relationships with other people are on a level where
only truth and honesty can survive and where even the mildest pretence
is a betrayal. In the remarkable episode in *Diary of a Country Priest*
when the young priest quite literally saves the soul of the despairing,
disillusioned Countess, the drama of their contact is terrible because
it is so bare. We are more accustomed to the heroic gesture, the tragic
stance or the defiant snapping of the fingers at fate; we are ill at ease
in a world of acceptance, an acceptance which, like Eliot's simplicity,
'costs not less than everything'. The priest speaks of evil and hell itself
to the Countess in the following, uncompromising terms: 'Hell is
judged by the standards of the world, and hell is not of this world, it is
of the other world, and still less of this Christian society. An eternal
expiation—! The miracle is that we on earth were ever able to think
of such a thing, when scarcely has our sin gone out of us, and one look,
a sign, a dumb appeal suffices for grace and pardon to swoop down, as
an eagle from topmost skies. It's because the lowest of human beings,
even though he no longer thinks he can love, still has in him the power
of loving . . . Hell is not to love any more.'

The eloquence here is of the same kind which was so apparent in
Bernanos's account of Chantal's apprehension of God. And, in *Joy*, it
is Chantal's death and submission that are responsible for the salvation
of the Abbé Cénabre, the embittered, clever priest who had lost his
faith, not only in God but in everything. But, before her death, she
joins battle with him in words wrung from the torment of her own
faith and simplicity: ' "Even if I were to die in ten minutes, I should
want to have Our Lord's permission first, like a child, no, not even a
child - like an innocent little animal that takes its last breathful of air,
its last drink of cool water, and walks to its death at the heels of its
master. The master holds the leash, one only has to follow . . . From
now on what difference does it make whether I am sane or insane, a
saint or a visionary, or even whether I am surrounded by angels or
devils - nothing can take me any farther out of my path than the length
of the leash!" '

In this spiritual combat, Bernanos employs every kind of image and symbol; his most simple characters are given the gift of tongues; language itself becomes something august, and almost sacramental. More important still, it is from prayer and from the uniqueness of a personal vision that his characters take their power and authority. Their experience is shared with and distributed to other men and thus gives a double sense to the word 'mystical' in the Christian conception of 'The Mystical Body of Christ'.

The world of Georges Bernanos is a world from which nothing has been omitted. His characters gaze with wide-open eyes at everything, from lust and horror to peace and happiness. Nothing is omitted but, paradoxically, the effect of his writing is one of starkness and essence. Everything has been considered and everything is compressed and integrated, in these two novels, into the vision of a single character. But that vision is itself a burning thing and reduces to ashes everything that is not vital and necessary. Bernanos's heroes and heroines bear the mark of the chosen victim and they are sent into their own wildernesses carrying, like men hurrying from a city on fire, only what is essential for life. But Chantal and the country priest bear the load of what is necessary not only for their own lives and salvation but also what is necessary for all mankind's.

A subsidiary theme in Bernanos's work is that of *exchange*; in his script called *The Fearless Heart* which was intended for filming and which is concerned with some Carmelite nuns at the time of the French Revolution, the terrified young novice finds in her own martyrdom the courage which her Reverend Mother lost on her death-bed. This profoundly Christian theme (so different from Scobie's bargaining with God in *The Heart of the Matter*) has another modern counterpart in the fiction of the late Charles Williams though Williams is more concerned with good and evil than in the attainment of the ecstatic joy which obsesses Bernanos. Yet both writers are referring to Christ's words, 'Greater love than this hath no man – that a man lay down his life for his friends.' With Bernanos this command, for it is more a command than an aphorism, is carried into the heart of the profoundest spiritual experience. But his characters do more than suffer on behalf of others; they also hand over *joy* to others, even a joy they may never have fully known themselves. His young priest's agonizing cry echoes through all Bernanos's work – 'The miracle of the empty hands – that we can give what we do not possess.' And this is something very like John of the Cross's 'Nada' and 'Toda', nothingness and

everything. 'He that seeks to lose his life shall find it.' It is this
finding, whose object is joy, that is Bernanos's prevailing theme and
obsession; and it is a perilous search because it is concerned with man's
life at its most intimate and profound point. He puts a rich and awed
imagination at the service of a total vision of life. And even in moments
of the acutest darkness and deprivation he can assert that 'Grace is
everywhere'.

# 14. THE USES OF ALLEGORY

## A study of the poetry of Edwin Muir

*What is essential in a work of art is that it should rise far above the realm of personal life and speak from the spirit and heart of the poet as man to the spirit and heart of mankind.*
JUNG

THE MOST STRIKING thing about the poetry of Edwin Muir is the slow sureness of its development. Outside literary movements, unswayed by fashions or passing tastes, he allowed his verse to grow as his own life grew. His poetry *was* his life not a marginal comment on it. The late verse, though shining with acceptance and more profound in meaning and interpretation than the earlier, is one with it; he could not have written his splendid last triumphant poems if the earlier struggling ones had not preceded them.

In this, Muir's development makes an interesting comparison with the mystic's experience of prayer. Perhaps a comparison with Teresa of Avila's Four Waters makes the most useful analogy for she, like Muir, appropriated every kind of natural image – corn, grass, fountains, streams, insects, birds – to encompass and express her experiences. The images objectified her subjective experience yet they did not dim it; there was no dilution, no misrepresentation. Everything she had seen, heard and felt was employed to express her vision of God and of the universe. With Muir, it was somewhat similar, but with this difference – since he was most completely himself when he wrote poetry, his poems were both the source and the fulfilment of his vision; they did not crystallize a past experience but embodied it even while it was being experienced. There was no question of feverishly seeking for appropriate imagery. The poetic, and also the visionary, experience came to him *in terms of* imagery. This is true of every poet but it needs to be remembered in any examination of the work of a visionary or mystical poet; for we tend to think that mystical poetry differs from other poetry in that the poet first experiences and afterwards searches for suitable imagery. This is not so at all. The vision *is* the words and images and only through them can it transcend them.

148

Edwin Muir was born in the Orkneys in 1887. The simple, primitive life of the soil, the immediacy of the changing seasons, the closeness of animal life, made a profound impression on him. Although, in his later life, he lived in many cities and many countries, it was this early natural life that gave him the foundation for his thought and his poetry. In his *Autobiography* he explains, 'The Orkney I was born into was a place where there was no great distinction between the ordinary and the fabulous; the lives of living men turned into legend.' And, as J. C. Hall has indicated in his Introduction to Muir's *Collected Poems*, 'As he grew up he saw all around him those "evidences of a past but strange life" which quickened in him the belief that our life is lived on two planes, the actual and the fabulous. This double vision is the central theme of Muir's poetry.' Muir saw the life of mankind as an endless journey through time, a journey continually repeating itself, continually reaching again the same stages. These stages were constant and so a kind of refutation of time. 'One or two stages in it (the journey) I can recognize,' he said: 'the age of innocence and the Fall, and all the dramatic consequences which arise from the Fall. But these lie behind experience not on the surface; they are not historical events; they are stages in the fable.'

The important words here are 'not on the surface' and 'not historical events'. They are crucial to all Muir's verse; they indicate that even when his vision was most personal it was at the same time an expression of the experience of the whole human race. All men know this, Muir believed, but only the poet can make it articulate.

Time itself, then, is one of the great themes of Muir's work. In one of his early poems, *Betrayal*, he concludes,

> He who entrapped her long ago
> And kills her, is unpitying Time.

Time is without compassion but is a fact as well as an abstraction. Muir writes of it here with a capital letter both to indicate its apparent supremacy and also to show that it *is* an abstraction, that it can affect but not subdue concrete things. In an early book of poems, *Variations on a Time Theme*, Muir wrote a sequence in which he examined time itself more closely. He speaks first of attempting to defy time:

> If I could drive this demon out
> I'd put all Time's display to rout.
> Its wounds would turn to flowers and nothing be
> But the first Garden.

Time is cold, pitiless – but it can be defeated; it can be defeated by being confronted with events outside time – by the Incarnation, the Passion and the Crucifixion of Christ. But time can only be defeated or won over if it is first accepted:

> Could Pity change the crown of thorns
> To roses peace would soon be fled.

In other words, Christ could only redeem man by entering time and becoming man himself. The crown of thorns is a crown of thorns still. To imagine otherwise would be to make a travesty of the whole Christian doctrine of Redemption. And so Muir concludes his sequence on time with these lines of quiet triumph:

> Here now heraldic watch them ride
> This path far up the mountain-side
> And backward never cast a look;
> Ignorant that the dragon died
> Long since and that the mountain shook
> When the great lion was crucified.

In this early work we can see the adumbrations of the large themes which were to inform all Muir's later poetry. He took the dogmas of Christianity and gave them a new and dramatic life. All is a movement yet all is also a stillness since repetition, renewal and regeneration are signs of permanence. The same things go on happening in every age and every life and are, in a sense, pursued by time; but they can never be finally altered by it, or harmed.

In the poems in *Journeys and Places*, Muir turned to a different aspect of his time theme. Instead of observing time, he studied what man does in time and how it affects his life and actions. He examined, therefore, the experiences of various great men:

> Saint Augustine gives back his soul
> To stumble in the endless maze.
> After Jesus Venus stands
> In the full centre of his gaze.

Many beliefs, many creeds are brought together (in much the same way as Simone Weil tried to integrate them in her syncretist approach to the great religions of the world); and yet, Muir continues,

> For there Immortal Being in
> Solidity more pure than stone

Sleeps through the circle, pillar, arch,
Spiral, cone and pentagon.

To the mind's eternity I turn,
With leaf, fruit, blossom on the spray,
See the dead world grow green within
Imagination's one long day.

There while outstretched upon the Tree
Christ looks across Jerusalem's towers,
Adam and Eve unfallen yet
Sleep side by side within their bowers.

Muir employs the changing yet recurrent seasons to illustrate not only the defeat of time but also the defeat of despair; he sees despair as an aspect of time and hope as an aspect of eternity:

Time led in chains from post to post
Of the all-conquering Zodiac ring.

In all the poems in *Journeys and Places* he follows the same theme yet he does not repeat himself. Every fresh examination of time and place becomes a closer scrutiny. For it is extremely important to bear in mind that Muir's obsession with time *is* an obsession, not in any pathological sense but in the sense of one man's urgent and often tormented inquiry into the meaning of change, rebirth, decay and changelessness. His verse is always lucid and sweet but there are darknesses and depths; the conclusions are never trite nor the triumphs easily won:

There the beginning finds the end
Before beginning ever can be.
And the great runner never leaves
The starting and the finishing tree,
The budding and the fading tree.

As I have suggested already, Muir never allows abstractions to have the last word. Always his poetry is rooted in the earth, in the earth of the land and of the seasons and also in the soil of history and legend. He considers the story of Tristram who

. . . among the shepherd's flocks
Often he lay so long, he seemed
One of the quiet rocks.

or the mad Hölderlin,

> So Hölderlin mused for thirty years
> On a green hill by Tübingen,
> Dragging in pain a broken mind
> And giving thanks to God and men.

The mind is broken but the man can still rejoice. Muir also considers Mary Stuart's plight in a beautiful, brief soliloquy:

> It was jealousy of the womb
> That let me in and shut him out,
> Honesty, kingship, all shut out,
> While I enjoyed the royal room.

The pain and the irony are apparent and they illustrate well the directness and honesty of Muir's attitude towards individual men and women.

But perhaps the lovely lyric called *Merlin* marks most vividly the stage which Muir's wrestling with time reached in *Journeys and Places*:

> O Merlin in your crystal cave
> Deep in the diamond of the day,
> Will there ever be a singer
> Whose music will smooth away
> The furrow drawn by Adam's finger
> Across the meadow and the wave?
> Or a runner who'll outrun
> Man's long shadow driving on,
> Break through the gate of memory
> And hang the apple on the tree?
> Will your magic ever show
> The sleeping bride shut in her bower,
> The day wreathed in its mound of snow
> And Time locked in his tower?

In this poem, the abstract and the concrete are perfectly balanced; 'the furrow drawn by Adam's finger' and 'man's long shadow' reinforce a phrase like 'the gate of memory' which might otherwise be rather vague. The day has its 'mound of snow' while cold, impersonal Time is shown as 'locked in his tower'. However abstract the ideas, the expression of them is always concrete; and, further, the vision is not complete till it is embodied in sensuous language.

Muir's treatment of time provokes some comment on his view of the meaning of life. Was the idea of human tragedy incompatible with his conception of time and eternity? Was the dignity of each individual human life,diminished in so august a conception of the human race as a whole? Yeats has said that tragedy consists in man finding himself confronted by an immovable object; he can only rail against that object, making his own gesture of defiance, something hieratic or symbolic. The beauty is all in the gesture not in the tragic conflict.

But Edwin Muir was a Christian though he admits in his *Autobiography* that, quite late in life, he suddenly became aware that he had been a Christian for a long time without fully realizing it. It has sometimes been said, I think wrongly, that the tragic sense of life is incompatible with Christian beliefs. It is certainly true that the Redemption, which was fulfilled by Christ's death on the Cross, saved man not only from damnation but also from despair; but those who hold too simplicist a view of this doctrine maintain that for the convinced Christian tragedy is thus impossible. The reason for this misunderstanding is that they tend to forget that the redemption only gives man the opportunity of salvation and eternal felicity; it does not take away his free will or his liberty to reject Christ. The most profoundly religious writers, of whom Dante, Milton, Claudel and Bernanos are four great examples, have always recognized this truth; and, what is more, they have realized that a Christian conception of tragedy, with all its terrifying consequences, can sometimes be far more effective than the Greek one where all wrong-doing was blamed on fate rather than on the individual and where death itself was an end rather than a threshold.

I think it is this entirely Christian conception of evil, death and tragedy that gives depth to Muir's vision of life. It is the shadow side of his verse, a darkness that can never be entirely cast off. His work is affirmative, yes, but there are no easy answers in it. Thus the state of pure acceptance which Muir expressed in his later poems was an acceptance won *through* suffering not by an evasion of suffering. Something of this conception of man's destiny is expressed in another poem from *Journeys and Places*; it is the last poem in the book and is called simply *The Unattained Place*:

> Once there we pored on every stone and tree
> In a long dream through the unsetting day,
> And looking up could nothing see
> But the right way on every way.
> And lost it after,

No foot knows where,
To find this mourning air,
Commemorative laughter,
The mask, the doom
Written backwards,
The illegible tomb
Pointing backwards,
The reverse side
Where strength is weakness,
The body, pride,
The soul, a sickness.

Critics have sometimes commented, with a certain amount of disparagement, on the modesty of Muir's verse, on its air and tone of traditionalism. It is true that Muir is a traditionalist in the sense that he made no violent experiments with form or language. He never attempted either to dislocate language or to violate it. He respected words as something much more significant than mere counters or approximations. His sense of the past was constantly with him and it included a sense of the value of past words. It was for Eliot and Pound to revivify language both for their personal ends and for the future of English poetry. Muir, on the other hand, accepted the traditional language of poetry and then transformed it by his own vision and insights. There is nothing of the staleness of an outmoded poetic diction about his work; his sensitive ear and fastidious taste give his poetry the effect of purity and transparency. Words are ciphers, but they are also windows.

His next volume of poems, *The Narrow Place*, is an advance in two ways. First, Muir's language has attained a new subtlety and strength, and, second, he is really beginning to get a full understanding and control of his subjects, subjects which he was to handle, in diverse ways, until his death. There are no adumbrations or promises merely in this book. In the first poem in it, *To J.H.F.* (*1897–1934*), Muir shows a quite new ability to use common and colloquial speech without in any way spoiling the dignity and austerity of his music:

Shot from the sling into the perilous road,
The hundred-mile-long hurtling bowling alley,
Today I saw you pass full-tilt for the jack.
Or it seemed a race beyond time's gate you rode,
Trussed to the motor cycle . . .

The same ease and colloquialism are apparent in *The Wayside Station*:

> Here at the wayside station, as many a morning
> I watch the smoke torn from the fumy engine
> Crawling across the field in serpent sorrow.

From such a casual opening Muir can move to the quiet grandeur of,

> . . . The lonely stream
> That rode through darkness leaps the gap of light,
> Its voice grown loud, and starts its winding journey
> Through the day and time and war and history.

One of the prevailing themes of *The Narrow Place* is the theme of return and recurrence, a theme which Muir himself saw most clearly in the interplay of story with fable, of the individual life with the life of the human race. In a poem called *The Recurrence* he writes,

> All things return, Nietzsche said,
> The ancient wheel revolves again,
> Rise, take up your numbered fate;
> The cradle and the bridal bed,
> Life and the coffin wait.

The poem ends with a consideration of history seen in heraldic or emblematic terms, and indeed the shield and the crest, with all their suggestions and symbols, had a special significance for Edwin Muir:

> But the heart makes reply:
> This is only what the eye
> From its tower on the turning field
> Sees and sees and cannot tell why,
> Quarterings on the turning shield,
> The great non-stop heraldic show.

The wonderfully effective use of the colloquial word 'non-stop' in that last line is worth remarking on.

Muir again treats the idea of return in a poem about Ulysses called *The Return*. But *The Narrow Place* is also notable for the emergence of another theme – the consideration of nature. This, like many of the ideas which Muir introduces into his poems, might be thought to be more the material of the philosopher or the metaphysician than of the poet. Yet, by seeing and depicting his world of ideas in terms of images, he escapes the dangers of abstractions and cold statements. Of nature he writes, in a poem called *The Ring*:

Nature in wrath broke through the grassy ring
Where all our gathered treasures lay in sleep –
Many a rich and many a childish thing.

.    .    .

And now, all new, for Nature knows no age.
Fatherless, sonless, homeless haunters, they
Had never known the vow and the pilgrimage.

*The Narrow Place* also contains a number of entirely personal poems which range from the lovely evocation of childhood in *The Gate* to the tender love poem, *The Confirmation*:

. . . Your open heart,
Simple with giving, gives the primal deed,
The first good world, the blossom, the blowing seed,
The hearth, the steadfast land, the widening sea,
Not beautiful or rare in every part,
But like yourself, as they were meant to be.

The book ends with the sort of poem Muir very rarely wrote – a meditation on the difficulties of being a poet and on the recalcitrance of language:

Oh give me clarity and love that now
The way I walk may truly trace again
The in eternity written and hidden way:
Make pure my heart and will, and me allow
The acceptance and revolt, the yea and nay,
The denial and the blessing that are my own.

These words which sound almost like an invocation show clearly that Muir viewed the vocation of the poet much as the priest views his vocation; it was something that demanded love, honesty and disinterestedness. In one important respect, however, Muir felt that the poet differed from the priest; where the man of prayer must always observe complete obedience and self-subjugation, the poet is permitted his own 'acceptance and revolt', his own 'denial' and 'blessing'. Yet the lovely words, 'whose service is perfect freedom' would certainly have been regarded by Muir as equally applicable to poet and priest.

In his next book of poems, *The Voyage*, Muir continued his exploration of the themes of journeys, returns, renewals and the overthrow of time. In poems like *Moses* with its wonderful last line,

White robes and sabbath peace, the snow-white emblem,

and *The Covenant*, he began to scrutinize more closely than ever before specific events or dogmas contained in the Old and New Testaments. This book also contains even more purely personal poems than the previous volume – poems such as *Song*, *Dejection* and *Sorrow*. Muir's skill in the handling of allegory, which was much more tentative in his earlier work, is displayed here with a new delicacy and power. Allegory for him was not a world of symbols set apart from the world we live in; it had nothing at all in common with the exquisite, escapist worlds of Chaucer's early poems or with Spenser's *Faerie Queene*. For Muir, allegory expressed and embodied a deeper level of experience than that at which we ordinarily live and feel. It had much in common with Jung's theory of archetypes and the collective unconscious, though there was absolutely nothing theoretical in Muir's conception and use of allegory. In *The Window* he presents, in lyrical form and by means of the concrete images of the tower and the window, a vision of man at peace and at war. It is, at one and the same time, a personal and a cosmic vision:

> There was a tower set in the wall
> And a great window in the tower,
> And if one looked, beyond recall
> The twisting glass kept him in thrall
> With changing marvels hour by hour.
> And there one day we looked and saw
> Marsh, mere and mount in anger shaken,
> The world's great side, the giant flaw,
> And watched the stately forests fall,
> The white ships sinking in the sea,
> The tower run toppling in the field,
> The last left stronghold sacked and taken,
> And earth and heaven in jeopardy.
> Then turning towards you I beheld
> The wrinkle writhe across your brow,
> And felt time's cap clapped on my head,
> And all within the enclosure now,
> Light leaf and smiling flower, was false,
> The great wall breached, the garden dead.
> Across the towering window fled
> Disasters, victories, festivals.

In *The Rider Victory* Muir returns to an examination of time but
now he sees it overthrown not only by the fable or the legend but also
by man's ability to make a lasting work of art. The statue of a mounted
charger is 'Suspended . . . leaping on air and legendary.' And in the
last poem in *The Voyage, In Love For Long*, Muir expresses with the
utmost simplicity the credo of his life, the conviction that the world,
however terrifying, brutal and tormented, is still 'a world of love':

> This love a moment known
> For what I do not know
> And in a moment gone
> Is like the happy doe
> That keeps its perfect laws
> Between the tiger's paws
> And vindicates its cause.

This is the kind of affirmation that could only be made by a man
who had himself suffered and been afraid.

In *The Labyrinth*, which is perhaps Edwin Muir's finest book, we
find a drawing together and merging of all his earlier themes and
preoccupations. What were mere foreshadowings in some of the early
poems are now clear, uncompromising statements. The nature of time,
the transitoriness of life on this planet, the abuse of power, the fall of
man – all these subjects are brought together and integrated. *The
Labyrinth*, even though it is in a much quieter key, has something of
the triumph, the affirmation of Yeats's last poems. And, like Yeats,
Muir now sees himself and his own life as part of the human predicament and he recognizes the fact with joy. He is no longer simply
meditating or observing but is himself living among the symbols he
has brought to life:

> Then suddenly again I watch the old
> Worn saga write across my years and find,
> Scene after scene, the tale my fathers told,
> But I in the middle blind, as Homer blind,
>
> Dark on the highway, groping in the light,
> Threading my dazzling way within my night.
>                                      (*Too Much*)

And in the title poem of this book, Muir is himself the wanderer
through the labyrinth; this is a true identification not a game of
impersonations. It has something in common with Rilke's superb gift

for *becoming* the objects or lives which he contemplated; but there is this difference – where Rilke drew outward symbols into his own mind and there transformed them by the power of his imagination, Muir moves outward *into* his symbols. Where Rilke was subjective, he is, in the most literal sense, objective:

> For once in a dream or trance I saw the gods
> Each sitting on the top of his mountain-isle,
> While down below the little ships sailed by,
> Toy multitudes swarmed in the harbours, shepherds drove
> Their tiny flocks to the pastures, marriage feasts
> Went on below, small birthdays and holidays,
> Ploughing and harvesting and life and death,
> And all permissible, all acceptable,
> Clear and secure as in a limpid dream.
> But they, the gods, as large and bright as clouds,
> Conversed across the sounds in tranquil voices
> High in the sky above the untroubled sea;
> And their eternal dialogue was peace
> Where all these things were woven; and this our life
> Was as a chord deep in that dialogue,
> As easy utterance of harmonious words,
> Spontaneous syllables bodying forth a world.
>
> (*The Labyrinth*)

That last line describes with great precision what Muir is doing in these later poems. The disparate symbols have come together and, in the light of a single personal vision, have created a world. The beautifully modulated blank verse of this poem and of many of Muir's later poems is reminiscent in cadence of the Wordsworth of *Tintern Abbey* or *The Prelude*. There is the tranquillity and assurance of an acceptance won after a lifetime of struggle both with life and with language.

It might be relevant to note at this stage that in spite of his dour Scottish upbringing there is nothing Manichaean or Puritanical about Muir's vision of the world; spirit and flesh are one even when they war against each other, and if there is a duality in the universe it is not an ultimate duality but simply a condition caused by the Fall and redeemed by the Incarnation. Muir, in the chapter about Rome in his *Autobiography*, reflects on this matter: 'The history of Rome is drenched in blood and blackened with crime; yet all that seemed to be left now was the peace of memory . . . But it was the evidences of another Incarna-

tion that met one everywhere and gradually exerted its influence . . .
During the time when as a boy I attended the United Presbyterian
Church in Orkney, I was aware of religion as the Sacred Word, and
the church itself, severe and decent, with its touching bareness and
austerity, seemed to cut off religion from the rest of life and from all
the week-day world . . . It did not tell me by any outward sign that the
Word had been made flesh . . . In Rome that image was to be seen everywhere, not only in churches, but on the walls of houses, at crossroads
in the suburbs, in wayside shrines in the parks, and in private rooms.'

This realization is at the heart of what I think is Edwin Muir's
finest poem, *The Journey Back*. It is an entirely personal poem yet it
also has deeper and wider implications than the experience of one man
at one time. In it, Muir perfectly balances description with reflection,
inquiry with exhortation:

> Seek the beginnings, learn from whence you came,
> And know the various earth of which you are made.
> So I set out on this calm summer evening
> From this my house and my father's . . .

The poet continues,

> But past it all is strange.
> I must in other lives with many a leap
> Blindfold, must lodge in dark and narrow skulls
> With a few thoughts that pad from wall to wall
> And never get out, must moulder in dusty hearts
> Inhabit many a dark or a sunny room,
> Be in all things.

Here, the identification is total and it is not only a poetic and
transitory identification of a moment's mood but an entirely Christian
conception, a real sharing and suffering with others. But Muir also
knows that each man is responsible for himself, that no one else can
live his life for him; so he writes, as if gathering together some of
Yeats's echoes and speaking them afresh in his own music,

> So I hie me back
> To my sole starting-point, my random self
> That in these rags and tatters clothes the soul.

*The Journey Back* ends with a vision of triumph won through striving
and also through arduous surrender. It is a Christian vision penetrated

with the light of Muir's intense awareness of it, and so brought to life anew. The image of the harvest is taken straight from the New Testament:

> There's no prize in this race; the prize is elsewhere,
> Here only to be run for. There's no harvest
> Though all around the fields are white with harvest.
> There is our journey's ground; we pass unseeing.
> But we have watched against the evening sky,
> Tranquil and bright, the golden harvester.

The vision is complete, yes, but the journey has to be made over and over again, renewed in each individual life and in the life of the whole human race. This idea of cycles, of returns and renewals, obsessed Muir to the very end and gave his poetry both its tension and its tranquillity.

Muir deals with many subjects in *The Labyrinth* – the conflict of good and evil in the wonderful poem, *The Combat*, political power and expediency in *The Usurpers* and *The Good Town*, an examination, made entirely in lucid imagery, of an event from the New Testament in *The Transfiguration*, and considerations of love and death. All these poems, perfect though they are by themselves, are a part of Muir's presiding argument – the continual struggle of good with evil, the necessity for each man to *use* the freedom which Christ's redemption won for him. These themes come together in *Soliloquy* which is a kind of meditative coda to *The Journey Back*. This poem contains all that Muir has himself discovered about life and in it he sees his own existence and experience both in historical and in transcendent terms:

> I have picked up wisdom lying
> Disused about the world, available still,
> Employable still, small odds and scraps of wisdom.
>
> .     .     .
>
> I have learned another lesson.
> When life's half done you must give quality
> To the other half, else you lose both, lose all.
>
> .  .     .
>
> I have watched
> In cheering ports the great fleets sailing out,
> And on another and a darker day
> Returning with disaster at the helm,
> Death at the prow.

There is nothing grandiose, nothing rhetorical here. The words amaze and hold the attention not because they are in themselves grandiloquent but because they appear in the context of a shining humility which can itself ennoble; this must surely be the grand manner in its only honest sense.

Muir published one more book of poems before he died, *One Foot in Eden*. Many of these poems show a new dexterity with rhythm and stanzaic form, notably in poems like *The Incarnate One*. The subject-matter is more overtly Christian than ever and all Muir's old themes are enhanced by their vividly concrete setting. There is no remorse, no regret; he writes, as he had done many years before, of Eden and the Fall of Man, but now the Fall is itself seen as a cause of joy:

> Strange blessings never in Paradise
> Fall from these beclouded skies.

But I think the last lines of *Soliloquy* from *The Labyrinth* make the most perfect ending to an examination of a poet who never postured or dramatized but saw life as itself a drama continually repeating itself. Muir's achievement is to have examined and appropriated that drama in intensely meditative but never merely abstract terms. The body of his work shows how a vision can often be most powerful when simplicity is at the centre of it – that simplicity which, as Eliot has said, costs 'not less than everything'. Edwin Muir wrote, at the end of *Soliloquy*,

> Set up the bleak worn day to show our sins,
> Old and still ageing, like a flat squat herd
> Crawling like sun on wall to the rim of time,
> Up the long slope for ever.
> > Light and praise,
> Love and atonement, harmony and peace,
> Touch me, assail me; break and make my heart.

# 15. ARTICULATE MUSIC

## *A study of the mystical content in the plays and* Four Quartets *of T. S. Eliot*

---

IT IS A commonplace that all T. S. Eliot's plays are religious plays. *Murder in the Cathedral* is overtly religious both in theme and in treatment, but *The Family Reunion, The Cocktail Party, The Confidential Clerk,* and *The Elder Statesman* are equally concerned with man's need for religion, his search for it in contemporary society, his moral problems, his sense of guilt and his desire for renunciation. They are all, in fact, plays about men and women who are searching for God. This is a truism which has been recognized by even the most hostile or undiscerning dramatic critics. What has not so often been noticed is that many of Eliot's characters are seeking God not simply, in the words of the catechism, 'to know, love and serve Him,' but to become one with him completely in this life — in other words to be united with him in the *mystical* experience. They enact the struggle, the purification and the surrender which have been described by mystical writers throughout the centuries. In *Murder in the Cathedral*, which is set and played out in the English Middle Ages, Becket's temptations and triumphs are perfectly in accord with those described by Julian of Norwich and the author of *The Cloud of Unknowing*. His most terrible temptation is that which suggests to him not only that he is seeking out martyrdom for his own glorification but also that he desires union with God out of a sense of personal power and pride. The Fourth Tempter taunts him thus:

> 'What can compare with glory of Saints
> Dwelling forever in presence of God?'

And Becket replies, as if violently thrusting away his own hidden thoughts,

> 'Who are you, tempting with my own desires?'

163

And he goes on to accuse the Tempter of offering him 'dreams to damnation'. This is indeed 'the last temptation' which is 'the greatest treason' – 'to do the right deed for the wrong reason'. Becket is deeply troubled by his own motives but in the Interlude which follows the temptation scene he preaches a sermon in which he indicates the essential humility of the martyr: '. . . the true martyr is he who has become the instrument of God, who has lost his will in the will of God, and who no longer desires anything for himself, not even the glory of being a martyr.'

Writers on prayer and contemplation have always stressed the especial danger which the mystic has to face and overcome – the sin of desiring to draw God down and possess him for one's own self-aggrandizement. In the Second Part of *Murder in the Cathedral*, Becket reaches, through the fires and torments of self-knowledge, a state where he can say simply,

'I have therefore only to make perfect my will.'

This connotes a perfect balance of striving and surrender, of activity and passivity. When his people cry out in anguish at the thought of his death, Becket replies,

'I have had a tremour of bliss, a wink of heaven, a whisper,
And I would no longer be denied; all things
Proceed to a joyful consummation.'

He recognizes that 'all things shall be well' once he himself has accepted God's plan for him. It is clear, too, from the words 'a tremour of bliss' and 'a wink of heaven, a whisper', that Eliot intends us to conclude that Becket has received some apprehension of God that is quite beyond both the senses and the reason.

I have dealt only briefly with *Murder in the Cathedral* and its mystical content because that content is so shiningly obvious. In the plays which follow it the content is there but it is more concealed. One reason for this partial concealment is, of course, the fact that the other plays are, on the surface, entirely contemporary plays. They deal with people living now, in a society which has largely lost contact with the Christian tradition. The plots are adapted from Greek plays but these plays are only springboards; they precipitate the action rather than dominate it.

*The Family Reunion* is a play about guilt. Eliot, with a remarkable humility and dispassionateness, has in his lecture called *Poetry and Drama* commented on what he now feels to be the flaws in this play: 'We are,' he says, 'left in a divided frame of mind, not knowing whether to consider the play the tragedy of the mother or the salvation of the son. The two situations are not reconciled.' This may be so, and it may also be true that, as Eliot himself thinks, his hero, Harry, is 'an insufferable prig'. Nevertheless, Harry's guilt and fear, if not his personality, do dominate the play; they give it both its mystery and its tension. In the great scene with Agatha, in which Harry speaks of, accepts, and finally exorcizes his sense of guilt, Agatha tells him that he is perhaps 'the consciouness' of his 'unhappy family' and that

> 'It is possible that you have not known what sin
> You shall expiate, or whose, or why.'

She speaks of Harry's suffering in terms which make it clear that Eliot wishes us to regard his torment and guilt as a purification, a kind of 'dark night', and, above all, as a *preparation*. Harry replies by speaking of 'a different vision', while Agatha names this vision 'a beginning'. In this dialogue there is something of the intensity we find in Hugh of St Victor's *Soul's Betrothal Gift* or in the conversations of Bernanos's young priest; spirit speaks to spirit removed for a moment, it seems, from the flesh. These are moments neither tragic nor comic but gracious and entirely human.

The garden is a favourite image with Eliot in his religious and mystical verse; it is dominant in the *Four Quartets* and also reappears in *The Confidential Clerk*. Here, in *The Family Reunion*, Agatha speaks of the garden she once discovered fleetingly; it is an image of peace and fulfilment and she introduces it to comfort Harry when he says,

> 'I have been wounded in a war of phantoms.'

It is important to note here that Harry is not a sick man or a psychopath; he is an ordinary human being who is atoning for his own sins and for those of others. His cure therefore will be found in prayer and penitence not in psychiatric treatment (we shall find the same cures advocated in *The Cocktail Party* but there they will be represented in *terms* of psychiatry – as a concession to the modern world perhaps); Agatha tells Harry of the garden she has sometimes been allowed a glimpse of:

'I only looked through the little door
When the sun was shining on the rose-garden:
And heard in the distance tiny voices
And then a black raven flew over.'

Harry enters Agatha's experience of this garden when he declares,

'O my dear, and you walked through the little door
And I ran to meet you in the rose-garden'

and again,

'. . . this is the first time that I have been free
From the ring of ghosts with joined hands, from the pursuers,
And come into a quiet place. Why is it so quiet?
Do you feel a kind of stirring underneath the air?
Do you? Don't you? a communication, a scent
Direct to the brain . . .'

What had seemed an entirely finite sense of affinity and love changes
now to a recognition and acceptance of the Eumenides themselves.
Agatha, at this point, changes her position and purpose; she no
longer directs Harry but follows him. In a mysterious brief poem, she
uses the language of the mystics:

'Accident is design
And design is accident
In a cloud of unknowing.'

Harry has now attained 'a moment of clarity' and by the end of the
scene he has also acquired an undeniable sense of vocation:

'To the worship in the desert, the thirst and deprivation,
A stony sanctuary and a primitive altar,
The heat of the sun and the icy vigil,
A care over lives of humble people,
The lesson of ignorance, of incurable diseases.
Such things are possible. It is love and terror
Of what waits and wants me, and will not let me fall.

Why I have this election
I do not understand. It must have been preparing always,
And I see it was what I always wanted.'

Here are the humility, the dedication, the wish to share, the power and the gentleness which have always marked the vocation of the Christian mystic throughout the centuries. There is, too, the willing acceptance of the unknown which rings out in Harry's last lines of this scene,

'I must follow the bright angels.'

Eliot does not tell us precisely who these angels are but it is clear now that the Eumenides have been changed from creatures of foreboding into guides and messengers. They have indeed something of the power and prescience of Rilke's angels.

In the last scene of the play, Agatha announces to the other characters that

'Harry has crossed the frontier
Beyond which safety and danger have a different meaning
And he cannot return. That is his privilege.'

In other words, Harry's vision has changed him entirely; however he responds to that vision he cannot remain unaffected by it.

It seems to me that unless we interpret the 'visions' of the chief characters in *all* Eliot's plays in a mystical sense, we cannot really understand them at all. The refusal to admit this mystical content is, I am sure, largely responsible for the failure of many critics to understand or appreciate the plays. They have complained of the sudden conversions, the violent alterations of mood, and because they have not interpreted these conversions in a mystical sense, as moments out of time, they have totally misunderstood Eliot's meaning and intention. It is, of course, true that a vision is only *dramatic* to the one who experiences it. To make his characters' visions acceptable dramatically Eliot has had to introduce them in dialogue; he has made his protagonists describe and bear witness to their visions in a context of discourse or argument. And for this he uses his most intense poetry. In *Poetry and Drama* he speaks of this heightened dramatic verse thus: 'It seems to me that beyond the namable, classifiable emotions and motives of our conscious life when directed towards action – the part of life which prose drama is wholly adequate to express – there is a fringe of indefinite extent, of feeling which we can only detect, so to speak, out of the corner of the eye and can never completely focus: of feeling of which we are only aware in a kind of temporary detachment from action . . . This peculiar range of sensibility can be expressed by dramatic poetry, at its moments of greatest intensity.' This is not only an admirable justification of Eliot's own practice but also a perfect exposition of the belief that only *poetry* is an adequate vehicle to convey mystical experience.

All Eliot's plays have this in common – each of them is about some aspect of acceptance. Each play has three points of focus – conflict, recognition, acceptance. It should be remembered that Eliot's chief characters resolve their conflicts by accepting and so by exorcizing them; and their spiritual life guides their emotional life rather than the other way round. In *The Cocktail Party*, for example, Edward and Lavinia Chamberlayne, who have had to face the appalling fact that one of them is 'incapable of loving' while the other knows that 'no one can love her', find that by accepting their tragedy they can accept themselves and each other. I do not think the dramatist intends us to believe that their whole emotional life is altered by their own willing admissions of their incapacity to love or be loved. What I am sure Eliot is implying is that even the most impossible personal relationships can be endured, and indeed transformed by endurance, when some kind of divine, transcendent love is admitted.

*The Cocktail Party* is about vocation, about the struggle to know precisely what one's vocation is. Based loosely on Euripides's *Alcestis*, the play presents a number of apparently 'ordinary' characters and places them in a contemporary setting. *The Cocktail Party*, it is generally admitted, has many of the attributes and properties of a West End success-comfortable upper middle-class life, parties, people who work in films, and, above all, the psychiatrist. The presence of such things should not, however, blind the spectator or reader of the play to its basic subject. One may, perhaps, criticize Eliot for intensifying the mystery of the psychiatrist, Sir Henry Harcourt-Reilly, by introducing a scene of prayer and libation into his consulting-room at the end of Act II, but this is a fault, I think, of too much ambition rather than merely a lack of judgment. In any case, it is beyond the scope and purpose of this study to explain or excuse all Eliot's dramatic devices.

As I have said, *The Cocktail Party* is concerned with finding one's vocation. It might almost be an extended illustration of St Paul's words about 'divers gifts'. It is, more than anything else, the story of one woman's search for God and of her struggle and surrender. The most profound and also the most poetic writing in the play is that which expresses Celia Coplestone's experiences. Her reported crucifixion on an ant-hill at the end of the play has horrified some readers and some audiences. 'Why,' they ask, 'did she need to die such a violent death?' Unless one sees Celia's vocation as essentially a contemplative vocation (the real contemplatives have always been the most practical people), such suffering is indeed unacceptable. But once her death is seen in the context of her calling, it becomes not only comprehensible but just. We may recall Teresa of Avila's gentle admonishment of God – 'No wonder you have so few friends when you treat them so badly,' but we must also recall the heroic surrenders of all the great saints and mystics. Their vocation of suffering does not make them less human but more human; as Aquinas has said, 'grace perfects nature'. To be appalled by death, however terrifying its form, is an animal instinct rather than a purely human one. To rail against death is another matter.

Sir Henry Harcourt-Reilly's role in the play is to show the other characters what their vocations are; he guides but does not coerce. In Act II, after he has shown Lavinia and Edward as much knowledge of themselves as they can bear, he talks with Celia. Their dialogue is on an entirely different level from that of the rest of the play. In it, Eliot employs that heightened dramatic verse which he speaks of in *Poetry and Drama*. In the course of the conversation Celia speaks of 'an awareness of solitude', that prerequisite of every contemplative. As the dialogue proceeds, it is as if we were eavesdroppers or on-lookers at the spiritual awakening of another person. This awakening is Celia's personal drama but it is shared with the audience by being presented in the form of a dialogue. One is reminded of the nakedness of the scene between Bernanos's country priest and the tormented Countess. The difference here, however, is that Celia is being drawn by nothing but her need of God; it is a need that has to be filled, not a desire that demands satisfaction or appeasement. She says of it,

> 'I have thought at moments that the ecstasy is real
> Although those who experience it may have no reality.
> For what happened is remembered like a dream
> In which one is exalted by intensity of loving
> In the spirit, a vibration of delight
> Without desire, for desire is fulfilled
> In the delight of loving. A state one does not know
> When awake. But what, or whom I loved,
> Or what in me was loving, I do not know.

And if that is all meaningless, I want to be cured
Of a craving for something I cannot find
And of the shame of never finding it.'

Here is the humility, the self-questioning which are notable in all
those who have received some form of mystical experience. There is,
too, the hunger to be possessed and to understand. But the desire to
understand lags behind the love; discursive reason is set aside, just as
we have seen it laid aside in the Fourth and Fifth of Teresa's Four
Waters.

Celia is not afraid of what her vocation may mean in terms of
mental and physical suffering and when Sir Henry declares uncompromisingly 'It is a terrifying journey,' she replies, 'I am not frightened but glad.' When he has sent Celia away, Sir Henry calls in the
two 'guardians', Alexander and Julia. Into Julia's mouth Eliot puts
the words which describe the life which Celia must now accept:

'Oh yes, she will go far. And we know where she is going.
But what do we know of the terrors of the journey?
You and I don't know the process by which the human is
Transhumanised: what do we know
Of the kind of suffering they must undergo
On the way of illumination?'

It is quite clear from this speech alone that Sir Henry, Alexander
and Julia are to be regarded as 'angels', as messengers, and not as
human beings. A little later, Julia goes on,

'She will be afraid of nothing; she will not even know
That there is anything there to be afraid of.
She is too humble. She will pass between the scolding hills,
Through the valley of derision, like a child sent on an errand
In eagerness and patience. Yet she must suffer.'

*The Cocktail Party* ends with the news of Celia's death, with the
reactions of her friends to it, and with the gentle submission to each
other of Lavinia and Edward. It is a quiet ending, a tranquil falling
away, a return to lives less lofty than that of Celia and to vocations
less severe than hers. If there is a 'moral' in the play (and 'moral' here
is too crude a word for so subtle a dramatist), then it is that every man
can perfect and save himself not only by acknowledging his own
limitations but also by accepting the possibility of a nobility which he
never dreamt he could attain.

In *The Confidential Clerk* the mystical element is much more dispersed than in either *The Family Reunion* or *The Cocktail Party*. The play does, however, contain a crucial scene in which the image of the garden again recurs. It appears in Act II in the dialogue between Lucasta Angel and Colby Simpkins. On the surface, this dialogue is very close to a preliminary to a conventional love scene; it depicts that gentle and most unpossessive moment when two people get to know each other by sharing their different pasts. The audience or the reader only knows at the end of the play that the garden about which Colby speaks is not one which he will share with Lucasta but one where he will meet God. The scene is therefore mysterious, ambivalent and full of dramatic irony. Colby says of his garden,

> 'And yet, you know, it's not quite real to me –
> Although it's as real to me as . . . this world.
> But that's just the trouble. They seem so unrelated.
> I turn the key, and walk through the gate,
> And there I am . . . alone, in my "garden".
> Alone, that's the thing. That's why it's not real.'

Colby is, as yet, unenlightened. He can lose himself in his music but it is some other kind of loss of self that he is really seeking. Yet he has a glimmering of what his garden might become:

> 'If I were religious, God would walk in my garden
> And that would make the world outside it real
> And acceptable, I think.'

Eliot obviously intends us to understand from this that whatever Colby's garden signifies, it is not an escape or a refuge. Later in this scene Colby speaks of 'the sense of desolation' one might have after leaving the garden. Unwittingly he is referring to the desolation, the dark night that the mystic must experience both before and after the moment of ecstasy.

*The Confidential Clerk* is a play about lost identities and mistaken parents. The idea which informs the whole play is that if you know who your father is, then you will learn who *you* are. In this respect, it is a more profound treatment of the subject of vocations than *The Cocktail Party*. And yet it is not such a satisfactory play. There are several reasons for this; in the first place, the verse is less taut and more pedestrian than that of the earlier play. It comes perilously near prose at times, and very flat prose at that. The second reason for the play's partial failure is a much more damaging one. There is an air of *contrivance* about it; one feels that Eliot deliberately constricted his imagination by forcing and holding it within the bounds of an extremely artificial plot. This has resulted in an apparent lack of conviction about the whole play. There is too little free play of the mind and the imagination, so that the scenes in which the characters do have a moment of freedom to live in their own right sound or read as if they came from another part of Eliot's work – from the *Four Quartets* perhaps. When, at the end of the play, Colby resigns himself (and the note of resignation is stronger here than the note of accept-ance) to life as an organist with the added possibility that he may take Holy Orders, we remain only half-convinced. The failure is perhaps the poet's more than the playwright's. There is a loss of intensity in Eliot's writing which indicates some opaqueness of vision. When a poet writes a play at the top of his bent, we are prepared to accept any number of inconsistencies and improbabilities (we do this constantly with Shakespeare), but if the verse fails, then the whole dramatic construction tumbles to the ground. Eliot's failure is not so absolute as this, for *The Confidential Clerk* is redeemed by a few moments of the utmost clarity. Such a moment occurs in Sir Claude Mulhammer's speech about his long-suppressed desire to be a potter:

'. . . When I was a boy
I loved to shape things. I loved form and colour
And I loved the material that the potter handles.
Most people think that a sculptor or a painter
Is something more excellent to be than a potter.
Most people think of china or porcelain
As merely for use, or for decoration –
In either case, an inferior art.
For me, they are neither "use" nor "decoration" –
That is, decoration as a background for living;
For me, they are life itself. To be among such things,
If it is an escape, is escape into living,
Escape from a sordid world to a pure one.
Sculpture and painting – I have some good things –
But they haven't this . . . remoteness I have always longed for.
I want a world where the form is the reality
Of which the substantial is only a shadow.'

The world of which Sir Claude speaks here is similar in kind to that of Colby's garden; it is not an escape or a refuge but a search for reality. The language is more explicit than in Colby's speech because Sir Claude is talking of something exact, concrete and self-evident — of art as a step towards ecstasy. He is not, however, substituting aesthetic experience for religious experience but presenting a feeling or talent for art, in this case the art of the potter, as itself a religious thing. This whole speech could usefully be annotated by some words of David Jones in his essay, *Art and Sacrament*: 'We are committed to body and by the same token we are committed to Ars, so to sign and sacrament,' and, 'For the painter may say to himself: "This is not a representation of a mountain, it *is* 'mountain' under the form of paint." Indeed, unless he says this unconsciously or consciously he will not be a painter worth a candle.'

These lines of Sir Claude's are, therefore, not only one of the most elevated moments in *The Confidential Clerk* but also central to this whole question of the relation between making and mysticism. When Sir Claude speaks of wanting 'a world where the form is the reality', we can assume, without in any way tampering with Eliot's meaning, that he is referring to some apprehension of God as 'pure Being' of which art may be both an analogy and a foreshadowing. The ground of both experiences, Eliot appears to be saying, is the same. It is, of course, dangerous to impute the words of one of a dramatist's characters to the dramatist himself, but in this case I think it is legitimate since the chief characters in all Eliot's plays express beliefs that he himself has affirmed elsewhere, either in his prose or in the *Four Quartets*.

In *The Elder Statesman*, Eliot's most recent play, the theme of acceptance has become an entirely moral matter. Moral issues reveal personal flaws, and self-knowledge in this play is displayed almost entirely in terms of morality. More than any of the other plays, *The Elder Statesman* reveals how little Eliot has in common with the French theatre of Sartre and Camus or with the American theatre of Arthur Miller. His characters are never searching for essence disguised under the name of integrity; they are reclaiming what has been lost rather than fashioning what has never before existed. The dilemmas of his protagonists are 'in and out of time', here and now but also set against an eternal order and a divine arbiter. They do not find their salvation either in an essentially frivolous doctrine of 'the absurd' or in an earnest quest for personal honesty alone. If there were more individual, fully-realized figures in the *Four Quartets* they would be

men and women like Harry, Celia and Colby. Eliot's work is a total
*oeuvre* and in his plays drama is put at the service of a vision which is
both personal and transcendent.

It is generally agreed that *The Elder Statesman* is a warmer, more
human, even, perhaps, more emotional play than those which preceded
it. There is a lyricism which manifests itself not so much in the words
as under the words. Yet in this play, Eliot's dramatic line (a line
previously fashioned both by technical experiment and by the needs
and conflicts of the poet-dramatist) is limper, more vacillating than it
was in *The Confidential Clerk* or *The Cocktail Party*. It may be that too
much personal material has appeared in this play in an unassimilated
form; or, and this is much more serious, it may be that Eliot has
exhausted the theme of acceptance. The moments of vision which
raise his best plays to a level which few modern dramatists even
attempt to reach are here very fitful indeed. The play, in effect, lacks a
centre and a *raison d'être* and no amount of warm, human emotion can
be a substitute for them.

Lord Claverton, the chief character of the play, is a man who in old
age is confronted with the results of his youthful misdemeanours –
misdemeanours, it should be pointed out, which are not much more
grave than the bogies which hide in everyone's past. Eliot's concern is
to show how Claverton is able to find forgiveness by seeing divine and
human love at work in all things – an echo, in fact, of Bernanos's
'grace is everywhere'. In Act III he says to his daughter, Monica,

'If a man has one person, just one in his life,
To whom he is willing to confess everything –
And that includes, mind you, not only things criminal,
Not only turpitude, meanness and cowardice,
But also situations which are simply ridiculous,
When he has played the fool (as who has not?) –
Then he loves that person, and his love will save him.'

By loving his daughter and by participating, at second-hand, in her
love for her fiancé, Charles, Claverton is able to exorcize his own
sense of guilt even about his mishandling of his son Michael. Unlike
Harry in *The Family Reunion*, however, he does not 'follow the bright
angels'; there is no vision, no mystical experience to descend from or
to return to. And since there is no lofty ideal to which Claverton can
dedicate his life, the play ends in the only way Eliot could end it in the
circumstances – with Claverton's death. But his acceptance and end

have nothing of the inevitability of Lear's death (though it seems as if Eliot intends his audience at least to recall *King Lear*) because Claverton's struggles and conflicts in the earlier parts of the play seldom carry any real conviction. They are too theoretical, with the result that when, at the end of the play, Monica speaks of her father in words suggesting that, even while still alive, he has entered a new dimension of experience, we feel that the words belong somewhere else, that they are true but not true of Lord Claverton's situation. Her speech deserves to be quoted, however, because it makes an excellent introduction to an examination of the mystical experience which pervades the *Four Quartets*; Monica says,

> '. . . He is close at hand,
> Though he has gone too far to return to us.
> He is under the beech tree. It is quiet and cold there.
> In becoming no one, he has become himself.'

And a moment later, in the final words of the play, she declares,

> 'Age and decrepitude can have no terrors for me,
> Loss and vicissitude cannot appal me,
> Not even death can dismay or amaze me
> Fixed in the certainty of love unchanging.
>                  I feel utterly secure
> In you; I am a part of you. Now take me to my father.'

As in *The Cocktail Party*, the play ends on a note of completely human, almost domestic, acquiescence. Yet it does not satisfy the audience. I think the reason for this failure is that the audience or the reader feel that something has been thrust upon them; they have been given a real answer to a problem which has been presented in the earlier part of the play in unreal terms; and unreality is fatally infectious. It may also be that Eliot has delegated to human love what can only be fully realized in divine love. As with *The Confidential Clerk* and, to a lesser extent, with *The Cocktail Party*, one feels that his selfconsciously contemporary setting and trappings have been a positive impediment to what he really wants to say; it is ironic that an attempt at realism has resulted in a feeling of unreality at a deeper level. And the modern dramatic voice, with its conversational conventions and clichés, appears to have drowned Eliot's meaning. What that meaning is, and has been in all Eliot's later work, is made perfectly clear if we re-examine the *Four Quartets*.

The *Four Quartets* are four movements in a poem which attempts to depict the way to an experience of loss of self and union with God. The form of the poem is impersonal and this helps to give it its authority. Eliot certainly at times introduces the 'I' but it is an 'I' divested of all egotism, a person with whom we can all identify ourselves. In his essay, *Tradition and the Individual Talent*, Eliot has spoken of the necessity of *impersonality* in all great poetry; he says, '. . . my meaning is, that the poet has, not a "personality" to express, but a particular medium, which is only a medium and not a personality, in which impressions and experiences combine in peculiar and unexpected ways;' and again, 'Poetry is not a turning loose of emotion, but an escape from emotion; it is not the expression of personality, but an escape from personality. But, of course, only those who have personality and emotions know what it means to want to escape from these things.'

This kind of 'escape from personality' is one of the two major themes of the *Quartets;* the other is the triumph over time – 'only through time time is conquered.' *Burnt Norton* opens with a delicate and entirely honest examination of time. In a bare and simple statement, which only *appears* complex because we are unused to poetry that is stripped down to essentials and essences, Eliot exposes the apparent domination of time:

> If all time is eternally present
> All time is unredeemable.
> What might have been is an abstraction
> Remaining a perpetual possibility
> Only in a world of speculation.

This poetry, which speaks of 'a world of speculation', is far from the definitions of the philosophers. It expresses a truth discovered by intuition (an intuition whose only vehicle is imagery, whose only master is the imagination) not by argument. Swiftly, Eliot moves from these reflections on time 'into our first world', the rose garden, the time of innocence. Yet that innocence cannot be entirely recaptured; there is still 'the deception of the thrush'. But the garden provides one of those moments that appear timeless to the conscious mind. Like the later 'music heard so deeply that it is not heard at all', the garden provides 'a formal pattern', an acquiescence in a life more real than our own. And the garden is not only full of *human* life ('full of children, hidden excitedly, containing laughter') but also of vegetable life; the flowers need the human eye ('the roses had the look of flowers that are looked at') to give them a greater reality just as, later in the *Quartets*, man will be shown to need the care and vigilance of God to have any reality at all. This is foreshadowed in the lines which immediately follow the description of the garden:

> human kind
> Cannot bear very much reality.

After the lyric which describes the unity of stars, trees and animal life, Eliot returns to his scrutiny of time. Time is now seen as a dance:

> . . . Except for the point, the still point,
> There would be no dance, and there is only the dance.

This is not yet 'the sudden illumination' of the saint but rather 'the unattended moment'. Nor are we yet in the dark night of the soul. Eliot speaks of the necessity of renunciation and withdrawal:

> The inner freedom from the practical desire,
> The release from action and suffering.

But there is still 'a white light' and 'a new world And the old made explicit'; there is still only 'the partial ecstasy'. In the third movement of *Burnt Norton* Eliot describes 'a place of disaffection'. This is still the world we all know and live in but, as if already touching on the great experience which the other three *Quartets* will make more explicit, he describes the sufferings which the mystic must undergo before losing himself in that later vision. Here these sufferings are seen negatively, though we ourselves have not yet attained the state of

> . . . darkness to purify the soul
> Emptying the sensual with deprivation
> Cleansing affection from the temporal.

We are still 'distracted from distraction by distraction', merely 'men and bits of paper.'

The world of the *Four Quartets* is a world of images; more than this, it is a world we know both from our maps and from our own experience. So now Eliot describes 'the gloomy hills of London', but even they have insufficient darkness. It is an inner darkness which we must enter, 'the world of perpetual solitude'. In this world we can only move in trust and hope: we must experience 'evacuation of the world of fancy' (not, be it noted, of the world of imagination; Eliot never repudiates *that*). But since we can bear so little of such reality, Eliot returns to the fitful, exquisite summer garden where 'The black cloud carries the sun away.'

*Burnt Norton*, in effect, depicts aesthetic delight and awe before natural objects as necessary preliminaries to a supernatural life. Grace perfects nature, so that the ineffable experience of union with God will not cancel out the love of natural or man-made beauty but rather gather it up and transform it. The only loss is the loss of the insignificant. 'The kingfisher's wing' and the 'Chinese jar' will always delight, will always be pointers to a loftier reality; they are adumbrations not illusions.

Towards the end of this first quartet, Eliot discusses the validity of language as a vehicle of truth. Such questioning increases the power of the total poem and is like the craftsman's constant and careful testing of his tools. It is imperative to note, however, that changing and imprecise as words can be, they are in themselves not only adequate but essential. It is only because they are vulnerable to 'Shrieking voices scolding, mocking, or merely chattering' that they can ever be in any real danger at all. To illustrate the power and supremacy he sees in language, Eliot at this point in the poem daringly echoes the beginning of St John's Gospel. Language is seen as Christ, the Word, the Second Person of the Blessed Trinity:

> . . . The Word in the desert
> Is most attacked by voices of temptation.

The end of the poem is purely lyrical but it is much more than a lucid utterance of sadness or felicity: it contains a hint of the pain which must be endured on the way to the full vision. We are exhorted to learn that

> Desire itself is movement
> Not in itself desirable

while 'Love is itself unmoving.' It only seems to us to be in motion because we view it in 'the aspect of time,' 'between unbeing and being.' To learn and know love completely, we have to become that 'nought' which the fourteenth century English mystical writers insisted so strongly upon. The poem ends on a note of nostalgia, on a sudden brief return to the rose-garden. When Eliot says

> Ridiculous the waste sad time
> Stretching before and after,

he is returning again, I think, to an earlier line of the poem – 'To be
conscious is not to be in time.' He means that our own lack of awareness makes time seem waste and sad. It is our shadows which 'stretch
before and after,' not our essential selves.

In *East Coker* Eliot widens and deepens his twin themes of time and
of escape from personality – only from the temporal aspect of
personality, however, or from what Jung calls 'the persona'. The
movement of the verse itself expands now to include prehistory,
history, tradition, and the natural life of the soil. This is a timely
moment to compare Eliot's treatment of time with Edwin Muir's; the
difference is in the approach rather than in the conclusion. Where
Muir sees the life of man on two levels, that of the story and that of
the fable, so that each human life repeats the great stages of the history
of the world, Eliot sees man feeling the domination of time and trying
to escape from it by ignoring it. Over and over again through the
*Quartets*, we are confronted with the apparent implacability of time.
'Only through time time is conquered' declares Eliot, but his insistent
message throughout these poems is to show man how he can reach
*the other side* of time, how he can arrive at a point where time itself
is meaningless. Muir also reaches this point but he does so in a
different way; he presents man living two lives simultaneously, each
one vindicating the other's cause. Man is only at war with himself
when he tries to live only at one level and it is this conflict which
provides the tension in Muir's best poetry. In Muir's vision, then,
man's struggle is cosmic and universal, in Eliot's, it is personal,
particular and expressed in the familiar terms of orthodox Western
mystical experience. And Eliot makes it clear that the full vision is
only to be attained in this life by the very few, by those who know
that 'to be conscious is not to be in time.' For Muir, the vision is open
to everyone, is, furthermore, lived out in each individual life.

In *East Coker*, however, Eliot comes close to Muir's conception of
human life because here he shows man as most near to reality when
closest to natural things and the elements:

> The time of the seasons and the constellations
> The time of milking and the time of harvest
> The time of the coupling of man and woman
> And that of beasts.

But the stress is still on time, and the word itself rings through this passage of the poem like a knell. *East Coker* continues with a brief reflection on the sea:

> Out at sea the dawn wind
> Wrinkles and slides.

This is a theme which will be taken up again later and elaborated on in *The Dry Salvages*. This second quartet now turns to an examination of the seasons – 'the disturbance of the spring', the 'creatures of the summer heat', all that moves in and through time, whose medium *is* time. Then Eliot goes back to the scrutiny of language which he touched on briefly in *Burnt Norton*. And it is relevant to state here that the *Quartets* have a cumulative effect, also a cyclic one. There is no debris, no abandonment, nothing is lost.

From his 'intolerable wrestle with words and meanings', Eliot moves on to a study of the value of old age and experience. His conclusion is disenchanted:

> . . . There is, it seems to us,
> At best, only a limited value
> In the knowledge derived from experience

and

> . . . We are only undeceived
> Of that which, deceiving, could no longer harm.

and again,

> . . . Do not let me hear
> Of the wisdom of old men, but rather of their folly,
> Their fear of fear and frenzy, their fear of possession,
> Of belonging to another, or to others, or to God.

The whole intent of the *Four Quartets* is beginning to disclose itself; the way to God is through

> . . . the wisdom of humility: humility is endless.

It is at this point of humble submission that Eliot shows himself at his most daring and most original; the dry, honest voice of the earlier poems speaks again but speaks now in a richer context. We are now entering the dark night not only of 'the vacant intersteller spaces', with its echo of Milton, but also the dark night of our own souls and our own troubled time – the world of 'the generous patrons of art',

(art alone, it is implied, is now not enough) and of 'the Stock Exchange Gazette'. Eliot depicts this world in dramatic terms and
employs an almost epic image of the theatre to illustrate it. After this
bold image, however, he returns to a theological context. The
humility essential to the mystic has already been stressed; it is now
the turn of the great theological virtues of faith, hope and charity:

> . . . the faith and the love and the hope are all in the waiting.

These words remind us of Becket's fear of becoming a martyr for
the wrong reasons. Eliot warns us,

> Wait without thought, for you are not ready for thought.

We are still in the early stages of renunciation, yet there is nothing
quietist about these words. We must still be active, even in the choice
of waiting,

> So the darkness shall be the light, and the stillness the dancing.

Now Eliot returns to the garden with 'the wild thyme unseen and
the wild strawberry.' There is still, and always will be, time for the
lyric moment, 'the echoed ecstasy'. And these things are made more
lovely simply because we know we must abandon them, at least
temporarily. After the moment in the garden, Eliot paraphrases some
vital words of St John of the Cross, as if to make quite sure that we
understand the burden of his message and the import of his meaning:

> You must go by a way wherein there is no ecstasy.
> In order to arrive at what you do not know
> You must go by a way which is the way of ignorance.

This is the way of the temporary rejection of images, yet images
are abandoned not because they are worthless in themselves but
because we need to be released from our adherence to them, from our
clamorous desire to possess them. And the dispossession itself hurts.
*East Coker* is, in fact, now entering a world of pain and suffering and
the fourth movement of it, which is a lyric written in a completely
regular form, stresses this. 'The wounded surgeon', 'the sharp
compassion of the healer's art', remind us that there can be no
salvation except through participation in the agony and death of
Christ. 'The whole earth is our hospital' and 'the ruined millionaire'
is both Adam, our first father, and ourselves. Like all true visionary
writers, Eliot stresses the importance of the Incarnation and, in

particular, the doctrine of the Holy Eucharist. All that seems hopeless and shameful is redeeemed and, in spite of all evidence to the contrary, 'we call this Friday good.' The vision is transcendent but it is also historic and dynamic.

The final movement of *East Coker* is quieter, more reflective. It is a point of rest along a journey of agony and travail. In it Eliot reconsiders the recalcitrance of language, 'the general mess of imprecision of feeling,' but he concludes, with a humble confidence,

> There is only the fight to recover what has been lost
> And found and lost again and again . . .
>
> .          .          .
>
> For us, there is only the trying. The rest is not our business.

The last lines of the poem refer again to old age but now age itself is transfigured:

> Old men ought to be explorers
> Here or there does not matter.

Stars and 'old stones' are again considered since we are still attached to the sky and the soil. But the poem ends on a great affirmation of a further experience, the experience of the mystic – something we can all prepare ourselves for though few of us may attain it. The sea is again introduced, the warning note of the chief subject of the next quartet:

> We must be still and still moving
> Into another intensity
> For a further union, a deeper communion
> Through the dark cold and the empty desolation,
> The wave cry, the wind cry, the vast waters
> Of the petrel and the porpoise. In my end is my beginning.

The loss of self in the mastery of self is a new birth and birth comes with the breaking of waters, the impulse of the tides.

In *The Dry Salvages*, water, especially the sea, is the key symbol. This quartet, which is perhaps the most perfectly articulated of the set, considers both the primal waters from which, according to Genesis, all creation came, and also the rivers and seas which man knows and uses but which remain forever 'untamed and intractable' with their 'hints of earlier and other creation'. The river, which is 'useful' but 'untrustworthy', is a 'conveyor of commerce'. But to early man, Eliot says, it was 'a strong brown god', a god who is now 'almost forgotten By the dwellers in cities.' In all the *Quartets*, as in earlier poems such as *The Waste Land* and *Preludes*, life in the city is seen as a bad thing of its very nature. It is bad because it has removed man from his natural context, from the earth where his roots were planted. Eliot's plea for the life of the land, however, is no cranky 'return to nature' protest; rather, it is yet another aspect of man's loss of tradition, a loss which he deplores in some of his best essays. He does not give any easy answers to the problems of our modern urban civilization but at the beginning of *The Dry Salvages* he states quite unambiguously that nature, in the form of the sea, will take her revenge on those who ignore her; she is the 'destroyer, reminder Of what men choose to forget.' It is significant, too, that the child always has this sense of affinity with natural things:

His rhythm [the river's] was presented in the nursery bedroom.

And further, Eliot is here exposing that side of mystical experience which moves *through* images and *through* the things which the senses affirm. As Traherne has said, 'You cannot love too much, only in a false way'; similarly, to reduce the things which satisfy the senses to the pleasures that can only be found in urban surroundings is to love in the wrong way, is to misuse the body entirely.

The poem goes on to show how the river and the sea are forms of life which we have come to regard only with the faintly curious eyes of mere onlookers:

> . . . Pools where it offers to our curiosity
> The more delicate algae and the sea anemone.

We must abandon this attitude and become participators, must lose ourselves in the people and natural objects which surround us. In effect, *The Dry Salvages* retraces the several steps towards contemplation, and this is true of all the first three quartets. Their movement is tidal, advancing and retreating; the poet's imagination works by reiteration and by a constant reshuffling of the same images. The first movement of this third quartet is almost entirely descriptive, yet it also has its momentary touches, not of didacticism but of explanation and elucidation:

> Between midnight and dawn,
>       when the past is all deception,
> The future futureless.

These, Eliot says, are moments which concern us all and not only 'the anxious worried women'.

The second movement of the poem is written in six extremely skilful stanzas which all rhyme with one another; it is a consideration, in terms of those who live by what the sea provides, of the agony of renunciation – not only the numbing agony which attends the failure of the emotions but the pain of negation itself, a pain which the flesh must experience completely when it is severed from the spirit at the moment of death. The only answer to this pain, the only *vindication* of it is 'the hardly, barely prayable Prayer of the one Annunciation.' Christ's Incarnation, Crucifixion and Resurrection, in other words, are the only facts which can make life and death endurable, and not simply endurable but also acceptable.

After this lyric, Eliot returns to the themes of time and age and to our own feeble attempts to disown the past, our own true beginnings, 'by superficial notions of evolution'. He then swiftly, but tentatively, refers to 'the sudden illumination' which is an experience shared by us all because it is the experience 'of many generations'. The implication is that this 'sudden illumination' is an awareness of God and therefore intended for all men. If we do not have this awareness, then it is because we have not prepared ourselves to receive it, and part of this preparation is the agony which 'abides'. Agony is expressed in terms of time but since time both preserves and destroys, suffering is neither fortuitous nor meaningless. It is part of the pattern not simply of the life of prayer but also of life itself.

*The Dry Salvages* continues by emphasizing the necessity of still trying, of still struggling and moving onward ('time is no healer: the patient is no longer here'). After another epic simile, that of the departure and journey of a train, Eliot exhorts us,

> Here between the hither and the further shore
> While time is withdrawn, consider the future
> And the past with an equal mind.

What is of absolute importance is to remember that 'the time of death is every moment' and, moreover, we must not cling to the fruits of all our separate actions throughout life but must 'fare forward' not expecting or demanding to 'fare well'. The kind of play which Eliot makes on words and phrases like 'farewell' and 'time is a healer' is an interesting characteristic of all the *Quartets*. It is a play of mind which is intended to shake our accepted and often ill-founded notions.

The fourth movement of the poem returns to the theme of the Annunciation, only here the Mother of God is herself invoked as the daughter of her son, the guardian of sailors and Queen of Heaven. The final movement is explicitly concerned with the stages towards mystical union with God. Eliot dismisses fortune-telling, seances, all the 'usual pastimes and drugs' which are man's attempts to palliate or else to ignore the fact of death. 'Man's curiosity,' he says, 'searches past and future And clings to that dimension.' We must abandon such curiosity and accept the 'unattended moment' of illumination which is given to us. It is at this point in the *Four Quartets* that Eliot aligns himself with those mystical writers of the past who have seen experimental union with God in this life as an experience that is only intended for the rare person, for the saint in fact. This is a perfectly orthodox viewpoint since there have always been two schools of thought in this matter *within* the Western Christian tradition. As we have observed, even the author of *The Cloud of Unknowing*, a man notable for his generosity of spirit, divided seekers after God into four classes – Common, Special, Singular and Perfect (we shall see how Eliot appropriates a line from *The Cloud* in *Little Gidding*). But Eliot also grants spiritual validity to aesthetic and natural ecstasies – 'The distraction fit, lost in a shaft of sunlight' and 'music heard so deeply That it is not heard at all, but you are the music While the music lasts.' These moments of self-losing are not only triumphs over time but are also fragmentary glimpses of God who is above time; and, as Augustine said, 'God made the world not in time but with time.'

But the aesthetic and natural ecstasies are only 'hints and guesses'; 'the rest Is prayer, observance, discipline, thought and action.' Yet discipline and asceticism are also essential for the saint, are, in fact, his vocation;

> . . . Something given
> And taken, in a lifetime's death in love,
> Ardour and selflessness and self-surrender.

At the end of *The Dry Salvages* Eliot declares that few of us can free ourselves from the tyranny of past and future because we are not sufficiently selfless. His doctrine of mystical experience has nothing in it of arbitrary election; Christian teaching has always stressed

God's desire to be completely united with every human being. But the movement must be reciprocal, must be a willing relationship between *persons*, and it is we who fail by refusing to play our part. This essential confrontation and mingling of personalities explains why so many mystical writers have used the language of secular love as an analogy of divine love. And it is our Puritanism, our deeply-engrained Manichaeism, not our human dignity, that flinches from such an analogue.

But most of us, too weak, too possessive to obey the commands of divine love, must fulfil ourselves by recognizing simply what we are (the theme of *The Cocktail Party* and *The Confidential Clerk*), and by not cutting ourselves off either from our roots or from our traditions:

> . . . content at the last
> If our temporal reversion nourish
> (Not too far from the yew-tree)
> The life of significant soil.

It must be stressed that the soil, and all that it implies, *is* significant, is a blessing. To think of it in any other way would be a blasphemy. The ascetic does not abandon the things of the senses and of the world because they are bad; on the contrary, he sacrifices them because they are *good* and, for that very reason, may distract him from a greater good which is God himself.

In *Little Gidding* Eliot comes, as it were, out into the open with the theme that has moved fugitively through the first three quartets – the search for God by means of self-surrender and love. But the city, the seasons, the soil, the sea are now caught up into the greater vision, the grander design; they are not so much subjugated to this vision as illuminated by it, and thus fall into their rightful place in the total pattern. Little Gidding is itself a place of prayer and so it too, like the full vision which permeates this poem, illuminates and humbles those who approach it:

> . . . You are here to kneel
> Where prayer has been valid.

The idea of tradition and continuity is also discovered in prayer itself since

> . . . the communication
> Of the dead is tongued with fire beyond the language of the living.

In the second movement of the poem which, like that of *The Dry Salvages*, is a lyric written in regular stanzaic form, the four elements are seen as agents of destruction. Our own wrong actions are responsible for the destructive power of the elements; Eliot writes,

> The death of hope and despair,
> This is the death of air.

And the last stanza of the lyric demonstrates the part we ourselves play in the destructive strength of the elements, our perversion of their powers for good:

> Water and fire shall rot
> The marred foundations we forgot,
> Of sanctuary and choir.
> This is the death of water and fire.

It should be noted that Eliot involves all creation in these acts of destruction. It is not death *by* water and fire but death *of* water and fire.

The poem continues with a long description of the poet's meeting with 'a familiar compound ghost' who has 'the sudden look of some dead master.' This passage contains echoes of Dante and its purpose seems to be both to confront the poet with his own past and the past of the whole race, and also to teach him again, and in no uncertain language, just how hard the way of surrender is. The pains of old age are vividly stressed – 'the cold friction of expiring sense', the 'bitter tastelessness of shadow fruit'. The things of the senses are again shown to be in time and therefore subject to time. Thus old men *can* be 'explorers' because their very condition has removed the power of the flesh even if it has not removed its shadow or regret.

The third movement re-enacts the stages through which non-attachment is reached. But this very detachment becomes a cause of joy:

> . . . See, now they vanish
> The faces and places, with the self which, as it could, loved them,
> To become renewed, transfigured in another pattern.

There is no loss, only an assigning of all things to their proper places. And now Eliot appears to have forgotten, perhaps deliberately, that mystical union with God is a special vocation. His vision widens to embrace all created being and he uses some words from Julian of

Norwich's *Revelations of Divine Love* to express an experience of joy and gaiety. Employing her words, Eliot now declares not only that 'Sin is Behovely' (since, like Adam's *felix culpa*, it was directly responsible for the merciful coming of Christ) but also that

> . . . all shall be well and
> All manner of thing shall be well.

Fire, suffering and pain are now also transfigured since the force that causes and drives them is love:

> Who then devised the torment? Love.

Love is the Second Person of the Blessed Trinity who, by taking on himself the sins and sufferings of the world, both redeemed them and gave them purpose. But the Second Person is also the Word and here, in the fifth movement of the last of the *Four Quartets*, language is also redeemed and transfigured:

> The word neither diffident nor ostentatious,
> An easy commerce of the old and the new,
> The common word exact without vulgarity,
> The formal word precise but not pedantic,
> The complete consort dancing together.

This passage, with its allusions to dancing and the marriage union, echoes the dance in the second movement of *Burnt Norton* and 'the association of man and woman' in the first movement of *East Coker*. All the threads are being drawn together so that finally the complete pattern may be revealed. 'We die with the dying' and 'we are born with the dead'; we are all part of a plan, and the ardour of the saint is linked, by hierarchy, with 'the moment of the rose and the moment of the yew-tree.'

In *Little Gidding* 'prayer has been valid' and it is valid because 'history is a pattern Of timeless moments'. Eliot's poem reclaims these moments but reclaims them only to show that we ourselves can add to them by continuing to explore and to struggle and by recognizing, and so sharing to some degree, the selfless ecstasies of the saints. With a line from *The Cloud of Unknowing* – 'With the drawing of this Love and the voice of this Calling' – Eliot demonstrates that we are all called to God though we are called in different ways. Our lives begin and end in God, but we are free to deviate from the divine will. Mystical union with God demands 'a condition of complete simplicity

(Costing not less than everything)', but we who cannot attain such simplicity can at least approximate to it; 'the children in the apple-tree', heard now 'between two waves of the sea', can give us glimpses of ecstasy, 'hints and guesses'. In the last four lines of the poem, Eliot wonderfully joins together, by means of symbols, the gifts of the Holy Ghost, the suffering of the saint, and the innocence of the child in the rose-garden:

> All manner of thing shall be well
> When the tongues of flame are in-folded
> Into the crowned knot of fire
> And the fire and the rose are one.

If we make the effort to pierce the surface complexities of the *Four Quartets* we cannot fail to find Eliot's own conviction that poetry is not only a medium for the expression of mystical experience but itself an experience of a similar kind. One proof of this is the delicate testing of the very validity of language which occurs again and again throughout the four poems. Words are subject to the attrition of time, yes, but they are constantly repaired and renewed by a sense of history and tradition. In one of his essays, Eliot commented dryly upon the arrogance of critics who say of ancient writers, 'We know so much more now'; Eliot's reply was, 'Precisely, *they* are that which we know.' And because the best poetry has this lasting quality, it can therefore embody and perpetuate the timeless moment of mysticism. The *Four Quartets* are both the record of the stages towards and the attainment of a total vision of life, and also an affirmation of the power of poetry to sustain that vision without the shadow of alteration or falsification. Eliot's achievement is well summed up in some words from a poem by W. H. Auden:

> The full view indeed may enter
> And move in memory . . .

# 16. THE RESTORATION OF SYMBOLS:

## A study of the poetry of David Gascoyne

*But it is not only on wood that the Redeemer is stretched out and crucified,*
*it is on the universe of which he forms the node, the centre, the* raison
*d'être, the heart, the pivot, the essential vital piece.*
PAUL CLAUDEL – A Poet Before the Cross

WITH THE DEATH of Edwin Muir, David Gascoyne is, I think, the
only living English poet, apart from Eliot, in the true mystical
tradition. If it is not directly influenced by it, his work undoubtedly
leads directly back to the visionary poetry of Vaughan, Herbert
and Traherne. Yet his work is emphatically of this time and this
place – concrete, rooted, exact. And this is true of all the finest
mystical poetry of the past: it takes the symbols and traditions of its
own time and then transcends them. John of the Cross's *Spiritual
Canticle*, as we have seen, is based on the imagery of the *Song of Songs*,
the cadences of Spanish folk poetry and the sophisticated forms of
sixteenth century court verse in Spain. From such traditions and
conventions it forms its own world and finds its own voice. Similarly,
in the seventeenth century in England, Vaughan and Herbert,
without any violent experimentation, appropriated the forms and
music in which conventional love poetry was written, and then
raised them to a higher power. Their verse was thus of its day yet
also outside its day. As Eliot has said,

Only through time time is conquered.

David Gascoyne started publishing verse as a very young man.
Much of his early work was surrealist in form and expression and
greatly influenced by French writers of the time (he is still only 44
years old). He has also written in French himself; I do not think,
however, that he really found his own voice or his own individual
means of expression until he started writing the poems which appeared
in the volume entitled *Poems 1937–42* – a book aptly illustrated by
Graham Sutherland, another visionary and tormented artist who also
had affinities with surrealism.

The prevailing themes in this book are war, suffering and the loneliness of modern man. These are the overt themes; beneath them, however, is the private voice seeking to express the poet's own struggle for meaning and for unity. The poems are profoundly Christian but, as Rouault, in modern times, has done with his paintings, David Gascoyne has revived and transformed the old symbols which bad 'religious art' so often renders lifeless, and displayed them, alive, in an entirely contemporary setting.

In the magnificent sequence of poems called *Miserere* which opens the book, the poet, in lines of extreme lucidity, examines the depths of man's guilt and the terror of life without God. The traditional 'dark night of the soul' is transferred to Christ himself – Christ who is both the victim and the conqueror:

> . . . God's wounds are numbered.
> All is now withdrawn: void yawns
> The rock-hewn tomb. There is no more
> Regeneration in the stricken sun . . .
>
> Thus may it be: and worse.
> And may we know Thy perfect darkness
> And may we into Hell descend with Thee.
> ( *Tenebrae* )

The poet sees himself as a part of Christ, prepared to endure intolerable suffering and even to touch the edge of despair, but never finally to become hopeless.

In the second poem of the sequence, *Pieta*, the tough, lithe quality of David Gascoyne's language and imagery begins to display itself. The tenebral cry of anguish turns to a vision of the Crucifixion:

> Stark in the pasture of the skull-shaped hill,
> In swollen aura of disaster shrunken and
> Unsheltered by the ruin of the sky,
> Intensely concentrated in themselves the banded
> Saints abandoned kneel.
>
> .           .
>
> The Mother, whose dead Son's dear head
> Weighs like a precious blood-incrusted stone
> On her unfathomable breast:
> Holds Him God has forsaken, Word made flesh

> Made ransom, to the slow smoulder of her heart
> Till the catharsis of the race shall be complete.

The last line of this poem shows the skill (except that 'skill' is too superficial a word) with which Gascoyne has involved the whole of mankind in the act of redemption and, in an entirely concrete way, has tethered past and future to the present moment.

The third poem is a prayer for faith spoken from the depths:

> Because the depths
> Are clear with only death's
> Marsh-light, because the rock of grief
> Is clearly too extreme for us to breach:
> Deepen our depths,
> And aid our unbelief.

The poet is not afraid to go even further into darkness and we are reminded of Vaughan's lines,

> There is in God, some say,
> A deep but dazzling darkness.

*Kyrie* explores 'the black catastrophe that can lay waste our world' and pleads

> Grant us extraordinary grace.

What is notable here is the complete lack of self-pity. In Milton's *Samson Agonistes*, Samson attained, after suffering and deprivation, a state of pure affirmation so that Manoa could say of him simply and honestly,

> Nothing is here for tears, nothing to wail
> Or knock the breast, no weakness, no contempt . . .

In *Lachrymae*, David Gascoyne affirms *through* tears; tears are a purgation and also a gift because they are man's tears mingled with Christ's:

> Thy tears were all.
> And when our secret face
> Is blind because of the mysterious
> Surging of tears wrung by our most profound
> Presentiment of evil in man's fate, our cruellest wounds
> Become Thy stigmata. They are Thy tears which fall.

The next poem, *Ex Nihilo*, is not a repetition of *De Profundis* but a development from it. It speaks of 'the revelation of despair' and the stubborn acceptance of temporary defeat:

> But kiss the hand that has consigned
> Me to these latter years where I must learn
> The revelation of despair, and find
> Among the debris of all certainties
> The hardest stone on which to found
> Altar and shelter for Eternity.

The word 'altar' is the key to the next poem. It is called *Sanctus* and though it never refers directly to the Mass or the Consecration, it is a vivid evocation of what the Consecration means and whence it moves. Let me put it another way: the Sanctus section of the Mass is, in this poem, like a pebble thrown into a pool. The pool causes wider and wider ripples and it is these ripples that Gascoyne is concerned with:

> . . . to understand
> Is to endure, withstand the withering blight
> Of winter night's long desperation, war,
> Confusion, till at the dense core
> Of this existence all the spirit's force
> Becomes acceptance of blind eyes
> To see no more. Then they may see at last;
> And all they see their vision sanctifies.

This poem is the heart of the sequence. It shows more completely than any of the other poems that it is the poet's vision itself which sanctifies and radiates. The vision is the end not the means and once it has been achieved, however fleetingly, it illuminates all things outside it while itself remaining locked in its own lyrical form and music. This is the hard-won triumph of all great visionary poetry.

*Ecce Homo* is a kind of coda to the whole sequence. It brings the passion and crucifixion down to human and contemporary terms; it refuses to ignore disgust and horror:

> Whose is this horrifying face,
> This putrid flesh, discoloured, flayed,
> Fed on by flies, scorched by the sun?
>
> .     .     .
>
> Behold the Man: He is Man's Son.

> Forget the legend, tear the decent veil
> That cowardice or interest devised.
>
> .            .            .
>
> He is in agony till the world's end.

The two thieves, crucified on either side of Christ, are depicted as ourselves or our own contemporaries, just as Stanley Spencer has shown them in his *Crucifixion*, except that in Gascoyne's picture there is nothing gentle or gracious. 'The decent veil' has been torn away:

> And on his either side hang dead
> A labourer and a factory hand,
> Or one is maybe a lynched Jew
> And one a Negro or a Red . . .

And Christ, 'who wept for Jerusalem',

> Now sees his prophecy extended
> Across the greatest cities of the world.

At the end of the poem he is invoked as 'Christ of Revolution and of Poetry' who has redeemed 'our sterile misery' in order

> That man's long journey through the night
> May not have been in vain.

Terrifying as the subject of this sequence is, Gascoyne has handled it with a dexterity that never deteriorates into mere smoothness, and with an unremitting candour and clarity. His subject is confusion and despair but his verse is easy and confident. The words embody the vision and the fact of being able to speak is itself a kind of small redemption.

The poems which follow *Miserere* in this volume deal with many subjects – light, landscape, music, the death of a friend – but even where Gascoyne is, on the one hand, most objective, or, on the other, most involved and personal, the mystical, visionary element is always present: if not in the lines, then between them. These poems are like brilliant chips splintered off a dazzling stone; they all come from, and belong to, the same thing, the same overriding preoccupation. In a poem which examines the idea of thought having 'a subtle odour', the poet moves, without any apparent straining, to a much deeper level of meaning:

> Nostalgic breezes: And it's then we sense
> Remote presentiment of some intensely bright
> Impending spiritual dawn, of which the pure
> Immense illumination seems about to pour
> In upon our existence from beyond
> The edge of Knowing.

These are large words and would be vague in the hands of a poet of less intensity, honesty and concern for language. With Gascoyne they convince because he only uses them when all other words have failed, when abstractions must overrule concrete images. It was the same with Dante when he was trying to describe Paradise. For the truth is that we have more precise words and images for horror and disgust than we have for ecstasy and vision.

The apotheosis of this volume of poems is reached not in the last poem but in the penultimate one, *The Gravel-pit Field*. Here, in beautifully controlled rhymed stanzas, Gascoyne conveys his own mystical experience. The poem starts with a description of a vacant lot beside the Thames:

> A stretch of scurfy pock-marked waste
> Sprawls laggardly its acres till
> They touch a raw brick-villa'd rim.

From an examination of pits, pools, grass, soil and weeds, the poem moves into its great subject:

> As with untold intensity
> On the far edge of Being where
> Life's last faint forms begin to lose
> Names and identity and fade
> Away into the Void, endures
> The final thin triumphant flame
> Of all that's most despoiled and bare.

The scene and the familiar objects which it contains still exist but they are now transformed, not by allegory or analogy but by the brilliance of the poet's sudden complete awareness of them as part of a larger whole. In this vision, 'the unclean mongrel's bones' appear to be 'the precious relics of some saint', while a Woodbine packet seems to have magical words written on it. The experience is entirely subjective but the poet's treatment of it renders it objective, as something we too can share. 'In a flash,' he ends,

Of insight I behold the field's
Apotheosis: No-Man's-land
Between this world and the beyond,
Remote from men and yet more real
Than any human dwelling-place;
A tabernacle where one stands
As though within the empty space
Round which revolves Lao Tse's Wheel.

One of the many interesting things about this triumphant conclusion is that even where Gascoyne is transcribing an ineffable
experience, he can still speak of the concrete; he introduces the wise
man's wheel, a concrete symbol but one quite different from the solid
setting of the gravel-pit field, yet it seems entirely fitting. It completes
the poem and also gives it a sense of timelessness, of something
continually going on both in the lines of the poem and in the reader's
own mind.

In his next book, entitled *The Vagrant and Other Poems*, published
in 1950, David Gascoyne made a more personal application of the
symbols which he had restored and revivified in *Poems 1937–1942*.
He is a poet who, while never repeating himself, continually returns
to the same themes and subjects. He finds them inexhaustible and
indeed they are since they are concerned with the most fundamental
problems of a man's life. In a very fine poem in *The Vagrant* called
*The Sacred Hearth*, he makes an affirmation of human, earthly love:

. . . we ought to know
That there can be for us no place quite alien and unknown,
No situation wholly hostile, if somewhere there burn
The faithful fire of vision still awaiting our return.

And again, in *Eros Absconditus* he speaks of a human love which,
though never completely attainable in this life, is nevertheless valid
and capable of fulfilment elsewhere:

Not in my lifetime, the love I envisage:
Not in this country, it may be. Nevertheless inevitable.
Having experienced a foretaste of its burning
And of its consolation, although locked in my aloneness
Still, although I know it cannot come to be
Except in reciprocity, I know
That true love is gratuitous, and will race through
The veins of the reborn world's generations . . .

The key-words here are 'aloneness', 'reciprocity' and 'gratuitous'. The poem is a gesture of relinquishment, of assigning to others what one cannot possess oneself. One is reminded of the heart-rending cry of Bernanos's young country priest: 'The miracle of the empty hands – that one can give what one does not possess.' In his sense of 'aloneness' Gascoyne is not inhabiting the kind of isolated world which Rilke created for himself; his loneliness is more akin to that of Hopkins – an acknowledgment of the existence of divine and human love even when both appear to be withdrawn temporarily from oneself. *Eros Absconditus* ends on a note of hope, a defiant recognition of the loveliness and transcendent power of friendship:

> The love of heroes and of men like gods
> Has been for long a strange thing on the earth
> And monstrous to the mediocre . . .
>
> .        .        .
>
> In blind content they breed who never loved a friend.

One of Gascoyne's most glittering and splendid poems appears in *The Vagrant*; it is *September Sun 1947*, a lyric in praise of light. Light has always been a favourite image with mystical poets. With a poet like Vaughan, as we have noted, it penetrates his entire work. After a triumphant tribute to the sun,

> Magnificent strong sun! in these last days
> So prodigally generous of pristine light . . .

Gascoyne moves on to a vision of the sun as an image of God himself:

> . . . with an angrier sun may He
> Who first with His gold seed the sightless field
> Of Chaos planted, all our trash to cinders bring.

As always, the language is precise and concrete, the music controlled and assured. Yet control does not preclude a rising pulse of excitement and the formal design of the poem stresses this excitement. Passion held in check is always more potent than passion at liberty.

In a sequence of poems called *Fragments towards a Religio Poetae* Gascoyne returns to a consideration of the themes he handled in *Miserere*, only here, as the title indicates, the approach is more personal, the setting more immediately contemporary. The two sequences might usefully be compared with St Augustine's conception of the Two Cities – the timeless City of God and the time-bound City of Man.

In *Religio Poetae* Gascoyne declares:

'The way to Life is through the entrance into Night.'

This is both the dark night of the individual soul and the dark night of the world at the present time. He continues,

> This world remains 'The World',
> An empire under rule
> Of a confederacy of lone wolf-hearted birds.

Later the poem becomes intensely personal and the movement of the verse seems, as Gide described Péguy's poetry, 'like the probing of a man in prayer'.

> Let me remember
> That truly to be man is to be man aware of Thee
> And unafraid to be. So help me God.

The penultimate section of the sequence is a return to a meditation on the Cruficixion and the two thieves who died with Christ. The tone, however, is more bitterly ironic than that of *Ecce Homo*. In the later poem Gascoyne writes,

> God's Son! Whoever heard of such a thing?
> There hangs our King, a thief on either side!
> For Christ was executed by the general will,
> Officially and popularly executed, thrust
> Out of this life in ignominy, put
> To death outside the righteous City's wall.

In *Ecce Homo* Gascoyne emphasized the terror and compassion of Christ's suffering and the way in which mankind was redeemed through it. In this poem he stresses our own guilt in killing Christ and this guilt includes not only our individual acts of evil but also the fact that we have tried to tame and reduce religion to small human terms:

> Jesus seemed a dangerously subversive Sabbath-breaker
>
> .          .          .
>
> To the most devoutly religious people in Jerusalem in Jesus' day.
> Let the dead continue to bury the dead as they did then,
> And let the living dead awaken and greet with joy the ever-living.

But the sequence terminates on a note of pure hope, of hope achieved through suffering and acceptance:

. . . the attic window-boxes above the market
Offer tribute of happy beauty to the omniscient Heavenly Eye.

Few writers could get away with a phrase like 'happy beauty'
and it is an indication of Gascoyne's power and perceptiveness that we
accept it so willingly. It is because, in all his work, he never gives the
easy answer or the facile half-truth, never stands outside either the
struggle to live or the struggle to communicate, that he is such an
important poet. Like all true visionary writers, he wishes to *share*
(Aquinas said that 'the fruits of contemplation were to be handed on to
others'); like Herbert or Vaughan or, to move further back in time,
like Walter Hilton or Dame Julian of Norwich, he is in the direct line
of English religious literature. He conveys a private vision in public
terms; his view of life is his own world but it is also rooted in ours.
The 'rain-gorged Thames', the gravel-pit field, the suburbs, the horse-
butcher – in things like these he finds his images, his 'objective cor-
relatives' and then transforms them.

In his most recently published work, *Night Thoughts*, a dramatic
piece written for broadcasting, David Gascoyne continued his theme
of man's loneliness in a world where he is rooted yet, paradoxically,
not at home. Part of this work is written in verse, part in prose.
Strangely, however, the dramatic device of using various speaking
voices is not entirely successful. Perhaps the reason for this is that
the necessary *overt* objectivity of creating voices and characters causes
a dilution of the poet's own intensity, a slight dimming of his vision.
It is the final passages of *Night Thoughts*, where Gascoyne resorts to
prose to speak of prayer and silence and loneliness, that are the most
successful. For the truth is that his lyric gift is an entirely personal not
a dramatic one. His subjects are always dramatic but his treatment is
meditative; he moves by monologue not by dialogue, he is more
interested in the fears and aspirations which men share than in those
emotions where they show themselves to be most diverse.

*Night Thoughts* should, I think, be regarded as an experiment, as a
marginal occupation. It would be something more than a cause for
mere regret if Gascoyne were to give us no more verse comparable
with the best in *Poems 1937–42* and *The Vagrant*. For he is a figure
outside literary movements yet perfectly within the English tradition.
His influences from French writers have been completely assimilated
in his own native English verse. His achievement is already formidable
and he is still only in his early forties. The radiance and honesty of

his poetry are matched by an integrity that will not permit him to force anything. He said himself, with a perfect poetic humility, in a poem called *Apologia*,

> Before I fall
> Down silent finally, I want to make
> One last attempt at utterance and tell
> How my absurd desire was to compose
> A single poem with my mental eyes
> Wide open, and without even one lapse
> From that most scrupulous Truth which I pursue
> When not pursuing Poetry. – Perhaps
> Only the poem I can never write is *true*.

David Gascoyne's powerful visionary poetry is itself a denial of that last line and it is with both patience and excitement that I await his next book of poems.

# 17.  VISION WITHOUT BELIEF

## *A note on the poetry of Wallace Stevens*

---

*A work of art presents feeling . . . for our contemplation, making it
visible or audible or in some way perceivable through a symbol.*
SUSANNE K. LANGER – Feeling and Form

WHEN BELIEF ENTERS poetry it must at once be absorbed by everything else which the particular poem contains; it must be neither
sediment at the bottom nor froth at the top. It must be entirely assimilated, entirely acquiescent. In every successful poem, belief is not a
by-product but a pervasion, or, to change the metaphor, not an offshoot
but the main branch.

Wallace Stevens is a poet without faith in the religious sense, nor
does he affirm in the familiar humanist sense. He would have agreed
only with the second half of Keats' dictum about 'the holiness of the
heart's affections and the truth of imagination.' But he pursued truth
*through* imagination with as much rigour and passion as mystics
seek God or philosophers seek meaning. Every poem he wrote is
fundamentally about the same thing – the search for reality by means
of imagination. His poetry enacts his philosophy; one cannot extract
the thought, the content, the meaning, without emptying out, as it
were, the whole poem. Yet there is nothing purely abstract in his
work. Indeed, a superficial reading might persuade the reader that
Stevens is a hedonist, a self-indulgent pleasure-seeker. His poems
abound in scents, sounds and tangible objects. Often his images arise
from paintings or *objets d'art*. Anything which appeals to the senses
may, in fact, be the springboard to his inquiries. But these things are
present for their significances not merely for their sensuousness. What
I want to attempt here is a portrayal of Stevens not simply, as he has
so often been regarded, as a philosophical poet, but rather as a visionary
poet. Where logic dissects and analyses, vision assembles and unifies.
And vision means not only seeing but also an inward and an outward
turning, a search for reality or what the Christian mystics would call
God. In *The Comedian as the Letter C*, Stevens makes this search

explicit and the explicitness takes on an absolute authority simply by means of the radiant audacity of the poem's language and imagery. In the third section of the poem he writes,

> . . . Shrewd novitiates
> Should be the clerks of our experience.
> These bland excursions into time to come,
> Related in romance to backward flights,
> However prodigal, however proud,
> Contained in their afflatus the reproach
> That first drove Crispin to his wandering.
> He could not be content with counterfeit.

Oddly perhaps, the tone of this whole poem is Shakespearean, Shakespearean in the imperious mastery of the blank verse and Shakespearean also on a purely verbal level. One could compile a glossary of words from this poem which are more characteristic of Shakespeare than of any twentieth century poet. 'Annealed', 'indulgences', 'parleying', 'blotched' are but a few examples.

Where Rilke, another modern poet much concerned with the overt search for reality, struggled for a vision, Stevens searched for his with an intense, an almost passionate calm. Like the mystic, he is unpossessive, wishing to gather things together not to gain dominion over them but to find a pattern in them. In a poem called *Of Modern Poetry* he speaks of 'the poem of the act of the mind'. This is metaphysics in the strictly philosophical sense, but with Stevens it is also something more. The poem which is 'the act of the mind' is created by the imagination working on the findings of the senses, and working on them not to elaborate them but to elucidate them. If Stevens's attitude is agnostic, if his answers are often negative, his poems are, nevertheless, a repudiation of chaos, a gesture against disorder. And where the mystics make contact with God through their wills and their intellects, Stevens makes contact with reality through his own poetic imagination. All poets do this, of course, but not all poets make this very search the prevailing subject-matter of their verse. In this sense, Stevens is a poet in the pure state, constantly reiterating and calling in question what most poets take for granted. And this search has its own torments since so much intrudes between the poet and his vision. As Stevens says in *The Comedian as the Letter C*,

> Crispin dwelt in the land and dwelling there
> Slid from his continent by slow recess

> To things within his actual eye, alert
> To the difficulty of rebellious thought
> When the sky is blue.

and again,

> Should he lay by the personal and make
> Of his own fate an instance of all fate?
> What is one man among so many men?
> What are so many men in such a world?
> Can one man think one thing and think it long?
> Can one man be one thing and be it long?

Stevens calls Crispin 'a clown, perhaps, but an aspiring clown.' *The Comedian as the Letter C* is an account of his search for meaning. Crispin discards the familiar philosophies of men one by one but he never finally repudiates the exquisite precision of his own imagination. The search has its own value even though it leads to the disenchantment of

> . . . what can all this matter since
> The relation comes, benignly, to its end?

The conclusion is stoical and 'death closes all'. Yet there is affirmation too since, through the fashioning of a 'mythology of self', Crispin has created a beauty comparable to that of the physical world. Stevens enlarges on this belief at the end of *Peter Quince at the Clavier*:

> The body dies; the body's beauty lives.
>                .                    .
> Susanna's music touched the bawdy strings
> Of those white elders; but, escaping,
> Left only Death's ironic scraping.
> Now, in its immortality, it plays
> On the clear viol of her memory,
> And makes a constant sacrament of praise.

It would be easy, too easy, to lay great stress on Stevens's use here of religious or ritual terms such as 'sacrament'. In fact, he appropriates such terminology for purely secular and utilitarian purposes. His tone, his personal voice, is created by an extraordinarily rich vocabulary. He draws his language from art, philosophy, poetry, nature and many other things. But he impresses these words not so much with his own personality (he is, in most ways, a remarkably impersonal poet) as with the colour and light of his own vision of the world. The vision is, as it were, trapped in this highly idiosyncratic yet extremely decorous language.

*Sunday Morning* is a poem about a world without faith yet it is neither a negative poem nor a despairing one. As with his language, so with his imagery – Stevens draws upon every resource of language to express his ideas. In this poem he uses the articles of Christian faith (the doctrine of the Resurrection in particular) to lend colour to his verse, to intensify his vision:

> Stilled for the passing of her dreaming feet
> Over the seas, to silent Palestine,
> Dominion of the blood and sepulcre.

The beauty of the world is here celebrated for its very transitoriness:

> She says, 'I am content when wakened birds
> Before they fly, test the reality
> Of misty fields, by their sweet questionings;
> But when the birds are gone, and their warm fields
> Return no more, where, then, is Paradise?
> There is not any haunt of prophecy,
> Nor any old chimera of the grave,
> Neither the golden underground, nor isle
> Melodious, where spirits gat them home,
> Nor visionary south, nor cloudy palm
> Remote on heaven's hill, that has endured
> As April's green endures.

Received religion is repudiated and replaced, first by a naked delight in sensuousness and, second, by the recognition of order in the natural world. God is absent from Stevens's world and yet his reality is sensed as something desirable,

> .    Not as a god, but as a god might be.

Stevens's final rejection of God is a melancholy one and yet, because he must have order, he makes the measure of his verse impose order even upon what he feels is without design or meaning:

> We live in an old chaos of the sun,
> Or old dependency of day and night.

But the movement of the mind is, like the 'casual flocks of pigeons'

Downward to darkness, on extended wings.

Stevens's view of the universe is not entirely unlike Rilke's. Both poets seek for reality by means of the imagination but where Rilke, at the end of the *Duino Elegies*, is prepared to admit a transcendent vision, Stevens remains content simply with the relation between the mind and the objective world. He needs no mediator but his own imagination and this limitation perhaps accounts for the repetitiveness (even though it is an exquisite and compelling repetitiveness) of his poems. His mind never rests but must always be teasing at his one great theme. He knows nothing of 'negative capability' or serene receptiveness. In a sense, Stevens is to his poetry what the God he himself cannot believe in is to the world of the Christian visionary. Yet Stevens's vision is quite without pride or megalomania; he celebrates only what he can affirm. The tension in his verse, that tension which is the life of all important poetry, resides in the struggle for something which he feels his intellect cannot accept. So he transfers the idea of divinity to the realm of art and in *To the One of Fictive Music* writes,

Unreal, give back to us what once you gave:
The imagination that we spurned and crave.

And in *Credences of Summer*, he touches on the same subject:

. . . The trumpet supposes that
A mind exists, aware of division, aware
Of its cry as clarion, its diction's way
As that of a personage in a multitude:
Man's mind grown venerable in the unreal.

This vision which permits no absolutes teases Stevens with continual questions. His mind proposes the idea of transcendence only to dismiss it, not so much as wishful thinking but rather as sublime invention. Thus in his most ambitious work, *Notes Towards a Supreme Fiction*, he examines, in breath-taking and ravishing imagery, the whole question of the purpose of poetry. Towards the end of the poem, he looks again at one of his prevailing images – that of angels – only, however, to relegate them to the area of the impossible. Where Rilke's angels represent what he himself could not explain, Stevens's bear the weight of his own incredulity:

What am I to believe? If the angel in his cloud,
Serenely gazing at the violent abyss,
Plucks on his strings to pluck abysmal glory,

Leaps downward through evening's revelations, and
On his spredden wings, needs nothing but deep space,
Forgets the gold centre, the golden destiny,

Grows in the motionless motion of his flight,
Am I that imagine this angel less-satisfied?

.          .          .

There is a month, a year, there is a time
In which majesty is a mirror of the self:
I have not but I am and as I am, I am.

These external regions, what do we fill them with
Except reflections, the escapades of death . . .?

Stevens continues by affirming the predominance of man's mind and
by discarding angels as ineffectual:

. . . I can
Do all that angels can. I enjoy like them,
Like men besides, like men in light secluded,
Enjoying angels . . .

He finds value in sensuous things not only for the beauty of their
very existence but also for the human mind's ability to recognize and
rejoice in that beauty:

A thing final in itself and, therefore good:

.          .          .

And we enjoy like men, the way a leaf
Above the table spins its constant spin,
So that we look at it with pleasure.

Existence is praised and is seen to have order but, unlike Traherne's
vision of creation as upheld and ordered by the love of God, Stevens's
vision is upheld and ordered by the mind of man. Yet there is struggle
and conflict too because, in Stevens's view, it is the poet's almost
godlike mission to discern and illuminate order even amid chaos:

. . . there is a war between the mind
And sky, between thought and day and night. It is
For that the poet is always in the sun.
Patches the moon together in his room

> To his Virgilian cadences, up down
> Up down. It is a war that never ends.

The poet, by means of his poetry, makes contact with reality and tries to maintain that contact. It is in this attempt at adherence, at unity, that Stevens's conception of the poet approximates to the Christian idea of the mystic. At the beginning of *Notes Towards a Supreme Fiction*, he makes poetry the embodiment of reality, the apex of truth. It is a lofty vision and also a supreme act of faith by a man who in all other ways would have regarded himself as an agnostic. Indeed, it may very well be that there is something at the heart of poetry which forbids the total gesture of agnosticism. Simply to write is, after all, some kind of affirmation, but to lay upon poetry, as Stevens does, all those things which other men have assigned to religion and philosophy, is a kind of enthronement of credence itself. In the early passages of *Notes*, he compares the priest's and philosopher's tasks with that of the poet, and then demonstrates what he himself feels to be the poem's power and purpose:

> The monastic man is an artist. The philosopher
> Appoints man's place, in music, say, today.
> But the priest desires. The philosopher desires.
>
> And not to have is the beginning of desire.
>
> .          .          .
>
> The poem refreshes life so that we share,
> For a moment, the first idea . . . It satisfies
> Belief in an immaculate beginning
>
> And sends us, winged by an unconscious will,
> To an immaculate end.
>
> .          .          .
>
> The poem, through candour, brings back a power again
> That gives a candid kind to everything.

The poem is thus seen not only as itself an aspect of truth but as a power which confers reality on everything outside itself, on everything which it touches.

In *Evening Without Angels*, Stevens takes up again a favourite and obsessive image, but while he again considers the idea of angels only to replace them with the physical powers and energies of man, they nevertheless move him, by their very absence, to a moment that approximates to ecstasy. Where the mystic comes from his contact with

God to find the whole world illuminated and meaningful, Stevens shows the poet's ecstasy as the sudden and fleeting awareness of order:

> . . . Bare, bare,
> Except for our own houses, huddled low
> Beneath the arches and their spangled air,
> Beneath the rhapsodies of fire and fire,
> Where the voice that is in us makes a true response,
> Where the voice that is great within us rises up.

This is that 'rage for order' which *The Idea of Order at Key West* explains and celebrates. Here, it is the voice of a singer which seems to impose meaning on apparent chaos,

> Fixing emblazoned zones and fiery poles,
> Arranging, deepening, enchanting night.

This sense of order is called 'blessed' and it is blessed because it comes from man's deepest instinct, his passion to create:

> Oh! Blessed rage for order, pale Ramon,
> The maker's rage to order words of the sea,
> Words of the fragrant portals, dimly-starred,
> And of ourselves and of our origins,
> In ghostlier demarcations, keener sounds.

I have suggested already that Stevens's world is, on the whole, an impersonal world. The people in it tend to be merely figures in a landscape or images to which the poet can attach his own meanings. They are, in short, his raw material and no more and no less august or important than the *objets d'art* or natural phenomena which he also incorporates into his verse. It is the *being* of his men and women, their mere existence, that Stevens is concerned with, not their emotions or conflicts – still less, his own. Paradoxically, Stevens's fastidious care for particulars is, in fact, only an exquisite mask over a passion for generalities. His work is highly sophisticated, yes, but it lacks the supreme sophistication of the great humanist poets (Chaucer, Shakespeare, Yeats) who are concerned not so much with meaning as with feeling. If there is tragedy in Stevens's work it is a tragedy not of individual emotions and sufferings but of a vision of the world as a place which can only be illuminated by the fitful insights of the individual imagination. Thus a poem entitled *God is Good. It is a Beautiful Night*, turns out not to be the celebration of a moment of human awe and reverence, but simply one more examination of order, revealed this time by the flight and song of a bird and the brilliance of the moon:

> The venerable song falls from your fiery wings.
> The song of the great space of your age pierces
> The fresh night.

Again, in a wonderful poem called *Less and Less Human, O Savage Spirit*, Stevens praises a particular time and place and finds rapture in the fact of its impersonality and transitoriness. The interesting thing about this poem is that in it Stevens postulates the kind of god he would revere if he could believe in a god at all:

> If there must be a god in the house, must be,
> Saying things in the rooms and on the stair,
>
> Let him move as the sunlight moves on the floor,
> Or moonlight, silently, as Plato's ghost
>
> Or Aristotle's skeleton. Let him hang out
> His stars on the wall. He must dwell quietly.
>
> He must be incapable of speaking, closed . . .
>
> .          .          .
>
> It is the human that is the alien,
> The human that has no cousin in the moon.
>
> It is the human that demands his speech
> From beasts or from the incommunicable mass.
>
> If there must be a god in the house, let him be one
> That will not hear us when we speak: a coolness . . .

This is stoic contemplation, a desire for a union that is divested of all sense of incarnation. Nothing could be less Christian, one would be inclined to say, and yet the beautiful poise and unpossessiveness here, the wish to let be, to let alone, are not far from the joy and reverence which the great mystics have always manifested. Stevens also display Simone Weil's passion to maintain a distance from the desired object, not in order to prevent union but to emphasize it by keeping all things on, as it were, a long and gentle thread. Or, to change the metaphor, Stevens wishes to stand back so that he may see a complete view, just as the painter must sometimes stand back from his canvas. And this very standing back is a sign of care not of indifference.

Stevens often writes of the sky, the stars, the moon, and the flights of birds; these things are constantly repeated images with him. But they *are* images not symbols; they are 'parts of a world' not objects weighted with allegorical significances. R. P. Blackmur has said: 'Mr Stevens has a notion often intimated that the sky is the only permanent background for thought and knowledge; he would see things against the sky as a Christian would see them against the Cross. The blue of the sky is the prevailing substance of the sky, and to Mr Stevens it seems only necessary to look at the sky to share and be shared in its blueness.'

The sky is indeed a prevailing image, an important décor, a background, but it is no more, and no less, *real* for Stevens than the inanimate objects which fill so many of his poems. His imagination invests vases, statues, pictures, musical instruments, tables, with a life that is valued simply for its remoteness from the commotions of men. He is, in a sense, a poet of stillness. As silence falls between the notes of the music he writes about, so stillness settles round the objects he depicts and describes. He would agree with Augustine, I think, in believing that 'peace is the tranquillity of order'.

This predilection for stillness, even for still lives, this search for serenity are attained by Stevens only momentarily and only after that teasing out of meaning to which I have already referred. As I have indicated, he probes with a kind of passionate calm. It all seems a matter of the intellect alone until one looks more closely at his images; when one does this, one sees at once the constant and restless play of the imagination and the agile logic of associations.

Stevens is a poet who finds a vision by asking questions. The mind inquires and the imagination answers. This dialectic concerns itself with discovering order and withstanding chaos. Stevens does not find reality in religion nor does he elevate art into philosophy. The successful poem itself is, for him, reality, containing as it does only what is essential, only what suffices and explains. In one of his last poems (he died in 1955), *Note on Moonlight*, Stevens speaks not only of the order which a poem both creates and imposes, but also of a desire for purpose, of the aching need for assurance:

> The one moonlight, the various universe, intended
> So much just to be seen – a purpose, empty
> Perhaps, absurd perhaps, but at least a purpose,
> Certain and ever more fresh. Ah! Certain, for sure . . .

As with the verse of Vaughan, light penetrates all of Stevens's poetry – sunlight, fire-light, and moonlight, especially moonlight. The sun is more than the sun of science for him; it sheds rays which the poem, as it were, gathers together and finds meaning in. But if it is not the scientific sun, nor is it a symbolic or analogical one. It has nothing in common with the light which the mystic uses as an analogy of union with God. Yet, for all its sensuousness, Stevens's is an austere art; it is severe and it is disciplined. It has that high seriousness, something so different from mere solemnity, that all major poetry must possess. He never allows himself, or his readers, easy answers or self-indulgent digressions. All his poems pose questions and often they find out only tentative answers; and they are tentative because Stevens is too honest to let his desires or his imagination cloud or conceal his intellect. He permits himself guesses, yes, but he never accords validity to guesses which, however delectable, do not really fit into his austere vision of the world; he will not trespass on the transcendent although he is always prepared to consider its implications, as in these lines from a poem called *A Thought Revolved*:

> Hymns of the struggle of the idea of god
> And the idea of man, the mystic garden and
> The middling beast, the garden of paradise
> And he that created the garden and peopled it.

He is a poet of *being* yet his doctrine of existence is closer to Plato's timeless essences than to modern existentialism. His infinite caution in proposing absolutes sometimes conceals not only a concern for but also an unawakened belief in absolutes. In other words, his poems sometimes go further than his severe beliefs would lead us to expect. It may be indeed, as I have suggested already, that poetry is of its nature antagonistic to complete incredulity or negation; a 'willing suspension of disbelief' is, perhaps, at the heart of poetry as well as at the heart of the perfect reading of poetry. Certainly, with Stevens, his poems appear sometimes to catch him off guard and amaze him with an affirmation. Art is, after all, more than a rational and logical process; it both takes possession and itself demands to be possessed. Like mystical experience, it cannot be sought, only prepared for and surrendered to; it is an invasion not merely a speculation. For Stevens, the imaginative faculty is august and autonomous and also, as Coleridge has said, 'the living power and prime agent of all human perception'. The senses supply it with material from which it shapes images and then gropes towards order.

Crowded with *objets d'art*, fastidiously selective, uncompromisingly honest, quick to detect error – Stevens's art is all these things. On the surface it appears, in his own words, 'less and less human', but this is only because he takes things at their source; he is concerned with perception, feeling, desire in their pure state, before they have become involved in passion or personal conflict. Yet his verse takes its tension from a battle between disinterestedness and self-expression, since all poems are made with feelings as well as with thought. Stevens's passion is a controlled passion but it is a passion nonetheless. He wishes to make contact with reality or, failing that, to *make* reality. His entire credo is well summed up in the last lines of *Holiday in Reality*:

> The bud of the apple is desire, the down-falling gold,
> The catbird's gobble in the morning half-awake –
>
> These are real only if I make them so. Whistle
> For me, grow green for me and, as you whistle and grow green,
>
> Intangible arrows quiver and stick in the skin
> And I taste at the root of the tongue the unreal of what is real.

# 18. VOICES OF EXPLANATION

*I have tried to show that we can hope for no progress on earth without the primacy and triumph of the* personal *at the summit of* mind.
PIERRE TEILHARD DE CHARDIN – The Phenomenon of Man

## I *Poetic Experience* by Thomas Gilby OP

*Poetic Experience* by Thomas Gilby is an attempt to define the nature of poetic experience and response in the light of the philosophy of Thomas Aquinas; that is to say, *The Summa Theologica* has been used to enforce rather than to prove Fr Gilby's own reflections on poetic experience. He carries his learning lightly and *The Summa*, far from being a weight round his neck, has provided him with a series of directions along a road on which he himself never stumbles.

This book deserves to be more widely known since, with Bremond's *Prayer and Poetry*, it is one of the very few serious attempts to explore the relationship between poetic and mystical experience. The acceptance or rejection of Aquinas's method of argument is not crucial to Fr Gilby's findings since he himself works from the object rather than from the idea, from intuition rather than from speculation. *Poetic Experience* is, in other words, as valid for the reader who is sceptical of the Scholastic system as for the one who approves it.

Fr Gilby begins this brief work by examining the nature of the problem before him. How, he asks, can *mind*, which only has direct knowledge of universals and abstractions, acquire *particular* knowledge of the concrete? For poetry, both in the writing and the reading of it, is nothing if not direct, immediate and concrete, and concrete here does not necessarily mean physical. He finds his answer in three different yet connected stages of thought. First, he examines the relationship between mind and will. The mind has a formal knowledge of things, it knows them by representation. The will, on the other hand, as Fr Gilby indicates, not only 'impels the mind to know', it also 'informs the mind'. It moves by love rather than by knowledge; it desires closeness and wholeness not remoteness or partial awareness. In this love-knowledge relationship, Fr Gilby sees not only the beginning of poetic experience but also the beginning of mystical union with

God. He then proceeds to the second stage of his discourse where he discusses the soul's knowledge of itself. We know our own identity, he argues, not by indirect means or formal likenesses but immediately and without the intervention of abstract ideas. This does not imply that our self-knowledge is perfect but rather that it is valid even if limited. Only God knows himself perfectly for, in him, knowledge and love are one and the same thing. And God's love-knowledge of us is also perfect. Perhaps I may here carry the argument one step further by saying that the soul's knowledge of itself is direct and concrete *because* it partakes, however weakly and imperfectly, of God's knowledge of it. And since, according to Aquinas, God is 'the act of pure being,' this knowledge is not static but dynamic, not in time but out of time, moving yet perpetual.

The third stage in Fr Gilby's thesis is that of the soul's knowledge of God. God is everywhere substantially, in everything and above everything, transcendent and immanent. He is present in every human soul but he is only *possessed* in the intimate awareness of love when that soul is in a state of grace. As Fr Gilby points out, a theologian may write admirable theology even if he is in a state of mortal sin; what he cannot do in that state is have the experience of complete union with God which is the heart of mysticism.

In drawing an analogy between the poet's moment of creation and the mystic's immediate awareness of God (and, in this sense, *any* good person can be a mystic), Fr Gilby is not concerned with illustrating all the likenesses between mystical and poetic experience. What he is doing is presenting the possible connection between the apprehensions of the poet and the apprehensions of the mystic. The fact that a poet can write a poem or a reader experience that poem while neither is in a state of grace is not to the point here. The crucial matter is that the poet has the *means* to immediate knowledge of concrete things for the very reason that that is the way the human soul (memory, understanding and will) is made; it has, in fact, a more direct method of knowing than simply a rational one, it is designed not for universals but for particulars.

Fr Gilby breaks down this third argument into three sub-stages – presence, action and experience or, in other words, the presence of God in the soul, God's workings and movements in the soul, and the soul's recognition of these things.

'Wholeness, harmony and clarity' were the three requisites which Aquinas demanded in a work of art. From Fr Gilby's exposition of the relationship between poetic and mystical experience, we can see how these three qualities are discernible both in the making of a poem and in the prayer of the mystic. Having established his philosophical ground, though never in the context of pure metaphysics since every statement he makes is supported by illustrations from music, painting and poetry, he concludes his book with a brief examination of the attitudes and dispositions which are shared by poet and mystic. He sees them as those 'who strive and suffer', as beings who are aware of constant struggle and continual fallings-away (not *moral* lapses) from the great simplifying moments when the poem is made or union with God realized. This participation in the very agony of creation (the seed struggling for air, the child's cry at birth, the bird's first clumsy flight) means that harmony and clarity are only reached after confusion and darkness and that when they are reached, they are held only fleetingly. This, however, neither invalidates their importance nor denies that sense of timelessness which I have already referred to.

In the learned fabric of Aquinas's thought, Fr Gilby has revealed the point where prayer and poetry meet. He has not chained himself to the language of philosophy nor, on the other hand, allowed himself to be carried away by rhapsodies about 'art' or 'inspiration'. He has given poetry a central and high place in human experience; he has shown how its moments of revelation are not simply amazing flashes out of darkness but are, on the contrary, the whole of man transcribing or responding to the most important function of life – knowing by loving and loving by knowing, grasping the whole of an experience not to possess but to be possessed, using the senses and emotions not denying them, releasing the mind from cold abstractions to free it for direct and close knowledge. This is the mystic's achievement and the poet's vocation.


## II *Prayer and Poetry* by Henri Bremond

Henri Bremond's *Prayer and Poetry*, first published in English in 1927, is a learned, witty and engaging examination of the relationship between mystical experience and the making of poems. More than this, it is a vindication of the supra-rational power of poetry, and a plea for the importance of aesthetic delight in human experience. In many ways it is still a daring and revolutionary book. Unlike Thomas Gilby's *Poetic Experience*, it does not use Thomist philosophy as a jumping-off ground; Bremond develops his study from a wide and deep knowledge both of the Christian religious tradition and also of Greek, Latin, French and English literature.

He opens his book with an assertion of 'the luminous night of poetry' as opposed to 'the clarities of reason' and goes on to attack Plato for casting poets out of his ideal city, and rebukes Aristotle for attempting to subdue the power of poetry to the activities of reason. He then proceeds to attack such French writers as Boileau for doing what Aristotle did, only for doing it with more violence and less humility – namely, for banishing the 'mystery' at the heart of poetry by attempting to explain the poetic faculty in purely rational terms. With great force and perspicacity, Bremond then exposes the fallacy at the centre of French eighteenth century classicism – its endeavour to remove poetry from the realm of serious purpose and relegate it to a kind of gentle entertainment. 'Poetry an amusement,' he says, 'that is the great discovery of the eighteenth century, such the crushing heritage of classicism.'

In the rise of so-called Romanticism, he detects a return to what he describes as 'the constant tradition of the human race in the matter of poetry, a conscious and reasoned reaction against the rationalist aesthetic of the eighteenth century and the senile humanism which had prepared the road for that aesthetic.' 'To take poetry seriously,' Bremond declares, 'as a free and splendid gift which lifts the poet above himself for his own and everyone else's greater good, is the very essence of romanticism.' He examines the poetic credos of such writers as Arnold and Shelley, and such critics as A. C. Bradley, and praises in them the reinstatement of poetry as a means of expressing experiences inaccessible to reason alone. He acknowledges his own debt to Bradley and says that he owes to him the solution to 'the unique problem' of poetry as a way of knowledge that bypasses the movements of the rational faculty. Bremond then investigates the belief, held by many Romantic poets, that poetry can teach or legislate, and repudiates this belief by quoting Bradley: 'The opinions, the reasoned convictions of poets have rarely the quality of their purely imaginative creations.'

Going more deeply into the question of didacticism in poetry, Bremond speaks of the poet thus: 'He takes the only imaginative means of entering into communication with us. But instead of this transmission of ideas, this didacticism being – as in ordinary language – the final and single purpose of the speaker, here it is only a means. By the intermediary of the ideas he expresses, or rather by the intermediary of the very expressions he uses, the poet designs, not to teach us anything whatever . . . but to communicate to us a certain shock, to train us to be worthy of a certain experience, to raise us to a certain condition. It is just in that the miracle of poetry consists, or, as we say, its magic.'

From these reflections Bremond moves, with great assurance, into the heart of his inquiry. Anxious to avoid the vaguenesses and misunderstandings which attend any use of the word 'inspiration' he nevertheless declares quite uncompromisingly that there *are* connections between mystical and poetic experience and, moreover, that the transcriptions of mystical experience may throw light on poetic experience. 'It so happens,' he says, 'that the mystics have described this psychological design, with all its springs and complicated mechanism, in a detail and with a penetration that may be sought in vain in the confidences of the poets . . . it is from the mystic that we can learn to understand the poet.' In order 'to calm . . . the scruples of those to whom the very idea of this assimilation seems scandalous,' Bremond quotes Maréchal, a writer on mysticism, to the effect that 'between the fundamental modes of human psychological activity and the various mystical realizations . . . there exist *analogies of form and communities of mechanism.* In other words, poetic and mystical experience share many of the same functions of the human mind and imagination, and both move towards an experience which may be different in *degree* but not essentially in *kind.*

In his next chapter, Bremond analyses the aesthetic experience and examines those moments (Eliot's 'moment in the rose-garden') when both time and reason seem to be in abeyance and we are possessed by an ecstasy which we cannot explain in rational terms. This ecstasy is proffered by the poet and is, in fact, a handing over to us of the experience he himself underwent in the making of his poem. With great lucidity, Bremond describes the nature of what he calls 'those profane mystical states'. 'Far from languishing, we were, on the contrary, in the throes of a high fever of meditation and research. Never was our curiosity more awake than when we were complaining of our torpor. Ideas are rushing in; one cannot express them . . . Then the spark shoots out, and there is a great peace.' This combination of intense peace with intense concentration has been alluded to by Robert Graves in a broadcast talk entitled *The Poet and His Public*: 'A poet finds himself caught in some baffling emotional problem, which is of such urgency that it sends him into a sort of trance. And in this trance his mind works, with astonishing boldness and precision, on several imaginative levels at once.'

Bremond continues his own inquiry by listing the stages through which the poet passes on the way to the achieved poem – 'first of all, a dull and painful gestation of mind and heart . . . then comes the spark, the inspiration; and then a joyful fertility of the mind or a gay decision of the heart.' We, the poet's readers, share at secondhand these experiences, but we, of course, stop short at the actual making of the poem; it has already been made for us. What we experience is beyond the senses, the intellect and the reason, yet it is not a denial of these things; rather, it is a fulfilment. Bremond concludes his chapter on *The Poetic Mystery* by questioning whether 'profane mystical states' are, in fact, wholly profane. They may be adumbrations of union with God and he quotes some lines of Wordsworth's to reinforce this conviction:

> . . . When the light of sense
> Goes out, but with a flash that has revealed
> The invisible world.

'All natural mysticisms,' concludes Bremond, '. . . show us obscurely and offer us the invisible himself, the ineffable, the Being of beings, who, unknown to us, often in spite of us, envelops and penetrates us with his presence.'

In his chapter, *Animus and Anima*, Bremond examines Claudel's beautiful little story about the interplay of Animus with Anima; Animus is rational knowledge, while Anima is mystical or poetic knowledge. The mystic, Ruysbroeck, notes Bremond, has called Anima 'the sacred region, our most hidden and intimate home, the extreme point and summit of the heart, the marrow of the soul.' We should perhaps, at this point, bear in mind Jung's use of the terms Animus and Anima in his analysis of the human mind. For him, Anima is the feminine portion of the mind, Animus the masculine. In the perfectly balanced psyche, the 'integrated personality', these elements do not conflict but rather complement one another. More limited in scope though Jung's use of these words is than either Claudel's or Bremond's, it is nevertheless not opposed to their definitions. Animus is masculine rational knowledge, Anima feminine poetic intuition. As Claudel writes in his fable, 'The soul is silent when the mind looks at it. Then Animus thinks that he will play a trick on her; he takes steps to make her think he is not present . . . little by little Anima reassures herself: she looks here and there, she listens, she sighs, she thinks herself alone, and noiselessly she goes and opens the door to her divine lover.'

This admirably describes the nature of both mystical and poetic experience and also shows the way in which now reason, now intuition dominate the mind. It demonstrates, too, the parts played by passivity and activity in both experiences. Bremond uses Claudel's story as a springboard for a close and careful study of the condition of mind of poet and mystic. 'Beyond ideas, images, the sentiments of sensation – but, of course, through the intermediary of all its surface activities –' he says, 'poetic knowledge attains and unites the poet to realities. Not directly to the sovereign reality, God – that is the exclusive privilege of mystical knowledge – but to all the created real, and underneath the created reality, indirectly to God himself . . .' In other words, the poet's experience is different from the mystic's not in kind but only in degree. What art seeks and sometimes finds, mystical experience *knows*, and it knows by affinity and love. Speaking of Racine, Bremond declares, 'he excels in the poetic knowledge of souls . . . Endowed as he is with a marvellous art which enables him to transmit to us something of what he feels himself at this apprehension, this contact, he renders present and sensible to our deeper self the deeper self of his personages.' What the mystic communicates of his own experience is, in the dramatic poet, transferred to his imagined characters. In the lyric poet, the poet who is speaking from the heights of his own supra-rational experience, the communication is immediate and personal. Poetry bridges the gaps and gulfs between the profoundest parts of the personalities of writer and reader.

Bremond goes on to show that the mystic comes away, as it were, from the intimate contact with God with his whole being enriched and enlarged. On this matter he quotes Teresa of Avila: 'But you will ask me how it can be that the soul should have seen and heard that she has been in God and God in her, if during that union she neither sees nor hears. I reply that she does not see it at the time, but she sees it clearly afterwards, when she has come back to herself, and she knows it, not by a (subsequent) vision, but by a certitude which God alone can give her, and which remains with her.'

This is a very remarkable and crucial vindication of the power of words to contain and embody a vision. In the state of ecstasy, the mystic knows a kind of 'wise passiveness'; after the ecstasy, he receives the power not only to understand it but also to communicate it, and to communicate without too much diminution. We are reminded of Shelley's words about the finished poem being like 'a fading coal' compared with the poet's initial experience; but the poem *exists* in its own right and is as truthful and as exact an account of his experience as the poet can manage, just as the mystic's transcription of his experience holds and sustains something of his mystical experience. Bremond sees the mystic's vision as in itself a veritable source of power rather than as an experience which the mystic must try to recapture and communicate before it is too late. The ecstasy, the contact with God, the vision, have, in fact, lasting effects.

Flooded as he is with new light and knowledge, the mystic has, nevertheless, to subordinate the vision to the potency of language. The communication can, therefore, as a rule only be effected imperfectly. But, Bremond affirms, 'there will be no lack of memories or literary matter to the mystic when he comes back to himself. To the poet still less and this leads up to the definition of the really original element in poetic experience.' We are, indeed, now at the very heart of this whole complex subject.

'The really original element in poetic experience' Bremond defines as 'an invincible need of translating, of communicating externally, the poetic experiences' and, he adds, 'it may be said, in a word, the specific quality of poetic experience is to be communicable.' After speaking of those people who, sensitive to other men's poetry are, in a sense, themselves poets but poets without a voice, Bremond examines Aristotle's concept of 'catharsis'. He declares that 'all poetic experience is Catharsis' and commends Aristotle for divining 'in those days mysteries which, thanks to mystical literature, seem to us today almost luminous.' And, he goes on, 'whatever be the reality to which our deeper soul is united, it is always by the Catharsis that this union is produced; or, rather, this union is the Catharsis itself, whether mystical or poetical, a simplifying inspiration.' To put it in another way, both poetry and the mystical experience have the effect of purging and releasing the poet's and mystic's mind and faculties.

Towards the end of *Prayer and Poetry*, Bremond makes a further and decisive affirmation of his belief in the likenesses between mysticism and poetry. He says, 'Poetic and mystical experience belong by their psychological mechanism to the same order of knowledge – real knowledge – not immediately conceptual but unitive.' However, he also asserts that the poet is 'but an evanescent mystic whose mysticism breaks down.' This breakdown occurs because of the poet's insatiable desire to communicate his experience, while, on the other hand, 'the more of a mystic any particular mystic is, the less he feels the need of self-communication.' And because the poet is so eager for communication, because 'poetic inspiration' is in such a 'hurry to find words in which to communicate its message to the world,' the poet's apprehension, says Bremond, is therefore 'more superficial than is that of the mystic, less solid, less unifying.' This is an assertion that will arouse much disagreement and it is, finally, an assertion that cannot be proved since the only materials we have to judge by are the statements of the *articulate* mystics. Bremond, nevertheless, provides some persuasive arguments for his belief when he declares that 'poetic experience does not permit the union of love which follows every normal mystic experience to take place. The poet *qua* poet only unites himself to the real in order to separate himself immediately from it,' i.e., his desire to communicate severs him both from total self-losing and from a complete and direct knowledge of reality. The poet, in effect, is in a similar condition to that of the ardent lover who is divided between his desire for fulfilment and his passionate need to put into words the ecstasy of which he has already had a glimpse. This does seem to be a just claim and it would certainly account for the poet's constant state of dissatisfaction with his past work and his longing to write another new and successful poem.

To sum up – Bremond sees an indisputable similarity between the stages that precede full union with God and those which occur before a poem is completed. First, there is the stage when the mind is thronged with conflicting thoughts (that moment when the mystic is unable to meditate in an orderly manner and is distracted by every passing thought and feeling, yet is still concentrated on the *desire* for clarity and peace). The next stage is what Eliot calls the moment of 'pure illumination' – that sense of being visited, possessed, the moment which Bremond calls 'the spark of inspiration'. This is the crucial moment for both poet and mystic and it is followed by a tremendous release of energy, a sense of order and fitness, of all struggle ended. It is now that the poet writes his poem and now that the mystic is aware of a unity and tranquillity beyond every argument of reason. Bremond rightly points out that this mystical sense of union necessitates 'a state of grace' in the recipient, and that it is also a Gold-given experience in its own right. The poet's moment of illumination, on the other hand, only enables him to *receive* the closeness of God, not to *apprehend* him. Yet, for Bremond, every visitation is a divine one.

The essential difference between the poet and the mystic, as he sees it, is that in the poet, the Animus, the reason, is continually searching for harmonious words to express the experience of the Anima, whereas, in the mystic, Animus and Anima are perfectly united in an act of love, in which the will, not the intellect, plays the supreme part. As Patmore says, 'The poet occupies a singular position in the hierarchy of beings: halfway between a saint and Balaam's ass.' And, as Vinet says, poetry is 'the paradox of the spring dispersed at its source.' And yet, as Bremond, who quotes these writers, himself adds – 'Strange and paradoxical nature of poetry: a prayer which does not itself pray, but which makes others pray.'

The value of Bremond's book seems to me to reside in its clear, closely-reasoned exposition of poetry as a way of loving knowledge which is not different in kind from the mystic's knowledge. He elevates poetry to a very high place in human experience, and resorts to psychology and philosophy, as well as to literature, to make good his claim. Neither antagonizingly didactic on the one hand, nor emotionally rhetorical on the other, his book makes a useful and reliable point of reference for all further studies of the connection between the experience of the poets and the experience of the mystics.

# 19. 'THIS GREAT WINK OF ETERNITY'

## The poetry of Hart Crane

*The essential is that everything should become simple, as for the child, that every act should be ordered; that good and evil should be arbitrarily, hence obviously, pointed out. And I'm all in favour, however Sicilian and Javanese I may be and not at all Christian, though I feel friendship for the first Christian of all. But on the bridges of Paris I too learned that I was afraid of freedom.*
ALBERT CAMUS – The Fall

I WANT TO end this examination of the relationship between poetry and mysticism not with any easy summings-up or laborious drawing of conclusions but with a study of a poet who, in the most unlikely and yet successful way, made poetry not simply a channel for mystical experience but the means to attain it. Hart Crane was an American, a homosexual, and he committed suicide in 1932 when he was still in his early thirties.

Crane, with his turbulent life and emotional excesses, reminds us a little of Rimbaud, but there is one big difference between the two poets; where Rimbaud managed to control, even to organize, his life and to maintain a cool, appraising distance between his actions and his poetry, where he sought out experience in an analytical, almost clinical way, Crane had no such powers or defences: for him, his life was his poetry and poetry meant first, sensation, and afterwards, vision. As A. Alvarez has perceptively remarked, 'He depends entirely on the spontaneity of his reactions and on his ability to fit words to them so as to leave the smallest possible gap between the language and the feelings.' Such an intense mode of living and writing eventually brought Crane into a state of despair; this happened when he thought he was finished as a writer and this fear was a kind of death since he had no other resources – intellectual, doctrinal or personal – in which to take refuge and find relief. With him, more than with most poets, there was a unity not only about his experience but also about his character. He put on no masks, had no public face; he believed, in Yeats's words, that

> There's more enterprise
> In walking naked.

But unlike Yeats, Crane was unable to shape a system of metaphors or beliefs. He could not create an ordered world but only release into words, sometimes into rhetoric, his inner world; and this world was a world of torment.

Hart Crane saw himself as a true descendant of Walt Whitman, as a man dedicated to creating an American myth and from it designing a truly American epic. But he lacked the intellectual stamina, the ability to select and order, those qualities which are quite as essential to the fashioning of an epic as noble ideas or reverberent language. Every poem Crane wrote was a wholehearted plunging into experience and, above all, a willingness, even a passion, to surrender. It is this willingness, together with his often repeated desire for loss of self in some transcendent experience or being, that brings him in line with the more orthodox mystical seekers after God. In Crane we have not only a perfect example of the poet in the pure state, a poet who works entirely by impulse and intuition, but also a type of man who embodies, and therefore represents, in his own personality both those attributes which poets share with mystics and also those in which they differ from them.

The most obvious difference between poets and mystics is that where the mystics, from the very beginning of their journey towards God, seek total surrender of self, the poet must first explore, even perhaps exploit, his own nature and capabilities. It is, of course, obvious that all mystics and mystical writers have stressed self-knowledge, and with it humility, as the vital first step towards God, but this kind of self-knowledge is of a different order from that of the poet. The poet, in effect, must plunder himself, must use all his thoughts, emotions and actions in order to make his poems. Bremond has indicated that perhaps the intrinsic nature and *raison d'être* of poetry is to be communicable. The poet, then, must know himself not in order to subjugate himself but to express himself; and he must believe in, take pride in this plundering, this self-expression. With the poet, the impulse comes first, the discipline afterwards. With the mystic the process is reversed for, as Augustine has said, 'Love God and do what you like.' The discipline is in the loving.

From all these comments and reservations it might be thought that Crane is the very opposite of the articulate mystic. In fact, it is only in his means that he differs, not in his end. His pain came from a desire to attain the kind of experience the mystics know, but to attain it entirely through the medium of poetry. Unity, Crane felt, would be found in the poems he wrote, and he meant something much more profound than either a surface smoothness of controlled thought and image or an order imposed on a sealed-off, autonomous poetic world.

Hart Crane was essentially a poet of his own time and of this century. Though some of his early language and imagery is 'Romantic' in the worst sense, his best work seeks meaning and unity by means of entirely contemporary symbols such as Brooklyn Bridge, modern buildings, ships, tunnels, and so on. Such imagery is not selected (as some of our own poets of the Thirties collected contemporary properties) to give an impression or provoke an awareness of modernity. Crane was as moved by iron machines or blocks of flats as Wordsworth, say, was moved by a lake or a mountain. They aroused his emotions, they were not carefully sought out to embody a feeling which would otherwise remain vague and inexplicit.

In the world of machines, then, Crane looked for a religious experience which would transcend that world and yet not destroy it. More than the work of any other modern poet, I think, his poems are poems of invocation and of incantation; they are written at the point of ecstasy, not as aftermaths of it. In *To Brooklyn Bridge*, for example, the poet cries out,

> O harp and altar, of the fury fused,
> (How could mere toil align thy choiring strings!)
> Terrific threshold of the prophet's pledge,
> Prayer of pariah and the lover's cry –
>
> .          .          .
>
> O Sleepless as the river under thee,
> Vaulting the sea, the prairies' dreaming sod,
> Unto us lowliest sometime sweep, descend
> And of the curveship lend a myth to God.

Almost every word Crane uses here feels as if it had just been made and just been spoken for the first time. This sense of newness, of directness, has little to do with the choice of the apt phrase or the precise image. The reader's response is not 'Yes, it *is* like that' but rather 'This is something quite fresh.'

Alvarez has suggested that Crane, whatever his overt subject may be, is always in fact writing about himself, and in particular about his own sensations. I cannot agree with this judgment. For me, the tension of

Crane's verse (and it is such a tremendous tension that the poet always seems perilously balanced on the brink of breaking point) resides in his desire, and his strenuous effort, to escape from himself and enter into communion with some life greater than his own. But Crane must do the whole thing himself, one feels; there is no sense of a reciprocated relationship between God and man such as we find in Herbert or Hopkins. Thus the poem called *The Tunnel* ends with a passionate attempt to lay hands on a vision, to possess and be possessed by it:

> And yet, like Lazarus, to feel the slope,
> The sod and billow breaking, – lifting ground,
> – A sound of waters bending astride the sky
> Unceasing with some Word that will not die . . .!
> A tugboat, wheezing wreaths of steam,
> Lunged past, with one galvanic blare stove up the River.
> I counted the echoes assembling, one after one,
> Searching, thumbing the midnight on the piers.
> Lights, coasting, left the oily tympanum of waters;
> The blackness somewhere gouged glass on a sky.
> And this thy harbor, O my City, I have driven under,
> Tossed from the coil of ticking towers . . . Tomorrow,
> And to be . . . Here by the River that is East –
> Here at the waters' edge the hands drop memory;
> Shadowless in that abyss they unaccounting lie.
> How far away the star has pooled the sea –
> Or shall the hands be drawn away, to die?
> Kiss of our agony Thou gatherest,
> > O Hand of Fire
> > gatherest –

Everything is exact, precise and concrete here. This is no allegorical or assumed world; the waters are real, the machines are made of solid metal. And yet the vision which these things disclose is as intangible as any mystic's sense of union with God. The point about Crane is that he catches the inexpressible by abruptly yet inevitably swerving, in his verse, from the adamant to the tentative. Even the way the words of his poem are laid out on the page (notably the end of the above passage) is an energetic, a dynamic attempt to catch the elusive thing and hold it down. The last eleven words of *The Tunnel* are strongly reminiscent of the scattered, unconnected words that Pascal wrote down after the extraordinary experience in which the nature of God seemed to be revealed to him through some other medium than that of his reason.

Kierkegaard said that the poet is a man who is 'unhappily in love with God'. It would be hard to argue or demonstrate this statement in regard to all poets, but in the case of Crane it seems to be exactly true. Much of his language has a religious, even a ritualistic or liturgical source, but much more important than this is the fact that his poetry is inward, spiritual at an extremely deep level. The words are, as it were, thrown up from some intensely personal excavation. When Wallace Stevens uses words like 'sacrament' or 'angel' or 'novitiate', one feels that these words are selected for their suggestiveness; Stevens coolly takes them from one context and places them in his own. The whole process is a matter of choice, of choice based on an exquisite sense of decorum. With Crane, it is quite different. He seems to be *used* by his language, not to be using it. And this is true of his most rigorously formal poems – *The Broken Tower*, for example:

> The bell-rope that gathers God at dawn
> Dispatches me as though I dropped down the knell
> Of a spent day – to wander the cathedral lawn
> From pit to crucifix, feet chill on steps from hell.
>
>           .          .          .
>
> Oval encyclicals in canyons heaping
> The impasse high with choir. Banked voices slain!
> Pagodas, campaniles with reveilles outleaping –
> O terraced echoes prostrate on the plain! . . .
>
> And so it was I entered the broken world
> To trace the visionary company of love, its voice
> An instant in the wind (I know not whither hurled)
> But not for long to hold each desperate choice.
>
>           .          .          .
>
> The steep encroachments of my blood left me
> No answer (could blood hold such a lofty tower
> As flings the question true?) – or is it she
> Whose sweet mortality stirs latent power? –

Here there is all the passion and anguish of Hopkins's last sonnets, but wonderfully fused and combined with these things is the kind of ecstatic precision and clarity we find in Vaughan and Traherne. Crane has rescued from oblivion and neglect not only the power of invocation and the delicate balance of statement with suggestion, but also the ability to know when the half-sentence, the gasp, even the murmur, will suffice. Over and over again he does what Shakespeare did when he made Leontes say, on seeing his wife come to life,

O, she's warm.

Crane's poems are often obscure but they are obscure because of their intensity, their compression. It is not an intellectual obscurity but an emotional one. And because we, the readers, are so quickly caught up into the momentum of the poet's feeling, we scarcely notice the obscurity until we attempt a strict verbal analysis afterwards. The poems work upon us long before we have any desire to pass judgment.

As I have suggested, Crane's images are concrete, vivid, and modern. His language is also often sexual but sexual at one remove, as at the end of *The Broken Tower*:

The commodious, tall decorum of that sky
Unseals her earth, and lifts love in its shower.

Or again, at the end of Part III of *Voyages*:

Upon the steep floor flung from dawn to dawn
The silken skilled transmemberment of song;
Permit me voyage, love, into your hands.

Here the sea, the voyage and all that they signify for Crane fall gently at last into a simple, yet not merely personal, expression of human love.

Mystics have, of course, often used the language of secular love to describe their experience of God. St John of the Cross and St Bernard are probably the greatest exemplars of this mode of expression. Like them Crane can use the most violently physical language to depict states which are wholly spiritual. But where the mystics use such language simply because it seems to come closest to a true transcription of mystical experience, Crane appears to start from physical sensation and then to transform it by the very act of writing.

Though he worked assiduously at polishing and perfecting his work, it is well-known that Crane needed a good deal of external stimulus out of which to get the first drafts of his poems – stimuli such as drink and music, for example. Where the man dedicated to God reaches full union with God through a long and arduous process of purification and self-mastery, Crane needed some objective, sometimes concrete, power to help him to attain that heightened awareness which his best poems demonstrate. It is interesting at this point to compare his use of drink and powerful music as an aid to expression and to a sense of wholeness, with what Aldous Huxley has to say about his own experiences while under the influence of mescalin: 'Mescalin,' he says, 'had endowed me temporarily with the power to see things with my eyes shut; but it could not, or at least on this occasion did not, reveal an inscape remotely comparable to my flowers or chair or flannels "out there". What it had allowed me to perceive, inside, was not the Dharma-Body in images, but my own mind; not archetypal Suchness, but a set of symbols – in other words, a home-made substitute for Suchness.'

This testimony, despite its inflated metaphysical tone, is a clear proof that under the influence of a particular drug, Huxley discovered some sort of heightened awareness into the nature of his own thoughts. The drug revealed something, yes, and revealed it with a startling clarity. What it did not do was *release* something. With a poet such as Crane (and one could also name others – Coleridge, for example, took drugs) alcohol was used to remove the various impediments that, temporarily at least, made the writing of verse impossible. Inarticulate men do not suddenly become poets under the influence of one stimulus or another, but some poets have used certain stimuli as a means towards expression. As Huxley himself says, 'The untalented visionary may perceive an inner reality no less tremendous, beautiful and significant than the world beheld by Blake; but he lacks altogether the ability to express, in literary or plastic symbols, what he has seen.' The drug, then, may set free a talent, it cannot cause or create a talent. Huxley is careful, too, not to equate the 'visions' produced by drugs with any kind of mystical experience: 'I am not so foolish,' he says, 'as to equate what happens under the influence of mescalin or any other drug, prepared or in the future preparable, with the realization of the end and ultimate purpose of human life: Enlightenment, the Beatific Vision.' He points out also that mescalin, even while it induces a sense of peace and order, at the same time relaxes the will and removes from the person who has taken the drug any desire to exploit his experience or, in other words, to *create* anything.

It may be that the sense of almost intoxicated energy which we find in Crane's poems has something in common with the passive state of ecstasy which certain drugs can temporarily produce. What is certain, however, is that the particularity, the brilliant detail, the care and craftsmanship of his work have nothing at all to do with the stimulus of alcohol. The fact that listening to music also helped Crane to write is, I think, quite a different matter. One art form often provokes another; a picture may suggest a poem, or music may be the secondary (seldom the first) cause of a painting or poem. In cases like these a relationship is set up between one work of art and another artist and from the fusion a second art form is fashioned. This is surely what we mean when we speak of tradition or influence, and this is undoubtedly what often happened with Crane.

If his poetry often seems at white heat, it is never chaotic; there is no sense of sprawling or anarchy. In their own way, Crane's best poems have as much formal perfection as those of Yeats or Wallace Stevens. What he often achieves most triumphantly is a sense of tamed violence, as at the end of *Repose of Rivers*:

> And finally, in that memory all things nurse;
> After the city that I finally passed
> With scalding unguents spread and smoking darts
> The monsoon cut across the delta
> At gulf gates . . . There, beyond the dykes
> I heard wind flaking sapphire, like this summer
> And willows could not hold more steady sound.

And again, in the last stanza of *Quaker Hill*, it is the sense of restrained power that gives the poem its intensity and visionary quality:

> In one last angelus lift throbbing throat –
> Listen, transmuting silence with that stilly note
> Of pain that Emily, that Isadora knew!
> While high from dim elm-chancels hung with dew,
> That triple-noted clause of moonlight –
> Yes, whip-poor-will, unhusks the heart of fright,
> Breaks us and saves, yes, breaks the heart, yet yields
> That patience that is armour and that shields
> Love from despair – when love foresees the end –
> Leaf after autumnal leaf
> > break off,
> > > descend –
> > > > descend –

The references here to Emily Dickinson and Isadora Duncan, the faint echo of Keats – such things as these do not conceal the attainment of a sense of ultimate peace and fulfilment. The agitation of the early lines of the stanza quietens down to an almost classic calm at the end of the poem. And where the mystic moves from desolation into serenity, Crane moves from excitement into ecstasy and its aftermath – calm and acceptance. Some of his poems, of course, remain on the level of alarm and agitation, but the best, the most fully achieved ones, seem suddenly to separate themselves from the fever of the senses and reach, however fleetingly, a spiritual point of rest – those 'spiritual gates' as Crane himself called this state. In a poem called *Legend* he makes a direct affirmation of this kind of experience:

> It is to be learned –
> This cleaving and this burning,
> But only by the one who
> Spends out himself again.

It is this 'spending' that contributed so painfully yet so fruitfully to the general torment of Crane's last months.

Many of the critics who have written about Hart Crane's verse, even some of the most sympathetic and perceptive ones, have suggested that there is something *manqué* about much of his work. Alvarez declares that Crane is a fine lyric poet who failed to be what he really wanted to be – namely, an epic poet. Allen Tate, Crane's critic and friend, sees him as a poet who embodied the agonizing failure of the Romantic spirit. Discerning as he is, Tate perhaps displays a fault common among even the best modern American literary critics; he is too eager to see a poet not as an individual but as a representative of a universal anxiety, a depersonalized tension. A poet thus becomes a symbol in a scheme of things, an embodiment of an idea, rather than a writer with a unique vision and a highly personal method of dealing with that vision. And yet Allen Tate has said some very valuable things about Crane as, for example, his remarks that 'The impulse of *The Bridge* is religious . . .' and 'Crane was one of those men whom every age seems to select as the spokesman of its spiritual life.'

What is baffling in Crane's work is, I believe, its odd mingling of tentativeness and boldness. His feeling, his emotion is always indisputably strong and direct; it is what this feeling drives him towards that sometimes makes his poems appear obscure and unfinished. He seems constantly to be trying to ensnare a sense of the transcendent, and it seems constantly to be eluding him. His poems enact this struggle, they seldom attempt to resolve it. Crane is thus a visionary who, unlike Vaughan or Traherne, can neither interpret his vision nor pass on its meaning exactly. But since his search seems to have been similiar in *intention* to that of the mystics, his tentativeness flowers into honesty; he will not say what he does not mean. What he hands on for his readers to share is an awareness of what is inexpressible;

and for this reason alone he has more in common with the mystic than with the overtly 'religious' poet who is more anxious to affirm his own faith than to depict his struggle towards God.

As I have said, Crane employed many Christian words, signs and symbols. But, as with Rilke, he removed these things from the realm of strict orthodoxy and gave them a free life of their own. His imagination unyoked them from the bondage of dogma in order to liberate them for a visionary but less easily defined activity. Thus in the section of *The Bridge* called *The Dance* he writes,

> We danced, O Brave, we danced beyond their farms,
> In cobalt desert closures made our vows . . .
> Now is the strong prayer folded in thine arms,
> The serpent with the eagle in the boughs.

In this highly compressed stanza, Crane unites some of the attributes of the ascetic life with an oblique reference to the Fall of man. He is, it is true, contrasting his own vehement search for reality with the stillness and surrender of the monk, but he is nevertheless still describing a *search*. The means are different, the end is the same.

We find the same kind of affirmation which, paradoxically, works by a method of repudiation, at the end of *The Visible the Untrue*:

> The window weight throbs in its blind
> partition. To extinguish what I have of faith.
> Yes, light. And it is always
> always, always the eternal rainbow
> And it is always the day, the day of unkind farewell.

Here is the Dark Night of the Spirit expressed in concrete, secular symbols.

Poets work upon and through each other; this is the real meaning of tradition and influence. They also work on and through the symbols and ideas of their own time. So it is not surprising to find that most modern religious poets, whether they are orthodox Christians or not, have often found their imaginations working through a sense of *duality*. They wish to convey a unique, personal vision in images that will communicate immediately. And since what was acceptable in the past – namely, symbols that sprang directly from accepted dogma – no longer have a wide significance, such poets have been forced to make a choice between two modes of expression; they must either refashion the old symbols (as Rilke did) or they must select the most appropriate ones from the life, idioms and ideas of their own time.

Crane is unusual in that he worked, sometimes simultaneously, by means of both these modes of expression. And because he did this with a passionate belief in the rightness of his method, he was able to inform his best poems with a deep sense of unity.

I have spoken of tradition and influence, of sacred and secular symbols. These things, however, are only peripheral to the subject of this book. What I have tried to disclose is a real union, a similarity of experience, between the activity of the poet and the activity of the mystic. To have hinted at such affinities is, I am well aware, not to have proved anything. One can only prove by particular examples and it is for this reason that I have, as far as possible, let the poets and mystics speak for themselves. I have no desire to proffer theories. What I am concerned with is experience and experience, it is sometimes forgotten, can be an intimation in the mind as well as a leap of the pulse. No critic, and certainly no poet, can be all things to all men and I have brought to this book all my own convictions, intuitions, enthusiasms – and uncertainties. I do not pretend to be disinterested though I hope that, on occasion, I have achieved some measure of detachment. But I have also brought my own conflicts to bear on these studies and perhaps it will be from this contact that truths will be grasped and relationships revealed.

Since Hart Crane is placed, for reasons I have already given, at the end of this inquiry, I shall let him have the last word. In the following extract, taken from a letter he wrote in 1922, he speaks of many of the problems which have exercised and excited me in the writing of this book. In his references to Eliot in this letter, Crane is, of course, speaking of the Eliot of *The Waste Land* not of the *Four Quartets*: 'There is no one writing in English who can command so much respect, to my mind, as Eliot. However, I take Eliot as a point of departure towards an almost complete reverse of direction. His pessimism is amply justified, in his own case. But I would apply as much of his erudition and technique as I can absorb and assemble towards a more positive, or (if I must put it so in a sceptical age) ecstatic goal. I feel that Eliot ignores certain spiritual events and possibilities as real and powerful now, as, say, in the time of Blake. Certainly the man has dug the ground and buried hope as deep and direfully as it can ever be done . . . After this perfection of death – nothing is possible in motion but a resurrection of some kind . . . All I know through very much suffering and dullness . . . is that it interests me still to affirm certain things.'  Oxford – Rome – London 1958–60

# A SELECT BIBLIOGRAPHY

A. Alvarez: *The Shaping Spirit*. (Chatto & Windus, 1958.)

Thomas Aquinas: *Selected Writings*. Edited by Martin D'Arcy. (Everyman.)

St Benedict: *The Rule of St Benedict*. Translated and edited by Abbot Justin McCann. (Burns Oates, 1952.)

R. P. Blackmur: *Language as Gesture*. (Allen & Unwin, 1954.)

Bernard Blackstone: *The Consecrated Urn, an interpretation of Keats*. (Longmans, 1959.)

Sir Russell Brain: *The Nature of Experience*. (Oxford University Press, 1959.)

Dom Cuthbert Butler: *Western Mysticism*. (Constable, 1951.)

Dom John Chapman: *Spiritual Letters*. (Sheed & Ward, 1935.)

S. T. Coleridge: *Biographia Literaria*. (Everyman.)

Donald Davie: *Articulate Energy*. (Routledge, 1955.)

T. S. Eliot: *Selected Essays*. (Faber, 1946.)

S. Freud: *The Relation of the Poet to Day-Dreaming*. (Hogarth Press, 1946.)

R. Garrigou-Lagrange o.p.: *The Three Ages of the Interior Life*. (Herder.)

E. Gilson: *The Mystical Theology of St Bernard*. (Sheed & Ward, 1955.)

Daniel Halévy: *Péguy*. (Dennis Dobson, 1946.)

Stuart Hampshire: *Thought and Action*. (Chatto & Windus, 1959.)

Alan Heuser: *The Shaping Vision of Gerard Manley Hopkins*. (Oxford University Press, 1958.)

Aldous Huxley: *The Doors of Perception*. (Chatto & Windus, 1954.)

Aldous Huxley: *The Perennial Philosophy*. (Chatto & Windus, 1946.)

Jolande Jacobi: *The Psychology of C. G. Jung*. (Routledge, 1951.)

William James: *Selected Papers on Philosophy*. (Everyman.)

David Jones: *Epoch and Artist*. (Faber, 1959.)

John Keats: *Letters*. Edited by Maurice Buxton Forman. (Oxford University Press, 1947.)

D. H. Lawrence: *Letters*. (Heinemann, 1956.)

Thomas Merton: *The Ascent to Truth*. (Hollis and Carter, 1951.)

Thomas Merton: *The Sign of Jonas*. (Hollis and Carter, 1953.)

Edwin Muir: *An Autobiography*. (Hogarth Press, 1954.)

Conrad Pepler o.p.: *The English Religious Heritage.* (Blackfriars, 1958.)

Conrad Pepler o.p.: *The Three Degrees.* (Blackfriars, 1957.)

St-John Perse: *The Anabasis.* Translated by T. S. Eliot. (Faber, 1959.)

Richard of St Victor: *Selected Writings on Contemplation.* Translated with an Introduction and Notes by Clare Kirchberger. (Faber, 1957.)

R. M. Rilke: *Correspondence with Princess Marie von Thurn und Taxis.* Translated and introduced by Nora Wydenbruck. (Hogarth Press, 1958.)

Stephen Spender: *The Creative Element.* (Hamish Hamilton, 1953.)

Wallace Stevens: *Opus Posthumous.* (Faber, 1960.)

Allen Tate: *The Man of Letters in the Modern World.* (Meridian, 1957.)

Victor White o.p.: *God the Unknown.* (Harvill, 1956.)

Yvor Winters: *On Modern Poets.* (Meridian, 1959.)

W. B. Yeats: *Autobiographies.* (Macmillan, 1955.)

R. C. Zaehner: *At Sundry Times.* (Faber, 1958.)

R. C. Zaehner: *Mysticism Sacred and Profane.* (Oxford University Press, 1957.)

# INDEX